The Vision of J. B. Priestley

Roger Fagge

B L O O M S B U R Y

LONDON • NEW DELHI • NEW YORK • SYDNEY

Bloomsbury Academic

An imprint of Bloomsbury Publishing Plc

50 Bedford Square   1385 Broadway
London   New York
WC1B 3DP   NY 10018
UK   USA

www.bloomsbury.com

First published by Continuum International Publishing Group 2012
Paperback edition first published 2013

British Library Cataloguing-in-Publication Data
A catalogue record for this book is available from the British Library.

ISBN: HB: 978-1-4411-0480-9
PB: 978-1-4725-1455-4

Library of Congress Cataloging-in-Publication Data
A catalog record for this book is available from the Library of Congress.

THE VISION OF J. B. PRIESTLEY

Contents

Acknowledgements

This project could not have been completed without the help of a number of individuals and organizations. Research was supported by grants from the British Academy and the University of Warwick Research and Teaching Innovation fund, and the study leave granted by the University of Warwick was invaluable in allowing the time to consider and write this book. I owe a big debt of thanks to past and present colleagues at Warwick, including Chris Clark, James Hinton, Trevor Burnard, and Margot Finn, who read and commented on earlier drafts of key chapters, and to Tim Lockley for numerous instances of help, and the other members of Comparative American Studies for being such good colleagues.

Thanks to fellow Priestley scholars, Chris Waters and John Baxendale, both of whose work and ideas made me look at Priestley in a different light, and to Tom Priestley who was supportive from the start, and willing to answer questions and help along the way. The book has also benefited from comments from the audiences at various conferences and seminars including those in Leeds, Bradford, Manchester, London and Boston.

Research was aided by the staff at the University of Warwick library, the British Library and the National Newspaper Library at Colindale. The Priestley materials in the Harry Ransom Research Center at the University of Texas at Austin and the Davison Correspondence in the Beinecke Rare Books and Manuscript Library at Yale have been particularly helpful in this study. All material pertaining to Priestley are quoted with permission from the Estate of J.B. Priestley. Thank you to Carol MacArthur of United Agents and to Tom Priestley for their help in this regard.

This book was originally commissioned by Tony Morris, at Hambledon, and then moved with him to Continuum. Tony was encouraging in the early stages of the project, before it was passed into the capable hands of Ben Hayes and more recently Claire Lipscomb. Claire has successfully seen the project through to completion and I have very much appreciated her interest, enthusiasm and willingness to be flexible on deadlines!

Finally, many, many thanks to Tara, Miles and Lewis for all their support.

Introduction

J. B. Priestley was a prolific writer whose work, including fiction, plays, travelogues, social criticism, journalism and autobiography, was published over a period of 50 years from the 1920s. This alone should have made him a significant figure in the twentieth-century literary history. Priestley, however, was more than simply a writer. His radical views lay at the heart of his writing, and the popularity of his work allowed him to intervene in debates concerning national identity and the meaning of "Englishness", social divisions, the Cold War and the impact of the mass society. Priestley became a public figure alongside his work – as *The Times* put it, 'he was the author as public figure'. [1] This was most obvious through his influential BBC radio postscripts following the Sunday evening news in 1940, where his Yorkshire accent and articulate presentation of a people's perspective on the war became a memorable part of the World War II cultural landscape. The later involvement in the formation of the Campaign for Nuclear Disarmament illustrated a similar willingness to get involved in politics, and Priestley's writing remained personal, critical and sometimes polemical, but above all engaged, through to the end of his life.

Given Priestley's importance, it is surprising how he struggled for the respect and recognition he felt he deserved during his lifetime, and he has been relatively lightly studied since his death in 1984. His northern roots, ordinary background and popular appeal no doubt played a role in this process. Born in 1894 into a middle class background in Bradford, Priestley encountered a strong sense of community and cultural vitality, combined with a principled labour and socialist politics. His relationship with pre-war Bradford was fractured by the brutality of World War I, which left a changed social and cultural landscape and, having served and been wounded on the front, a changed Priestley. A less than happy experience at Cambridge after the war, which exacerbated his political radicalism, was followed by a move to London and becoming a full-time writer. Priestley remained to large extent a Yorkshireman, albeit exiled, and this grated with elements of the literary establishment, as did the fact that, having no private income, he had to write and publish regularly to pay the bills and feed his family. His belief that art should be accessible, not elitist, created further problems, not least when it was combined with the runaway success of *The Good Companions* (1929). There was nothing like success to alienate the purveyors of high art, and Priestley found himself unfairly designated, damningly as a "middlebrow". As Virginia Woolf (in) famously put it, he was, along with Arnold Bennett, 'a tradesman of letters'.[2]

Although Priestley received more credit later in his life, and particularly fulsome tributes when he died, for a long time subsequently he received neither the attention he deserved, nor was he seen as a particularly significant thinker, particularly when compared with other figures on the left, like George Orwell. There have been several biographies over the years, most of which have taken a conventional narrative line about Priestley's life, as well as literary and critical studies. The best of these, including Braine and Brome, were well written and informative.[3] Much of the writing also saw Priestley's Bradford upbringing and his experiences in World War I as being the defining factors in the shaping of his personality. Priestley had been dogged during his life with suggestions that his work was "nostalgic", and this continued after his death, leading some to see his views as representing an ossified rural Englishness.[4] More recently, however, alongside a more positive interest in British intellectual life generally,[5] historians and others have begun to reassess Priestley's importance, including John Baxendale, who argued that 'no one did more' than Priestley 'to think through England's twentieth-century experience, or strove harder to shape its national imaginary'.[6]

Drawing on private letters and published works, this study builds on this renewed interest in Priestley and provides an original intellectual biography, which argues that his views were perceptive and important, as well as sometimes idiosyncratic. It explores his formulation of a radical Englishness and his preference for popular rather than class politics. It also sees Priestley as more than an English writer, viewing him through a transatlantic perspective. Often seen as Anti-American, Priestley was, in fact, well-travelled and outward looking, and his experience of the United States shaped his thinking about the emerging mass society and post-war politics. As the book suggests, Priestley should be seen as a major thinker in the Anglo-American context.

Chapter 1 explores Priestley's relationship with politics and class in the inter-war year. It looks at his emergence as a writer following his unhappy sojourn at Cambridge and explores the way his views evolved in response to personal and political change, often exhibiting a tension between realism and idealism. In this period, Priestley's views operated under the umbrella term of Liberal Socialism, which drew heavily on nineteenth-century radicalism. From this came an uneasy relationship with class and a preference for the populist notion of the people.

Chapter 2 focuses on Priestley's relationship with England and Englishness. The latter lay at the heart of much of Priestley's work, and this chapter explores the writer's discussion of a radical Englishness in the 1930s. Challenging the association of Priestley with the conservative notion of 'Deep England', it argues that he valued both town and country and saw a democratic Englishness as a potentially unifying force for the people and an example to the wider world. However,

Priestley's England was an idealistic construct, which imagined a degree of unity, and a nation "asleep" that could be woken up with energy and enthusiasm. Explicit within this was the idea that people's torpor was in part caused by political conservatism and the spread of patterns of mass consumption, which Priestley saw as inimical to the radical English project.

Chapter 3 explores how Priestley became an influential public voice during World War II, via his radio postscripts. It shows how he slipped comfortably into this role, believing that the British people had received the wake-up call he had long argued they needed, and would go on, with his and others' encouragement, to build a new England. However, this optimism was not to last and his influence lessened as the experience of war led to a change in the public mood. Unbowed, Priestley argued in favour of reform and encouraged the people to become active in shaping their own future. However, his part romantic, part pragmatic approach to politics left him, by 1945, with doubts as to whether the new order he dreamed of would emerge. This chapter also places Priestley's vision of a radical England in a wider context and, in particular, offers a comparison of his views with those of another wartime radical, George Orwell.

Chapter 4 shows how, post 1945, Priestley's remaining hopes for a more radical future began to dissolve. Although a long-time Labour supporter, Priestley was unimpressed by the Labour Party's reforms after 1945, not least the enhanced role of the state, and he moved to a more pragmatic, centrist position on the political spectrum. He was also a critic of US foreign policy and the emerging Cold War, as he was of the further spread of the mass society. Despite this sense of disillusionment, Priestley still made several important contributions across the arts and was also involved in the creation of CND, blowing the dust off his wartime arguments about active citizenship. However, as Priestley himself came to realize, the time was passing for his vision of a radical England.

Chapter 5 examines Priestley's relationship with the United States and how the latter influenced his thought. It begins by looking at *Journey Down a Rainbow* (1955), co-written with Jacquetta Hawkes, which marked a key transatlantic intervention in the debate about the mass society. Echoing in varying degrees the arguments of US social critics, Priestley created the term "Admass" to describe a system that had spawned what he described as the "mass man". Admass was, he argued, "the great invader", spreading its tentacles around the globe. Priestley had travelled widely and had a genuine engagement with the United States since the 1930s, seeing democratic potential in its social, cultural and political framework. However, Admass underlined a shift to a more negative view of the mass order, and the book also reignited a longstanding argument about Priestley's alleged Anti-Americanism – something the author vigorously denied.

Chapter 6 looks at *Late Priestley*, suggesting that Priestley's work remained vital and relevant into his seventies, including his remarkable *Literature and Western*

Man (1960). There were continuities in his thinking on politics, the United States, the Cold War, the mass society and time, and he also found a somewhat warmer reception from critics as a "Grand Old Man" of English letters and was awarded an Order of Merit in 1977. His unease at the mass order, however, remained undimmed.

By the time of his death in 1984, Priestley had left a significant body of work in various media and made a number of important interventions in public and political debates. His influence was felt in the world of theatre, television, film, journalism, literature and politics, where his articulation of a democratic Englishness cut across more conservative conceptions of the national identity. It also enabled him to provide an influential critique of the American-orientated postwar world. For this and the best of his writing – which enshrined his sense of humanity – Priestley, as this book suggests, deserves to be remembered.

1

Priestley, Politics and Class

J. B. Priestley was a complex person – a creative, driven and idiosyncratic individual nurtured in the vibrant culture of pre-war Yorkshire. Needless to say, these factors impacted upon Priestley's political views and the way he negotiated the turbulent inter-war years. Some have characterized Priestley's thought in these years, and beyond, as "nostalgic" and rooted in the past, while at the other extreme, some have suggested that his views approximated to a Gramscian vision of "Anglo-British modernization".[1] In fact, while there is a stronger grain of truth in the latter than the former view, Priestley was less rigid than these approaches suggest, and he often thought on his feet, responding in different printed mediums, aimed at different audiences. As he once openly admitted, 'consistency is not one of my virtues, or vices'.[2] His views evolved in response to personal and political change and often exhibited the common tussle in an artist's view between the realist and the idealist. Journalistic realism, at times, was followed by flights into romantic idealism at others. These occurred under the umbrella of a commitment to Liberal Socialism that was really only a partially modernized nineteenth-century radicalism. From this came an uneasy relationship with class, or more appropriately, the divisions caused by class, and a preference for collapsing the latter into a populist notion of the people. As we shall see in the next chapter, this became intertwined with Priestley's passionate and unfashionable espousal of Englishness.

J. B. Priestley was not seen as a political writer from the outset. In the immediate aftermath of the war, he left the army like many others among his generation 'with no great resolutions', keen to return to civilian life and leave the horrors of the war behind them.[3] After 3 years at Cambridge, he sought a career as a writer in London. Lacking a private income, married, and by 1923 a father, Priestley's overriding imperative was to make a living – a significant struggle until the remarkable success of *The Good Companions* in 1929.[4] Seen as a popular, middlebrow writer at that point, Priestley's writing began to gradually exhibit a stronger line on social and political issues. *Angel Pavement* (1930) provided a critical portrait of a troubled London; *Faraway* (1932) mixed escapism, with an awareness of the corrupting impact of modern values on the developing world, while *Wonder Hero* (1933) marked a more dramatic shift into the political, which, in Priestley's own words, set out 'to satirise the popular press, the publicity nonsense, the sillier and seamier side of the West End, and then throw into high relief...the plight of the people in one of the depressed areas.[5]

English Journey (1933) took the genre of travel writing and provided a perceptive analysis of the state of the nation, not least the social consequences of the Great Depression, a theme explored in fictional form in *They Walk in the City* (1936). Forced to defend the latter, which critics and friends considered one of his weakest works, Priestley told a sceptical Hugh Walpole that 'I have certain quite strong convictions, and I tend more and more to bring them into my writing'.[6] From thereon, politics continued to play a prominent role in most, although not all, of Priestley's writing, and he sought to position himself as a commentator on contemporary affairs. Hence, on lecture tours to the United States, his biography announced that 'his subjects have less to do with literary themes than with the larger political, social and philosophical themes of the day'.[7]

The move to a more politicized form of writing as the 1930s progressed seems straightforward enough and can be related to the political circumstances of the decade. Priestley later described how had he lived 'in another age, I might never have written a line about political concerns', but as 'half artist and half a damaged man of action', he felt compelled to write about politics.[8] The damage had in large part been caused by the war, and the shift towards a more political line should not blind us to the fact that Priestley's work, even prior to the 1930s, while not openly political, engaged with the contemporary world. This is clear in *The Good Companions* where poverty and the hardship of working-class life are an important part of the fabric of the novel. For example, the Midlands town of Tewborough is described as 'like an engine with a burst boiler lying on the side of the road; it was a money machine that had almost stopped working', a town 'too much' even for the Bruddersford born and bred Jess Oakroyd.[9] Similarly, Susan Cooper has pointed out how in essays such as 'T'match' Priestley explored themes that would be expanded upon in *English Journey*.[10] And Priestley himself was somewhat bemused by critics who saw him as a sentimental novelist who had only just discovered political issues in the early 1930s. Pointing out that he had written for socialist papers prior to World War I and had often referred to social conditions in his novels, he told Eugene Saxton that 'it makes me smile when these reviewers greet me as a man who has just wakened up to what life is really like'.[11] It is clear, therefore, that Priestley's writing always had an undercurrent of social observation but that the changing political environment made these more central within his work.

Priestley's politics were influenced by his father's socialism. Bradford was the birthplace of the ILP, and Priestley's schoolteacher father and friends were enthusiastic supporters of the latter's brand of ethical socialism. Priestley was drawn through 'tradition and filial piety' to share such beliefs, but he also admired the enthusiasm and honesty of the Bradford socialists and their tendency to be 'life-seeking, and life enhancing' rather than, like other leftists, 'men of steel'.[12] Priestley recalled his father's willingness to speak out on political issues, some-times with such conviction that he 'bristled and blazed like a lion',[13] and he viewed his father as 'the ideal socialist citizen'. 'Of such', he wrote, 'could be made the best kingdom yet on this earth'. Priestley, however, adapted his political inheritance to his own experiences and character. 'There was', he wrote, 'more wilful individual-ism in me than him...I set more store by independent lines of thought'.[14]

Ethical socialism and liberalism shared similar roots and ideas, and Priestley's own views came to express strong elements of both[15] – 'Liberal Socialism' as he put it, in part because of the limited role ascribed to the state and the related emphasis upon the rights of the individual. In *Midnight on the Desert* (1936), he described his ideal socialist state as owning and distributing free 'all the vital necessities of life', with small private retailers supplying luxury goods (he characteristically chose cake and wine as two examples of the latter!). People work to buy these luxuries, but money could not be saved or traded – 'there are no financiers, money jugglers in my country'. Work itself was divided between 'co-operative labour for the community' and 'private' work that people chose to do. Crucially, although the state played such a vital role in distributing the necessities of life, Priestley saw it as having 'no mystical significance' – it was simply a 'convenient arrangement that enables us to pool our resources and co-operate'. Nor would it be allowed to inter-fere in people's lives: 'Nobody wants to be told how to feel, to think, to pray...we do not allow it to be the guardian of our private morals'.[16]

This dismissal of the monolithic state ran counter to the thought of some on the Left in inter-war Britain but was shared by many others. As has been shown elsewhere, voluntarism had long and firm roots in English radical thought, and although the Left now viewed the state in a more positive light, many remained cautious about its potential for bringing about change.[17] Priestley's views, in many ways, reflected this cautious acceptance of limited state activity.

Part of Priestley's suspicion of an unbridled state came from his passionate belief in the rights of the individual and his scepticism about the way govern-ment and other large organizations sought to classify people as economic units, shearing away their humanity. As Professor Kronak put it in *Let the People Sing* (1939), 'Civilisation is more than producing and owning things'.[18] This was one of the central arguments about the dehumanizing impact of the Depression,[19] but it also related to the growing bureaucratization and loss of identity in ordi-nary life. 'When I was a youth', Priestley wrote in an article in 1936, 'I visited five foreign countries, and I had never seen a passport or a visa.... Now we are all passported and visa-d up to the neck'.[20] For Priestley, individual freedom was not an optional extra but an essential element of a civilized society, without which we would 'perish or dwindle into bees or ants. That is why', he argued, 'in spite of my strong feeling of community, and my belief in some form of collectivism, I was ready to fight for liberty not only of expression…but also in the manner of living, which is in itself a form of expression'.[21]

Priestley believed firmly in the value of' "community", without which, he argued, 'we should live like brutes',[22] and favoured the local organizations that sprang from them. The localized institutions of his native Bradford were a constant touchstone, particularly those related to the arts. Priestley wrote proudly of how, in his memory of the vigorous world of pre-war Bradford, cultural life was enlivened by two local theatres, two music halls, a concert hall and a full music programme, an arts club and a playgoers society, not to forget pubs and cafes.[23] During the depression, it was also noticeable how Priestley was encouraged by activities at the community level, and Settlement houses were singled out for praise, for their role in fighting the corrosive impact of poverty.[24]

Other organizations and ideas, outside of the local culture, were viewed less sympathetically. While Priestley appreciated that workers had to struggle to secure a decent position in society, he had little enthusiasm for Trade Unions in general, particularly in the world of theatre and entertainment. Priestley was irritated by what he saw as their pettiness over job differentiation and their lack of respect for individual rights, tending to treat employees as economic units like the employers.[25] He was also critical of their role in the Labour Party and national politics principally on grounds of democracy: 'There is no more reason why we should be governed by railwaymen and transport workers, just because they belong to large and powerful unions, than that we should be governed by rich employers and landowners because they are paying the most taxes'. He also had 'a more fundamental objection' concerning his belief that trade unions 'produce a certain type of mind, admirable within its own limits, but not a deeply creative statesman-like mind'.[26]

Priestley's liberal socialism developed organically from his upbringing, and despite what critics sometimes alleged, he had little time for communism. In *English Journey*, Priestley described meeting 'militant communist' Bob, who helped at the People's Theatre in Newcastle. Priestley saw Bob as 'a kindly, lively, but forceful sort of chap', who had been turned into a communist by his experience of the Depression and his desire to rise above his situation. Priestley described how Bob saw the world as a set of conspiracies, where employers and officials could not be trusted and consistently plotted to 'trick him and his mates'. The cynicism about other classes was accompanied by a utopian belief in the cleansing value of communism:

> His communism is not a reasoned alternative to a social machine that is wobbling and running down, is not a transition from an obviously incompetent and unjust system to an

order of society that embodies our ideas of competence and justice: it is the entrance into a Human Paradise, and a new Golden Age, from which, by some mysterious means all the selfish wickedness of the present world will be banished.[27]

Priestley believed that Bob was typical of thousands of others in similar circumstances who embraced communism in an unthinking manner.

Priestley similarly contested the arguments of the middle class communists of the inter-war years. Disputing Ivor Montagu's claim that the Soviet Union 'has always been the land of the free', Priestley dished out a stern lecture on the need for both economic and democratic rights. After all he suggested that political exiles, including Marx and Lenin, would never have been able to formulate their ideas in the British Library if it had not been for 'paper freedoms' in Britain.[28] He had even less time for younger poets who signed up for the communist cause: 'It's silly for young men to announce themselves as new types of humanity…and then give you nothing but stale communism', he wrote to Hugh Walpole, adding 'Old H.G. Wells has more new ideas than the lot of them.'[29]

Priestley's opposition to communism, and suspicion of trade unions, was related to a broader, liberal approach to the language and meaning of class. In many ways, this again reflected his roots in the longstanding tradition of English radicalism, although Priestley was not always at his clearest when it came to dealing with this issue. His views were also presented at a time when class had become a more significant factor within British society – both as a social and cultural division and as a political strategy.[30] This was most apparent with the rise of the Communist Party at one extreme and the Conservative Party's use of anti-working class propaganda to shore up their support on the other.[31]

The increasing presence of the language of class within political debate made Priestley uneasy. Again he associated it with a lack of respect for individuality and difference. Writing after hearing protestors at a fascist meeting in Bristol, Priestley commented, 'I heard something about "the rising of the masses". And why is it always "the masses"? Who cares about masses? I wouldn't raise a finger for "the masses". Men, women and children – but not masses.'[32] A similar sentiment was present when Jess Oakroyd fell out with a communist shop steward when he described the word 'Proletariat' as 'a bloody daft word.'[33] Oakroyd's comments are given extra significance by the fact that the character was partly based on 'Mr. W', the father of one of Priestley's friends. Priestley described how he used the latter's 'mixture of simplicity and real shrewdness, of independence and deep affection' when creating Oakroyd.[34] The stress on independence is significant as it reinforces the role of the individual as an active agent, neither acting within a class nor accurately described as a member of such. Indeed, Oakroyd and his real-life source represented Priestley's ideal worker, so different to the paranoid communist Bob. In language similar to that in which he described his own father, Priestley enthused that he would like to see England full of people like 'Mr. W,' which would create a 'very different' nation, where men 'stand on their own feet, do their jobs with a will, stoutly resist stupid opposition but give way to affection...and are grand lumps of character'.[35]

Part of this suspicion of the language of class was related to Priestley's interpretation of his Bradford youth, which was spent in an environment where 'the social hierarchy was invisible'. Priestley recalled how wealthy employers in the Wool industry left Bradford for the country, where they embraced a rural lifestyle, making Bradford relatively free of class differences. It was only later when he served in World War I that he "discovered" the true nature of the "class structure".[36] This depiction of his largely classless upbringing, however, does need some qualification.

In later life, Priestley had a tendency to paint a romanticized picture of his hometown, but even within these works, it is clear that class or status issues clearly had some bearing on his early years. His mother, who died in October 1896, came from what he described as 'the careless and raffish side of the working class', although there is some debate as to the exact nature of her background. Priestley certainly became aware later that part of his father's strict morality might have come from a desire to prevent him from slipping down into the less respectable ranks of Bradford society. [37] His father's promotion to the post of headmaster also allowed the family to move in 1904 to 5 Saltburn Place, an 'ultra respectable suburb'[38], which they shared with other better off citizens of Bradford. This contrasted with the 'wretched little "back-to-back" houses in the long dark streets behind the mills', where some of the young Priestley's relatives lived.[39]

Among the fellow residents in Saltburn Place were the managers in the mills, who incurred the wrath of Priestley and others for their treatment of the mill women and girls under their employment. In *Margin Released*, which generally paints an Arcadian vision of Bradford, Priestley recalled how certain managers vigorously opposed pay rises for their employees, while 'turning the prettiest and weakest of them into tarts'.[40] This provided the basis for the time play *An Inspector Calls* (1947), which was set in 1912, and told the story of the industrialist, Tory, and middle-class Birlings, who are, in varying degrees, responsible for the suicide of mill girl, Eva Smith. That the callous disregard for Eva is based on class differences is clearly illustrated when Mrs. Birling tries to dismiss her daughter Sheila's desire to find the reasons behind the suicide by suggesting that it would be impossible to understand 'girls of that Class'. Sheila responds that they 'mustn't try to build a kind of wall between us and that girl'. Her realization that the mysterious Inspector will see through this artificial social distinction is confirmed by the Inspector himself.[41] Interestingly, Priestley also saw the mill girls as a separate group, although he held them in much higher regard than the fictional Birlings.

The mill girls were, he suggested, 'no models of feminine refinement' with their boisterous language and behaviour that made the young Priestley's 'cheeks burn'. Priestley clearly admired their energy and honesty, but his picture of them is resonant with a sense of social difference.[42]

It is clear, therefore, that Priestley's pre-war Bradford was not as immune from class differences as he sometimes suggested. However, it is also apparent that it was only in the army that the full 'tangle of superiorities and inferiorities' of class became apparent, not least because the independent thinking Priestley sometimes found himself at odds with the 'jackasses' in the senior officer class.[43] Indeed he initially rejected the idea of becoming a junior officer, although he accepted a commission in 1917.[44] Junior officers, however, were, in his eyes, less responsible for the chaos he had encountered than their senior colleagues. Over 40 years later, his anger at this group remained undimmed and underscored his belated introduction to the class system: 'The tradition of an officer defying both imagination and common sense, killed most of my friends as surely as if those cavalry generals had come out of the chateaux with polo mallets and beaten their brains out. Call this class prejudice if you like', he argued, but 'remember ...I went into this war without any such prejudice, free of any class feeling'. He added, with intended irony, that he came out of the war 'with a chip on my shoulder: a big heavy chip, probably some friend's thigh-bone'.[45]

The introduction to the class system that Priestley suggested he discovered in the army was reinforced by his time at Cambridge. Offered an ex-serviceman's grant, he decided to take the opportunity to attend university this time around and arrived at Trinity Hall in 1919; he soon felt like 'neither fish nor fowl'. His experiences during the war, the fact that he was in his mid-20s and his Yorkshire accent (and background) left him out of step with the public school climate he encountered. This was reinforced by the frugal standard of living he endured, surviving on £120 per annum grant, supplemented by teaching and writing. This left him reliant on a meagre diet, including frequent boiled eggs, while his younger counterparts put on expensive 'monster' teas. His marriage to Pat Tempest in June 1921, after which he returned for a postgraduate year, placed further pressure on his income and led, following the successful publication of *Brief Diversions* (1922), to the departure for London. [46] Even the flat fenlands irked one who took so much pleasure in the landscape of his native Yorkshire. As he later concluded on his time at Cambridge, 'I didn't much like it, and it never liked me'.[47]

Priestley left Cambridge with a stronger sense of the dynamics of class, and it began to make an appearance in his work. This often took the form, as we have already seen with *An Inspector Calls*, of an exploration of the experiences of the middle classes, sometimes considering their social and cultural prejudices. In *Angel Pavement*, for example, the Dersinghams are presented as a shallow, acquisitive couple, who shored up their own social position by looking down on others. This was clearly illustrated by Dersingham's reaction to the appearance of the mysterious potential business partner, Golspie: 'A few terms at Worrell would obviously have made a great difference to Golspie, who now, in his middle age, showed only too plainly by word and deed that he was not a gentleman. From that there was no escape: Golspie was not a gentleman.'[48] Dersingham reconfirms this opinion later on, having discovered that Golspie has departed. 'He isn't a gentleman – never looked like one', he tells Smeeth, making light of the latter's discovery that Dersingham had tried to cut Golspie out of the deal with Mikorsky's, the Russian veneer suppliers.[49] By contrast, Mrs. Dersingham's response to the randomness of the crisis that hits them was to rediscover her humanity, and empathy with other people, and look beyond her shallow middle-class values. 'She understood now how millions of people live. It was a moment of revelation.'[50]

Shallowness associated with class is also apparent in other works, including *When We Are Married* (1938), where the protagonists see themselves as having risen up the social scale, where they sit, self-satisfied, judging others. The superiority is punctured when the put upon servant, Mrs. Northup, having pointed out the women's ordinary backgrounds, informs Clara and Maria that the couples' marriages were not in fact legal. The tables now turned in the respectability stakes, Mrs. Northup informs them 'I was going to say I'm as good as you, but the fact is I'm a damn sight better, 'cos I'm a respectable Married woman an' that's more than any o'you can say'.[51] Of course, the marriages turn out to be legal after all, but not before the couples have had the chance to re-examine their relationships and their values.

There was little comedy in the bleaker *Time and the Conways* (1937). Although principally a time play, it also explores the middle-class experience – in this case, a family forced to face up to the difficult reality of the post-war order.[52] On the surface a seemingly happy family, their optimism in 1919 gives way to a much darker outcome by the 1930s. Although social and economic changes have played a role in their predicament, the play also suggests that snobbery, greed and shallow complacency have also been significant. The casual dismissal of the younger Ernest Beevers, in part because 'his social background is rather lower' than the Conways, later costs the family in personal and financial terms.[53] Likewise, Mrs. Conway's cruel interruption of Gerald and Madge's heart to heart ('The generous mood is shattered. Madge might have been hit in the face' – as the stage notes put it) blights both of their lives and alienates Madge from her mother and the family.[54] Only the innocent Carol, who dies tragically young, is able to approach life in a more genuine and honest manner. She is the one member of the family who is welcoming towards Ernest Beevers, and in her passionate avowal of life at the end of the play, she proves that she is capable of seeing through the snobbery and pretensions of the others. 'The point is', she tells them, 'to live. Never mind about money and positions and husbands with titles and rubbish – I'm *going to live*'.[55]

Carol's embrace of life, ironic given her fate, reaches beyond the less appealing aspects of middle-class family life. Similarly in *Angel Pavement* and *When We Are Married*, Priestley presents a learning process through which people discover a greater depth within themselves than their social position seemed to allow. In reclaiming their essential humanity, and independence, they join the ranks of Jess Oakroyd who never subscribed to a simplistic class identity in the first place. In these and other fictional works, we can see that Priestley saw class as an essentially cultural issue, an attitude or a set of attitudes, not necessarily an economic criterion. In this regard, Priestley certainly did not hold to the usual socialist position of an inevitable contradiction between employer and worker. His picture of the virtually 'classless' Bradford is one example of this, as was his praise of the Potteries, where he argued that the nature of the trade allowed family businesses to remain 'in which the employer is well acquainted with all his workpeople'. When combined with work that demanded 'personal skill and quick judgement', this left a largely 'contented' labour force.[56]

As Priestley admitted, the Potteries were probably "unique", and other workers faced different situations, ranging from unemployment through to modern, mechanized factories that were 'really an enormous machine in which the workers are simply cogs and levers'.[57] Interestingly, even here, Priestley did not necessarily identify class differences within the workplace. Writing about the Imperial Typewriter Company in Leicester, he noted how a group of engineers in executive positions operated at a level giving them both control and job satisfaction. In one sense, he argued, this corresponded to a class division, where 'there is a drop from them to the mass of employees, all caught in monotonous routine work'. However, Priestley argued, this was not 'a question of the capitalists and the proletariat, the bosses and the workers. The men I call the masters of the machines may not have a penny of capital and they are workers too.... It is not a question of economic status at all'. Instead of class, Priestley argued that the division was increasingly along gender lines, as 'the masters of the machines are men, and the routine workers, the servants of the machines, are recruited more and more from girls and young women'.[58]

Priestley's somewhat tentative engagement with class was inevitably shaped by his own social position. Thanks to his modest roots, Priestley believed that he was particularly well qualified to speak on behalf of ordinary people in general. 'I really do know about these people', he told Walpole in 1928, while writing *The Good Companions*, 'because I've spent a lot of time in pubs and low music halls, and at football matches – especially in the early, impressionable years'. This was something, he argued, that marked him out from most other novelists who 'have not an extensive acquaintance with the people and life of this country'.[59] The first quote implies a particular knowledge of the working classes and the middle class outsiders who become part of the Good Companions theatre troupe, while the second quote implies a wider demographic. Eleven years later, Priestley argued that 'he grew up with the proletarians in one of the grimmest industrial regions and indeed their blood is mine just as, I hope, their dreams are mine', while also stating a few pages earlier that he was 'essentially bourgeois and middle class' himself.[60]

Priestley obviously saw no contradiction in this position, and he genuinely believed he could provide a voice for the powerless within the nation. However, the actual experience of class inevitably left open to question whether his "dreams" or at least reality was somewhat different from some of his poorer counterparts. We have already seen him recall the sense of social difference between himself and the mill women while growing up in Bradford, and when he left Cambridge, he soon began to adopt a middle-class lifestyle. His marriage to Jane in 1926 encouraged this tendency, and with the success of *The Good Companions*, the family were able to live in the style of the wealthier sections of the middle class. As early as 1927, he wrote to Edward Davison complaining that 'the servant problem is ruining country life here'.[61] The 1933 move to the 15-acre Billingham Manor Estate on the Isle of Wight, with another residence in London, cemented a style of living a long way removed from his Bradford origins. Under Jane's direction, the house was "exquisitely decorated" and frequently filled with eminent guests and friends.[62] Edward Davison's son, Peter, who visited the smaller Brook Hill, where the Priestleys moved in 1948, wrote that the 'baronial establishment' was 'teeming with family, friends, servants'. As an American-born Harvard graduate, Peter found the 'English country house atmosphere' made him uneasy.[63] He was not the only one. Jane had also been instrumental, by this point, in the family's move into farming, which she believed would provide a good financial return. Priestley had opposed this from the outset, and with the marriage fragmenting, he told his daughter Mary 'the last thing I thought I would ever become was a farming type'.[64] Reluctantly, therefore, Priestley had become an unlikely member of the 'landed gentry'.[65]

Although the nature of Priestley's work left him semi-detached from the class system, and his democratic instincts and plain, unpretentious writing style all leant towards an ability to give voice to the dreams of both the working and the middle classes, an inevitable gap appeared at times, not least with Priestley's growing critique of popular culture. Similarly, perhaps realizing that the nation of sturdy independent Mr. W's was now no longer an option, by the end of the 1930s, Priestley was an increasingly vocal supporter of the enlightened middle class. As he put it in 1939, 'when they are not tangled up in snobbery and false values, the ordinary English bourgeois middle-class are grand people', going on to describe the benefits the middle class have given to the world, suggesting that their creativity and talent could remake the nation in the shape of 'a bourgeois democracy'.[66] Priestley's enthusiasm for this middle class vanguard was, no doubt, influenced by the fact that he credited the intelligent middle class with fully understanding his experimental plays such as *Johnson over Jordan* (1939).[67]

Priestley's attempt at speaking for the breadth of the people was a noble aim, and one he occasionally achieved. However, the very class system he despised, the effects of which were the subject matter of some of his works, made it difficult for him to truly imagine and represent the entire experience of his working class readers. It illustrated the difficulty in marrying a hard analysis of the political reality of the inter-war years with an artistic sentiment that sought a vision that was 'life seeking and life enhancing'. The process became more complex still, when "the people" were placed within the context of an over-arching Englishness.

2

Priestley and England Between the Wars

An integral part of Priestley's social and political vision in the inter-war years, and indeed after, was concerned with the state of England and Englishness.[1] His two major statements on the subject in this period were presented in *English Journey* (1933) and a chapter in *Rain Upon Godshill* (1939) (Priestley described the latter as the 'best thing in that line I've ever done on…England and the English.').[2] However, these were by no means his only comments on this subject, and England was at the heart of many of his plays, novels and non-fiction.[3] Given his interest in this sub-ject, there has been a move among historians and critics to tie Priestley's views on England in with a broader assumption about the conservative nature of the English identity. The latter argument suggested that by the end of the nineteenth century, the ruling elite had, in an attempt to resist the rising tide of modernity, constructed a dominant view of the nation based upon a nostalgia for a mythical rural past. This southern 'Deep England' of landscape, village and country gentlemen, it was argued, became the ideal for rural and urban dwellers alike and acted as a brake on a genuine engagement with the reality of the modern world, condemning England to social, cultural and economic decline.[4] Various individuals, agencies and pub-lications were cited in support of this argument, including J. B. Priestley, who got bracketed in as the theory gained a more general currency. Historians like Angus Calder, Philip Dodd and David Smith all identified what they saw as rural nostal-gia in his writing.[5] The latter, for example, wrote of 'rural themes' being 'prevalent' in Priestley's inter-war novels, while the wartime postscripts 'reconstituted images of the past…it was for the countryside, the essence of England' that Britain was fighting.[6] Chris Water's well-written and intriguing article on Priestley also makes similar claims. In a broader argument characterizing Priestley's nostalgic romanti-cism, he suggests that 'Priestley's rural nostalgia' could be compared to contempo-raries like Leavis and Baldwin, but his thought was able to move beyond this into a broader interpretation of Englishness.[7]

More recently, historians have begun to challenge the hegemony of the broader 'Deep England' thesis. Peter Mandler, for example, has pointed out that rural nos-talgia was much less influential than has been suggested and that it remained the preserve of a small elite. In fact, he argued, prior to World War I, 'English culture as a whole was aggressively urban and materialist', and in the inter-war period, a

growing interest in the countryside was practical rather than romantic or nostalgic. Suburbanization, for example, was less about respect for rural ways than taking the city into the country, reflecting a belief that the countryside should not be
preserved but 'put to good use'.[8] Others have also contributed to the debate, offering an interesting picture of Englishness, and even the rural nostalgia of Baldwin and the Conservative Party has been called to question.[9] John Baxendale has
also responded to those who allied Priestley to the 'Deep England' bandwagon.
He situated Priestley 'in the overlap between the two force-fields of radical dis-
sent and modernist planning', making 'his relationship to the rural consequently
ambivalent and complex'.[10] Baxendale also underlined the important qualification
of the association of an interest in the countryside with rural nostalgia, pointing out that 'we cannot "read off" anti-modernism from a liking for the English
countryside'.[11]

The above point is particularly relevant when considering Priestley, as throughout his life he had a profound love of the countryside. It was the love, however,
of 'a townsman born and bred',[12] an artist and a down-to-earth Yorkshireman,
and Priestley was an avowed critic of those in his own time who tied the countryside in with a rural conservatism. For many urban dwellers, particularly in
industrial areas, neighbouring countryside offered a sense of space, beauty and
clean air, which had little or nothing to do with intellectual constructs concerning
ingrained conservatism.

Priestley's love of his native Yorkshire was well documented, but it is important
to underline how he and other Bradfordians saw the countryside around them
as a contrast to their urban environment. Juxtaposing the two worlds, Priestley wrote, 'I spent my childhood and youth in the West Riding, where trams go
groaning on through miles and miles of dark streets, where the very houses look
like little factories and the factories themselves look like great grim fortresses, and
all the works of man are formidable and forbidding'. The local people, however,
'had a genuine passion…for the high moors and deep green dales of the Pennine
region. They were great walkers, these people, and would trudge on for hours to
catch another glimpse of a favourite bit of moorland or dale. The roughest fellows, whom you might imagine to care nothing but for beer and football, would
surprise you with their fine appreciation of the countryside'.[13] Nor was Priestley's
aesthetic respect for landscape only restricted to Yorkshire, or even England, as he
also fell in love with the landscapes of the United States. As we shall see later, this
formed part of his ambivalent relationship with the United States.

Priestley saw the countryside with an artist's eye, where the weather and
nature of light suited the famous water-colourists like Girtin, Turner, Colman and
Clome, and he appreciated this art for the beauty that it presented.[14] And it was
the destruction of beauty that he railed against when he began writing about and
campaigning for the environment in the mid-1930s. He wrote, for example, of

the 'mild and friendly' countryside of the Midlands, which had been 'ravished' by Industry. 'Drunken storm troops have passed this way; there are signs of atrocities everywhere; the earth has been left gaping and bleeding; and what were once bright fields have been rummaged and raped into these dreadful patches of waste ground.'[15] The 'commercial greed' behind such destruction of an earlier time was also, he argued, affecting the environment in the 1930s, where lack of planning, inferior buildings and roads built without respect for the countryside were further breaking down the 'old happy compromise between nature and man'.[16] Balance was an important factor as Priestley saw the landscape not as an untouched Eden but one whose 'moderation' was 'born of a compromise between wildness and tameness' as well as between man and his environment.[17] 'Britain is in Danger', he wrote in 1939, as this balance was being eroded with the spread of roads and the subsequent construction of factories, shops and housing alongside them. This meant that 'instead of stopping properly and giving the meadows and woods a chance', towns 'now straggle on mile after mile. The new houses and shops look a mess. The road is more congested with traffic than before. And some nice bit of the real England has gone forever'. Towns themselves were not the problem, he claimed, but 'the stupid half-and-half' of suburban developments,[18] and even the car, if used appropriately, could enhance the appreciation of certain types of countryside.[19]

Priestley supported the 'Council for the Preservation of Rural England' and 'National Trust' in their campaigns to protect the environment and suggested that Britain should follow the example of the United States and establish National Parks. Calling for such a move in the Lake District, Priestley attacked the way beautiful areas were advertised, attracted development and disinterested crowds, and then 'it is no longer a little place, and has no beauty, remoteness or peace.'[20] He made a similar argument in *English Journey* when describing the Cotswolds, which contained not only 'enchanted valleys' but also traditional crafts and skills, which Priestley believed should be preserved as an 'experiment' – one that was needed 'when everybody is being rushed down and swept into one dusty arterial road of cheap mass production and standardised living.'[21]

In some ways, the protection of this 'Real England' would seem to suggest something more than a defence of beauty and instead an elitist rejection of the modern, mass society corresponding to the minority described by Mandler.[22] However, this would be an inaccurate representation of Priestley's views. In his call for National Parks, he did condemn 'crowds who do not want remoteness or peace, who come roaring up', but he also argued that 'the Lake Country…should belong to the nation, to the world, to every man everywhere who can come and enjoy them properly.'[23] In other words, 'Rock climbers, fell walkers, lovers of the picturesque, literary tourists', who wanted to experience the Lakes in their natural beauty, were welcome; those who wanted a commercialized version were not. This was very much in keeping with the US vision of National Parks and had less to do with elitism than a common-sense approach to natural beauty and protecting the environment.

In a similar vein, Priestley had no interest in a ruralism controlled by or working in the interests of the elite. He was consistently critical of members of the middle class who moved into the country and tried to recreate a gentrified existence (notwithstanding his own unexpected entry into country living). In an argument that anticipated the later Englishness debate, he believed this furthered the gap between the classes and the 'guns, dogs and bridge tables' brigade created a brake on social and political change.[24] Even in his beloved Bradford and Yorkshire, 'the industrialists were busy turning themselves into country gentlemen and are leaving the cities to the professional, clerking and working classes'.[25] Priestley also resented the political manifestation of this process, in the way the press worked with the Tories to push a 'kind of life – with its country houses', while Labour failed to present 'a steady vision of a new urban civilisation'.[26]

For despite his love of the countryside, Priestley the townsman did not accord rural England a primacy, nor did he seek a return to rural values. His writing across the genres presented social change and modernism, and the cutting edge lay within the realm of the urban. This was clearly presented in his fullest statement on Englishness, presented in *English Journey*. Here, at the end of his travels, he considers the different 'Englands' he has encountered. The first of these was 'Old England', 'the country of the cathedrals and minsters and manor houses and inns, of Parson and Squire; guide-book and quaint highways and byways', advertised to American tourists. There is beauty here ('the best cannot be improved upon in this world'), and the tourist may find comfort, but, crucially, he argued, 'it has long ceased to earn its living'. Consequently, it can only play a minor role in the contemporary nation, where Priestley was all for 'scrupulously preserving the most enchanting bits of it', such as the Cotswolds, cathedrals and colleges, but the rest had 'to take its chance'. Taking on the conservatives who believed that there could be a 'mysterious return' to 'Old England', he mocked that even the first step would require killing off 90% of the population. 'The same people', he suggested, 'might consider competing in a race at Brooklands with a horse and trap'. The 'right course of conduct' towards 'Old England', he suggested, was not to 'brood and dream over these almost heart-breaking pieces of natural or architectural loveliness' as this would be done 'at the expense of a lot of poor devils toiling in the muck'. Instead, it was to 'peep' and 'thus steel your determination that sooner or later the rest of English life, even where the muck is now, shall have as good a quality as those things'.[27]

The important aspect of relevance in 'Old England', therefore, was its beauty and the quality of its buildings and products, not the impractical social model proposed by the rural romantics of the 1930s. Priestley found less to praise in his second England, which was anything but rural and presented little of the quality he valued in 'Old England'. 'Nineteenth Century England' was largely situated in the industrial heartlands of the North and Midlands, where it had been responsible for the environmental destruction that we have already seen Priestley deplore. It produced good literature and was 'not a bad England' to the more fortunate. However, it encouraged 'tough, enterprising men' who, confident of Britain's economic strength, made their money and could then, in what we have already seen was another of Priestley's bugbears, retreat to the 'older, charming' world where they aped aristocratic, country living. By contrast, the 'less fortunate classes were very unlucky indeed in that England' because although they had a level of 'security' that many contemporary workers lacked, this involved 'monstrously long hours of work, miserable wages, and surroundings in which they lived like black-beetles at the back of a disused kitchen stove'.[28]

Moreover, they were meant to be thankful for, and unquestioning of, their conditions, which even their contemporaries living in these areas were not expected to do. Priestley concluded his consideration by attacking those in the 1930s who sought a return to the individualism of the nineteenth century: 'I felt like calling back a few of these sturdy individualists simply to rub their noses in the nasty mess they had made. Who gave them the right to turn this country into their ash-pit?' He continued, 'the more I thought about it, the more this period of England's industrial supremacy began to look like a gigantic dirty trick'. Then making a link with empire, 'at one end of this commercial greatness were a lot of half-starved, bleary-eyed children crawling about among machinery and at the other end were the traders getting natives boozed up with bad gin'. He concluded that 'cynical greed – *Damn you, I'm all right*' lay at the heart of this England. 'You can see as much', he argued, 'written in black letters across half England. Had I just not spent days moving glumly in the shadow of their downstrokes?'[29]

Priestley's anger at the waste of 'Nineteenth Century England' gave way to a more ambivalent reaction to his 'third England', which emerged after World War I. In a perceptive comment that identified one of the emerging traits of the twentieth century, Priestley noted how this England belonged 'far more to the age itself than to this particular island. America, I supposed, was its birthplace'. Most obvious in the South, this was the modern, mass England of the new roads, modernist architecture, bungalows, movies and consumerism. Illustrating why he was neither a nostalgic who rejected the modern nor pro-modern whatever the cost, Priestley suggested that 'care is needed' when considering this England 'for you can easily approve or disapprove of it too hastily'. On the positive side, making a point relevant to his rejection of the British class system, he believed that it was 'essentially democratic' and open to all. 'In this England, for the first time in history Jack and Jill are nearly as good as their master and mistress; they may always have been as good in their own way, but now they are nearly as good in the *same way*'. Blackpool, he argued, showed the way in this regard in earlier times, and now 'modern England is rapidly Blackpooling itself'. Goods and services were now cheap and available to the majority, and outside of the rural areas, young people looked to film and sports stars as heroes, rather than their social 'betters'.[30]

The problem, however, was that the quality he valued in 'Old England' was missing, and this England 'without privilege' 'was a bit too cheap....too much of it is simply a trumpery imitation of something not very good even in the original'. Moreover, there was 'a depressing monotony', a lack of character and individualism, a growing standardization in work and leisure patterns and a lack of genuine involvement and choice. Outside influences 'probably....astute financial gentlemen, backed by the press and their publicity services' were wielding an unwelcome influence on this life, telling people what they should and should not like. 'I cannot help feeling', he wrote, 'that this new England is lacking in character, in zest, in gusto, flavour, bite, drive, originality, and that is a serious weakness' – a deficiency that could open the way for an 'iron autocracy'.[31]

Priestley's discussion of modern England illustrated perfectly the mixed feelings he had about it. For although pointing out the democratic side of mass society, something which he valued, his language is much harder when dealing with the negatives, as the individual and 'originality' also really mattered to him. The extent to which the latter undercut the former is left unsaid, although as time went on, he had more to say on this subject. It is left unsaid because the discussion of these three Englands, which he saw 'variously and most fascinatingly mingled in ever part of the country', was framed within the context of a fog-bound car journey from Norwich to London.[32] This, with its mixture of the personal and political, and the looser discursive structure particularly suited Priestley's style of writing.

His argument builds along a discussion with himself and follows various tributaries along the way, before coming to a set of conclusions. In many ways, this could be seen as representing an example of his supposed 'intuition over intellect' approach in practice, which, as we have seen, represented part of Priestley's self-deprecatory armoury. However, it also represented an interesting dimension of his social criticism, making it accessible and enjoyable to read, while avoiding a rigid framework for the analysis of ideas. This approach often worked in Priestley's favour as his skill as a writer allowed him to build a close connection with the readers, inviting them think, without coming across as doctrinaire or following a party line. This was generally the case with *English Journey*, which presented themes that had been apparent in Priestley's work prior to 1933 and that he would return to long afterwards.

The discussion of different Englands was part of a more general analysis of the state of the nation and the meaning of Englishness in the 1930s. One of the strongest themes within this was 'the England of the dole' and what that meant to the nation. *English Journey* levelled an unflinching eye on the suffering in industrial areas and the human consequences of the Depression. 'We ought to be ashamed of ourselves', he argued, lambasting the lack of planning and thought on this issue and the lack of care for those suffering as a result.[33] One of the most harrowing examples of this was Rusty Lane in West Bromwich. Priestley came across this when he visited the warehouse of a Black Country businessman with whom he had been having lunch, and the shock remained with him: 'I have never seen such a picture of grimy desolation as that street offered me. If you put it, brick by brick, into a novel, people would not accept it, people would condemn you as a caricaturist and talk about Dickens. The whole neighbourhood is mean and squalid, but this particular street seems worst of all'. When some of the children living there threw stones at the roof of the warehouse, Priestley condemned not their behaviour but the environment in which they had grown up. 'They need not to have run away for me, because I could not blame them if they threw stones and smashed very pane of glass for miles'. 'Indeed', he went on, 'nobody can blame them if they grow up to smash everything that can be smashed'.[34]

Similar scenes were described in other parts of the Midlands and the North, where people lived in communities that were poorly planned – 'insects could do better than this', he wrote about Gateshead – and now faced economic hard times.[35] In the Potteries, where trade was difficult, and unemployment increasing, it was 'either work or misery', and a similar fate befell communities in Lancashire, Yorkshire and the North East.[36] Priestley encountered inadequate food, poor housing, a crumbling social infrastructure and widespread poverty and hardship throughout these areas. 'If T. S. Eliot ever wants to write a poem about a real wasteland instead of a metaphysical one', Priestley wrote about the road between Wallsend and North Shields, 'he should come here'.[37]

Priestley was particularly effective at capturing the way poverty frequently drained the humanity out of people and eroded their citizenship. In Jarrow, 'the men wore masks of prisoners of war', while older workers 'felt defeated and somewhat tainted'. [38] In a similar vein, he described how several, particularly poor, ex-servicemen failed to attend a battalion reunion in Bradford – 'they felt their clothes were not good enough'. He continued, 'I do not like to think then how bad their clothes, their whole circumstances, were', contrasting their commitment during the war with their shabby treatment in the years that followed.[39]

Poverty was not simply morally wrong; therefore, it represented a failure to pay back the efforts and commitment of the ordinary people whether in war or otherwise. 'We have marched so far', he argued, 'not unassisted in the past by Lancashire's money and muck, and we have a long long way to go yet, perhaps carrying Lancashire on our backs for a spell'.[40] Focusing on what he saw as one of the causes of the crisis, namely, the City of London, 'which is treated as if it were the very beating red heart of England', he noted that it 'must have got its money from somewhere...it could not have conjured up gold out of Threadneedle Street'. In reality, he argued that this money came from 'that part of England which is much dearer to me...namely, the Industrial North. For generations, this blackened North toiled and moiled so that England could be rich and the City of London be a great power in the world'.[41]

This sense of obligation, which, incidentally, conveniently sidestepped the issue of class, by raising the banner of North versus South, was tied in with Priestley's understanding of what constituted the nation and the meaning of citizenship. 'Was Jarrow still in England or not?' he asked. 'Since when did Lancashire cease to be part of England?' he queried after considering the crisis facing the Lancashire cotton communities, and referring to a family he had met in Blackburn, 'under what flag are little Joyce and Muriel and their parents in that Blackburn street?' Poverty and the lack of concern and planning therefore undermined the citizenship of individuals, and England itself – a situation that was 'unworthy of a great country'.[42]

The City of London was a traditional target for English radicals, and it clearly rankled with Priestley, who echoed populist rhetoric when he depicted the production process as authentic and financial interests as parasitical. 'I distrust this money-lending England', he wrote in 1939, 'and I should like to see it receive such a set-back that the other, the producing England, came to be given another chance'.[43] Its geographic location was also significant in his eyes, beyond the Yorkshireman's mistrust of the capital, because it meant it was too far away to *see* the suffering it was responsible for in the industrial districts, while in contrast, it was 'much too near Westminster: they can hear each other talking'.[44] Priestley believed that the city had been given too much power following World War I and that it had an undue influence on politics, even to the point of individual MPs following their own financial interests as opposed to the nation's.[45] The city also moved outside the national orbit, into the Empire, exploiting abroad, while benefiting the rich and a conservative section of the nation who lived on private incomes and pensions. Priestley believed that latter, many of whom 'were half-alive', acted as a brake on social change and did 'not know or understand England'. Interestingly though, Priestley had not entirely given up on this group who, despite his vigorous criticism, he felt could rediscover their energy and help take the nation forward.[46]

The City of London was also at the heart of changes in the economic structure of the nation aside from the Depression, which encouraged centralization and a more national, business-centred ethos. As we have already seen, Priestley valued the individual, community and region, but these changes worked against all of these factors. After World War I, Priestley believed that 'regional self-sufficiency' and provincial culture came to an end with London assuming a much larger importance for business and social and cultural trends. The press represented one example of this process, and Priestley recalled how his father 'never read' a London newspaper as he had no interest in events in the South.[47] Priestley believed that the local papers knew their readers and offered a 'Fleet Street' in 'Bruddersford', while the real post-war Fleet Street was obsessed with gossip and trivia and helped foist a set of dangerous myths upon the nation.[48] Writing of the popular press in 1928, he accused it of 'throwing more and more limelight upon the silliest and idlest people in the country' and presenting an unrealistic portrait of society.[49] This became one of the central themes of *Wonder Hero*, which presented, through Charlie Hubble's temporary fame in London, a satire of the frivolous nature of the London press and its inability to report on more serious issues facing the nation.

The move away from the local also affected business and ran against Priestley's belief in a localized harmony between employers and workers. On returning to Bradford on his journey around England, he found that the Depression had ended the wool trade as he had known it in his youth, a pattern repeated elsewhere across the Depression-hit areas.[50] As he discovered, changes in the scale and organization of industry shifted ownership and control from locally based families to either absentee owners or shareholders. Priestley disliked this, believing that it contributed to the loss of identity and control of ordinary workers and their classification as economic units. He also felt that the current owners neither understood nor were truly committed to industries or the people who worked in them. This was illustrated in *Wonder Hero* when Hubble's uncle surveys the desolate yards of the closed-down Sturks' engine plant:

> When I first started working there, lad, Old Sturk himself was still on the job. And a hard old devil was, too...(but)...old Sturk would never have seen them works closed down. Any rate he'd have gone down fighting with us. But he'd two sons. They made a limited company out of it. Put a manager in. Then, as far as I can make out, one o' these clever Dicks from London bought it, lock, stock and barrel: and then they pushed the shares up and up until Sturks' five pound shares were fetching five and thirty pounds. And then the slump comes – and bang!

By which time the two sons were wealthy men who 'very likely' put their money in 'war loan and whatnot', and one of them became an M.P. 'Conservative, of course.... Pity we couldn't have sold out, isn't it lad', he concluded, 'but the old man wouldn't have done that. He'd have kept them works going till he bust. Well, that's Sturks. In Memoriam. RIP.'[51]

The fictional decline of Sturks illustrated the themes of Depression, the growing hegemony of London and the increasingly capitalist ethos among a newer generation of business leaders. Priestley's faith that the older Sturk, 'old devil' that he was, would not have let the plant close without a fight presented his belief in a non-class-based set of principles shared by those outside the ruling elite. For Priestley, the longer history of England, and more specifically the contemporary crisis, was related to the influence of this elite, with the City at its heart and the press as its chorus boys, whose interests ran against those of the people. This group had betrayed the hope of a brighter future after World War I and, instead, had tried to take the country back to before 1914. The 'faked financial crisis' of 1931 and the 'bogus' National Government only made things worse, and by the late 1930s, Priestley believed that the country was not a genuine democracy but 'a plutocracy roughly disguised as an aristocracy' where aristocratic values still cast an unhealthy shadow encouraging deference and Priestley's much disliked country house culture.[52] The social pyramid was 'nothing more than a gigantic sham' with an undemocratic constitution, honours bought and sold and power following 'private' rather than public interests.[53] 'All our real Government is done by the Right People', he wrote, 'not only in Parliament…but in all the various positions of authority, in the Civil Service, Finance, the Church, the fighting services…'. Secretive government and the partisan and destructive media encouraged apathy and disinterest among ordinary people and played into the hands of the Tories and the Right.[54]

England could only be saved from this malaise, Priestley argued, through the agency of the people. He believed that, by nature, the English people were creative and decent and that if they could wake up and see through the myths and lies being peddled by the 'Right People', then a new England would be born. Despite 'all our nonsense', he wrote to Edward Davison, 'we have something precious in England – a non-hating, decent spirit – and we must preserve that'.[55] Tolerance, humour, creativity, fairness and independence were all important constituents of this Englishness, channelled through the local, and community. Shakespeare, Dickens, local theatre, the Dales and characters like Mr. W. and Jonathan Priestley were repositories of this spirit.

This Englishness had been under threat for many years. The emotional side of the English had, he suggested, been quashed 150 years earlier by the 'ruling classes' who 'adopted the pretence of being the new Roman stoics…The public schools learnt and taught the trick. The Empire builders carried on and widened the tradition. And now we are seen as an unemotional race'.[56] World War I further illustrated this problem when the actions of the military underlined how 'official England' could be cruel and lacking in tolerance.[57] The inter-war years had then brought things to a head. Part of the reason for the hegemony of the elite's uncaring England lay in the tolerant, private nature of the 'people's' Englishness, which displayed strong moral idealism but was more interested in character than the cut and thrust of politics. 'We are a nation of idealistic simpletons frequently governed and manipulated by cynics', Priestley suggested.[58]

What was needed, therefore, was a creative idea that would wake the people up, reigniting Radical England and taking the country forward.[59] Priestley, who as we have seen, saw himself as a product of, and a spokesperson for, the people, believed that it was his responsibility to help wake the English up: hence his various writings on the subject. *Let the People Sing* is interesting, if rather blunt in this regard, revealing a light, humorous story of such a change. It showed how the people of Dunbury are awakened by a group of enthusiasts seeking to reclaim the town's concert hall for music, turning their back on the local elite's false alternative of a museum, or a showroom for the powerful local business, United Plastics.

That these are metaphors for the different choices facing England is made clear with Priestley offering his third way of energy, creativity and the local community as opposed to ossified aristocratic England or Americanized England. The rebels included the music hall comedian Tommy Tiverton and the perceptive Czech refugee Professor Kronak, both of whom were outsiders in contemporary England but very much central to Priestley's people. Similarly, the spirited Hope Ollerton represented the younger generation, formed by, but partially alienated from, contemporary society but confident and committed enough to challenge the elite. Reprising his belief, aired in *English Journey*, in the potential of members of the younger generation, Hope is described as 'a spirited member of the genuine democracy, now rapidly growing up within the false democracy we are always congratulating ourselves on in England'.[60] The irony was, of course, that *Let the People Sing* first aired on radio the day war was declared, and what was to follow provided a more bloody wake-up call for the people than anyone had imagined.

Priestley also saw this 'decent' Englishness as a force for good in the wider world. Commenting on the Great Depression in the United States, Priestley suggested somewhat unrealistically that 'it was a good thing for humanity', as it would 'end the spell of a mechanical material hog-philosophy'. The solution would come from England and Englishness – 'quality against quantity, men against machines, poetry and fun against dreary materialism'.[61] 'We have led the world, many a time before to-day', he wrote in *English Journey*, 'on good expeditions and bad ones, on piratical raids and on quests for Hesperides. We can lead it again'.[62] Six years later, with the world facing the spectre of fascism, Priestley's faith was undimmed, and he still believed that Englishness could benefit the world. 'We have been – and still are, at heart – a great race', he wrote, arguing that English principles were 'perhaps even more valuable now to the world than they have ever been before'.[63] This went hand-in-hand with an opposition to Empire. 'I wish I had been born early enough to be called a little Englander', he wrote, suggesting that 'Big Englanders' were 'red-faced, staring loud-voiced fellows wanting to go and boss everybody about all over the world'. 'They should pay attention instead to poverty at home', he suggested, 'to the likes of Jarrow, Hebburn and Rusty Lane, West Bromwich'.[64]

As we have already seen, Priestley understood the economic exploitation that tied in with Empire, and he wanted England to influence the world instead through the export of the values he located at the heart of Englishness. Priestley was less critical of the colonial presence, however, when he visited Sudan in 1937. Witness-ing the efforts of the British in the area, he attacked 'other novelists who go jeering round the empire'. 'Instead of a fit of disgust', he wrote, 'all I got was a tennis elbow, the result of trying to keep up, afternoon after afternoon, with so many still young and recent Blues'. He praised the efforts of those he met, 'some excellent specimens of our Race', suggesting that they were more successful than the Indian service, and 'if anybody retorts that they should not be there at all, bossing the blacks, I would advise a brief study of local conditions when the Madhi reigned in Omdurman'.[65]

Priestley's pragmatic response to Sudan did not contradict his broader critique of Empire, as the end result of the British presence, in his eyes, produced a bet-ter outcome for the Sudanese people. The language he used, however, and the assumptions made illustrate the in-built sense of superiority that went hand-in-hand with Priestley's romantic vision of England's role in the world. In this, of course, he was no different to earlier generations of English idealists, from Milton's 'God's Englishmen' through to the nineteenth-century radicals who saw Britain as a force for good in the world, and sought to use British power to this end rather than the 'evil' of Empire.[66]

Time had moved on, however, and Priestley's dreams of England leading the world again came more from the heart than the head. Others, like Priestley's friend and fellow idiosyncratic radical, H. G. Wells, were able to see a more com-plicated and divided world. Wells, for all his idealistic blueprints, understood the significance of the United States and accepted that it could play a role in a pro-gressive new world order.[67] Priestley was also out of step with many on the Left for most of the inter-war years, as the latter were suspicious of patriotism and radical nationalism, linking it with jingoism, and the rising tide of fascism. Their pacifism, however, was to prove no more appropriate in such troubled times, and the Left became more appreciative of the language of national identity when faced with the prospect and then actuality of war with Fascism. [68]

Priestley's use of the word "Race" might also imply that racial superiority played a role in his judgements. However, he used the word in a descriptive sense, usually when referring to the English, and did not imply a clear superiority based on skin colour. Indeed, Priestley was, for his time, relatively progressive in his approach to different racial groups, relating it to the tolerance he believed lay at the heart of Englishness. Part of his love for pre-war Bradford came from the cultural mix caused by international connections of the wool trade and the German-Jewish liberals who 'acted as a leaven' when they settled in the city. 'They were so much part of the place when I was a boy', he wrote, 'that it never occurred to me to ask why they were there'. He also praised their influence in helping make pre-war Bradford an exciting and vibrant place to live, 'determinedly Yorkshire and pro-vincial, yet some of its suburbs reached as far as Frankfurt and Leipzig. It was odd enough, but it worked'.[69]

As the 1930s progressed, Priestley wrote in defence of the Jewish community, concerned by the rising tide of anti-semitism.[70] However, there were qualifications in his defence. While attacking the stereotypes put forward by anti-semites and pointing out the diversity of the Jewish community, he did suggest that there was a 'Jewish Problem' with regard to whether the community assimilated or not. 'The problem will never be settled until the Jew decides either to move further away or to come nearer'.[71] Seeing himself as a decent and tolerant Englishman, he was also touchy when accused of unflattering references to Jewish characters in the novel *Angel Pavement*. Replying to Mrs. H. Laski, who raised this issue, he complained that 'I have no prejudice whatever against Jews. I know and admire many people of your race', arguing that no one complained when he satirized characters who represented 'types of Englishness' and that he was not responsible for the opinions of his characters. He asked in conclusion whether 'you are not too sensitive about this'.[72]

This allegation rankled with him so much that he mentioned it 5 years later in another generally supportive article 'The Jew Business', leading him to suggest that 'many Jewish people, are unduly sensitive, find slights, insults, anti-semitic prejudice where they do not exist'.[73] Ironically, Priestley probably committed the greater error by projecting his personal pique at being criticized onto the whole Jewish community, as there was some justification in his original defence of the book. *Angel Pavement* has few references to Jewish characters, and although those that are there lack subtlety, and border on stereotypes, within the context of the novel, which takes a satirical, Dickensian approach to character, and the climate of the 1930s, they are not noticeably anti-semitic.[74]

Priestley's tolerance also extended to other ethnic groups. He was intrigued, for example, by the 'wonderfully mixed' race children he found in a Liverpool school, speculating that he had probably seen 'a glimpse of the world of 2433, by which time the various root races, now all members of a great world state, may have largely inter-married and inter-bred'.[75] Likewise, he commented how, in the same city, the Chinese community had declined due to poor trading conditions and 'too much interference' in their cultural pursuits. 'After all', he wrote with intended irony, 'I suppose if our countrymen who carry the white man's burden in the East suddenly found themselves prevented from indulging in sport, meeting in clubs, and drinking gin and whisky, they would not linger long in exile'.[76]

Given the generally compassionate and tolerant tone in Priestley's writing, especially in *English Journey*, it is somewhat surprising that shortly after writing these comments on mixed race children, and the Chinese, he launched into a bitter denunciation of Liverpool's Irish community. 'A great many speeches have been made and books written on the subject of what England has done to Ireland', he wrote, and 'I should be interested to hear a speech and read a book or two on the subject of what Ireland has done to England'. He continued, 'if we do have an Irish Republic as our neighbour, and it is found possible to return her exiled citizens, what a grand clearance there will be in all the western ports, from the Clyde to Cardiff, what a fine exit of ignorance and dirt and drunkenness and disease'. The argument carried on in a similar manner, digging at the Irish Republic and criticizing the failure of the Irish in England to try and improve their lot. 'The English of this class generally make some attempt to live as decently as they can under these conditions', but the Irish 'have settled in the nearest poor quarter and turned it into a slum, or finding a slum have promptly settled down to out-slum it'.[77]

Such views were not, of course, uncommon at the time, and Priestley's view linking what he believed was the arrogance of the Irish Republic with the attitude of the Irish in Liverpool would have been shared by some of his readers. However, given his ability to see the humanity of individuals mired in poverty and to turn his guns on those he held responsible for such conditions, they reveal an inconsistency in his approach. This was not the tolerant, decent Englishness that illuminated the vast majority of his writing.

With the exception of his comments on the Irish in Liverpool, Priestley's Englishness was an idealistic, romantic and sometimes inconsistent vision of possibility in a world busy tearing itself apart. In international terms, this could be problematic, inflating the power and reach of England to a point where it was boxing far above its weight, in a world where more determined and powerful alternatives were hogging the limelight. As a set of intellectual ideas, it also cherry-picked the parts of the English tradition that fitted with the liberal, democratic philosophy that lay at the heart of Priestley's thought. Of course, it was not unusual in this regard, as all nationalisms are creative or destructive acts of selective memory and argument, whether taken up by radicals or conservatives. That, after all, was one of the reasons why many on the British Left had difficulties with radical nationalism in the difficult terrain of the inter-war years. However, Priestley was more perceptive than that, and like radicals across the Atlantic and his counterparts in Britain like Wells and Orwell, he understood that national identities mattered to people and that ordinary, democratic voices needed to contest the ruling elite's version of the national story.

Priestley's liberal socialism drew on his Bradford roots, and the radical nationalism of the nineteenth century, and was mixed with a large measure of pragmatism. He was not a philosopher, or a political scientist, and generally eschewed detailed political programmes, preferring to emphasize spirit, character and the potential of the people. This may have lacked polish and been inconsistent, but it offered an explanation for Britain's problems and had faith in the agency of ordinary people – the likes of Mr. W., his father, Tommy Tiverton and Hope Ollerton – and that, at a time of oppression, economic suffering and emerging slaughter, had considerable merit. The problem, however, was that Priestley's people, like his Englishness, was an act of observation and imagination, and it assumed a level of unity and common purpose that would only be apparent, in his eyes, during wartime. In the longer term, Priestley was destined to be disillusioned, and 'the dusty arterial road of cheap mass production and standardized living' carried the British nation to a different destination.

3

Priestley, the 'People' and the Second World War

When Priestley read the first instalment of *Let the People Sing* on BBC Radio on 3 September 1939, the day war was declared, he may have hoped, but could hardly have expected the turn that his life was about to take. For within a few months Priestley was to move from being a moderately famous writer to a position where, via the Radio Postscripts, he was considered by some to be second only to Churchill in the public's mind. As one historian would later put it, he was 'in many ways *the* voice of the 1940s'.[1] Priestley not only slipped comfortably into this role, but did so at a time when he believed that the British people had received the wake-up call he had long argued they needed, and would go on, with his and others encouragement, to build a New England. As he put it in May 1945 'in the magnificent summer of 1940... I think I felt better than ever before or since. We lived at last in a community with a noble common purpose, and the experience was not only novel but exhilarating'.[2] However, this optimism was not to last, as life did not imitate the learning processes and happy finale of *Let the People Sing*. His influence lessened, and the long, hard experience of war led to a change in the public mood. Unbowed Priestley wrote furiously and spoke across the country, vigorously arguing in favour of reform and encouraging the people to become active in shaping their own future. However, his part romantic, part pragmatic approach to politics left him, by 1945, with doubts as to whether the new order he dreamed of would emerge, and the English nation would learn to sing with a unified, radical voice.

Priestley's belief in the steadfast spirit of the people, and his own role as their tribune, seemed to be confirmed on the outbreak of war. He volunteered to work for the Ministry of Information, and was soon given the task of travelling 'up and down the country as a kind of super-reporter of the new wartime England'. The articles were to be published in the *News Chronicle* and then, he hoped, syndicated around the world. Priestley felt impelled to carry out this task because he wanted to provide a 'human picture of what is happening' rather than 'the rather depressing stuff' currently provided by the Ministry and the BBC. He conceded to Walpole that this task would be 'a financial smack in the mouth', as it interrupted his normal work routine at a time when the theatre and book trade was in a state of confusion.[3]

Given his disdain for the 'Right People' who he believed occupied the positions of power within the nation, it was not surprising that before long Priestley became frustrated with his role. Less than a month after telling Walpole of his plans, he wrote to Edward Davison suggesting that he 'may soon cut short the tour.' He complained that the Ministry of Information was 'extremely badly organised' and lacked an effective control of the presentation of the war to the public. 'Deep down', he wrote, 'they have the mandarin's contempt for the general public.' He contrasted this with his own position: 'in any other country than this', he argued, 'a man of my experience and knowledge of the English public mind would at least have been consulted at some time or other, but neither I nor any other author has been asked.' Instead 'they turn these matters over to lawyers, Treasury officials and the like.' Interestingly, Priestley added a handwritten footnote to the typed letter, in which he suggested that he was aware that the above comment 'sounds pompous and conceited', but 'I don't mean it that way. Took myself as nearest example.'[4]

In the same letter Priestley also told Davison, who was anxiously watching events unfold from across the Atlantic that, just over a month since war was declared, the country was largely united and sober about the future. 'The whole atmosphere is quite different from 1914', he wrote, 'no jingoism, no flag-waving, no bands, none of that hysterical Bank holiday feeling.' He added 'this is a clear refutation that human nature doesn't change, for I never saw such a change.' The 'tiresome restrictions' of wartime had been tolerated, but were now beginning to be resented in the uneasy calm that prevailed. However, he argued 'fifty bombs would clear all those grumbles away'. Still alluding to a people who were awaiting their call onto the historical stage, he told Davison 'this war puts us all on desert islands, upon which, at six thirty, total darkness descends. But a bit of darkness won't do us any harm. Perhaps we can find ourselves in it.'[5]

Priestley's involvement in the civilian side of the war effort obviously placed pressure on his usual work pattern. By January 1940, he had already travelled 3,000 miles for the MOI, and was planning work on a propaganda film, plays, as well as keeping an eye on his recent publications and theatre performances — Music at Night, for example, was the first play to open in London after war was declared, when it started a run at the Westminster Theatre. It was clear to Priestley, however, that it would be impossible for him to concentrate on his own work in his usual manner whilst the war was in progress. He wrote, 'it takes twice as much effort to do the work now, like running a car on two or three cylinders instead of six. One part of one's mind is permanently occupied by queries and anxieties about the world's madhouse.'[6] By the end of April, a novel set in the preceding ten years and dealing with the experiences of an actor was shelved after 30,000 words. Although Priestley suggested the potential audience was a problem, he admitted that 'at a time like this the choice of subject is very difficult'.[7] Under such circumstances Priestley's concern over the conflict, and his desire to contribute to a successful prosecution of the war effort and reconstruction, led to official publications, including *British Women Go to War* (1943) and *Manpower* (1944), various journalism, political interventions including *Out of the People* (1941) and *Here are Your Answers* (1944), five plays and three novels. The novels *Black-Out in Gretley* (1942), *Daylight on Saturday* (1943) and *Three Men in New Suits* (1945) were all set in, and directly concerned with, the war, whilst of the plays, *Desert Highway* (1944) was produced for the Army Bureau of Current Affairs, *How are they at Home?* (1945) for ENSA and *They Came to a City* (1944), an examination of utopian ideas, an intervention in the political debates ensuing during the conflict. Alongside these print publications, Priestley also found the time for radio broadcasts, work on several propaganda films and documentaries, including 'Britain at Bay' (1940), a five-minute documentary for the GPO film unit, 'For Our Russian Allies' (1941) and 'The Foreman went to France' (1941).[8] It was only towards the end of the war that Priestley was able to return effectively to writing which had a different focus.[9]

Priestley's contribution during wartime was accompanied from the outset by a belief that the conflict should act as a 'bridge' to a better future. This argument became most apparent in the 'Postscripts' and later writings, however as early as November 1939 he remarked, reprising his rather ambitious dismissal of American power and influence, that he 'would like to see Western Europe step out of this war morass, federate itself on a decent democratic basis, and then produce a civilization that made America look like a rusty Ford car.'[10] With more specific regard to Britain, he explained in early 1940 that 'many of us feel here that the testing time will come just after the war...I anticipate great social change here, much greater than after the last war.' His faith in the potential of the British middle class to institute change was underlined by his belief that 'the professional and technical classes should have a great chance to assert themselves, and under modern conditions it is more and more they who run a highly organised country.' The destination, he argued, should be 'a liberal socialism, of the type toward which the Scandinavian countries have been moving.' This was all straightforward enough, however, Priestley cited 'long-continued and murderously high taxation' as one of the factors leading to social change.[11] Given that socialist programmes, Scandinavian or otherwise, rarely advocated or practised reductions in taxation, this subject was more the territory of the political Right. For Priestley, however, tax had always been a bugbear, and would become something of an obsession in the years following the war, however inconsistent it may have been with his belief in liberal socialism.[12]

By the summer of 1940, the fall of France, the accompanying evacuation from Dunkirk and by July, the start of the Battle of Britain had changed everything. Britain now stood alone, facing a more powerful adversary and the possibility of a bloody and irretrievable defeat. It was appropriate that in that tense and remarkable period Priestley succeeded in becoming the voice of the people. His non-elite Yorkshire accent, his down-to-earth approach to language and life, and his ability to conjure the dramatic and inspirational out of the ordinary all struck the right note at the right time; as did his thinking on England and Englishness that had been fashioned in the previous decade, and was now presented to a nation whom Priestley believed had woken from the apathy and demoralisation of the interwar years. When the BBC were looking for a speaker to enliven their Postscripts to the Sunday evening Nine O'clock news, which were designed to coun-ter Lord Haw-Haw's (William Joyce) broadcasts from Hamburg, Priestley fitted the bill. The first broadcaster on the Postscripts, in March 1940, the eminent lawyer Maurice Healy, had been a limited success and the BBC were looking for someone with a more popular touch. They turned to Priestley who was keen to work in the medium of radio, and was already proving himself an adept broadcaster to an overseas audience, most recently on the 'Britain Speaks' programme transmitted at the end of May to the US, Canada, Australia, New Zealand, South Africa and India among others.[13] The first of these proved a great success, portraying the resilience of the ordinary people, ('the temper of the ordinary easy-going English folk is rising. Any attempt at invasion will only send it up a few more degrees. I haven't met anyone yet who's particularly worried about it, ') and the way the war represented a battle between an imperfect but civilized world, and the 'other kind of life, which has spread like a foul stain over half Europe, (and) is simply evil'.[14]

Six days later, on 5 June 1940, and the day after Churchill made his defiant 'we shall fight on the beaches' speech in Parliament,[15] Priestley made his first post-script broadcast to the domestic audience. It presented a perfectly pitched analysis of the recent evacuation from Dunkirk, to a public shocked by the fall of France but drawing strength from the nature of the rescue of over 350,000 people. 'What strikes me about it is how typically English it is', Priestley told them, 'both in its beginning and its end, its folly and its grandeur.' Against the 'vast machine' of the enemy, which 'has no soul', the British succeeded thanks in part to the decidedly non-efficient, non-machine-like or soulless 'little pleasure-steamers' that previ-ously plied the holiday trade. 'We've known them and laughed at them, these fussy little steamers, all our lives', but 'these "Brighton Belles" and "Brighton Queens", left that innocent, foolish world of theirs – to sail into the inferno, to defy bombs, shells, magnetic mines, torpedoes, machine-gun fire – to rescue our soldiers.'

Mentioning the 'Gracie Fields' which he knew well from the Isle of Wight ser-vice, and was lost in the battle, he spoke of how 'never again will we board her at Cowes and go down into her dining saloon for a fine bacon and eggs.' However, 'this little steamer...is immortal. She'll go sailing proudly down the years in the epic of Dunkirk.' He concluded, 'and our great grand-children, when they learn how we began this war by snatching glory out of defeat, and then swept on to victory, may also learn how little holiday steamers made an excursion to hell and came back glorious.'[16] This evocation of a national context, the contrast between the everyday and the horror of war, the way the ordinary could defeat a more powerful opponent, and the suggestion of an ongoing history all struck a chord in the audience of the summer of 1940. The 'little boats' would become entwined with the memory of Dunkirk, and also acted as a metaphor for the nation itself and the emerging struggle. Priestley, along with Churchill, had played his part in the construction of the 'Dunkirk Spirit'.

Another postscript followed on Sunday 9 June, and they continued at weekly intervals until Sunday 20 October (with the exception of week's break in mid-August). These broadcasts followed a similar format, and explored some of the same themes. The second broadcast, for example, offered a paean to the beauty and continuity of the English springtime, before contrasting it with the violent disruption of wartime. 'I had to remind myself that the peaceful and lovely scene before me was the real truth; that it was there long before the Germans went mad, and will be there when that madness is only remembered as on old nightmare.'[17] A quotation from Tennyson followed, whilst Hardy concluded the third postscript, which described a night on the watch with characters representing 'a good cross-section of English rural life'. Continuity again, and Priestley's belief in community as opposed to the 'black hearts' of the Nazis are emphasized: 'I felt too up there a powerful and rewarding sense of community: and with it too a feeling of deep continuity. There we were, ploughman and parson, shepherd and clerk, turning out at night, as our forefathers has often done before us, to keep watch and ward over the sleeping English hills and fields and homesteads.'[18] In many ways these postscripts invoked the classic images of 'Deep England', and may explain why Priestley is sometimes seen as a writer in that mould.

However, we have to recall that Priestley was an imaginative writer, providing a morale-boosting message to a nation at war, and the use of ruralism offered a comforting story and message about continuity. As we have already seen, Priestley himself had a more complex view of England, and, indeed, repeated in a later postscript his definition of himself as a townsman who loved the country.[19] As the postscripts went on, the rural images lessened, and the other Englands came into view.

The evil of Nazism was a regular theme in the broadcasts, but Priestley made it clear that it was the philosophy and its supporters, rather than Germany itself, that was the problem. On 23 June 1940, he told listeners that he had always believed that the Nazis were 'evil' and that 'we must destroy them or they would destroy us', as 'they emerged from the underworld'. The root of this evil was not solely German, but the 'growing corruption, the darkening despair of our modern world, shaping it into one vast dark face – a German dark face that would call to other dark faces elsewhere'. 'Every nation has two faces', he told his audience, recounting his own experiences and love of German music and philosophy, but, 'the bright face has gone, and in its place was the vast dark face with its broken promises and endless deceit'. The presence of fifth columnists in Britain and elsewhere were no surprise therefore, as Nazism was 'an attitude of mind' belonging to those 'who can't find their way out of their adolescence, who remain overgrown, tormenting, cruel schoolboys'.[20] In a similar vein, on 4 August 1940, he told listeners that 'this isn't 1914. It isn't simply a question of Germans fighting for Germany and Britons for Britain...reduced to its simplest, but profoundest, terms, this is a war between despair and hope.' The Nazis he added came 'like their vile creed from an underworld of despair and hate'.[21]

Priestley was by no means alone in seeing the war as an historic and fundamental battle between two civilizations – one evil, and the other good, if not perfect – however, he drew a number of radical lessons from the situation.[22] These first made an appearance in the postscripts at the end of June 1940, and were a consistent message in the broadcasts that followed. He argued repeatedly that the conflict could only be won with the full involvement of the ordinary people, the practice of democratic methods and the subsequent unleashing of the English spirit. Moreover, he gave full voice to his belief that the war had arisen due to the failures of the interwar years, and that there could be no going back to the old ways. The only way forward was to a new Britain and a new World.

In this vein on 30 June 1940, stressing his own credentials as a voice of the people, he told listeners that, 'sometimes I feel that you and I – all us ordinary people – are on one side of a high fence, and on the other side of the fence under a buzzing cloud of secretaries are the official and important personages... and now and then a head appears above the fence and tells us to carry our gas masks, look to our blackouts, do this and attend to that.' These officials had 'their place in the wartime scheme of things', but they did not appreciate the potential of the people, and were in danger of 'creating a rather thick, woolly, dreary atmosphere in which that national character of ours couldn't flourish and express itself properly'. Instead, giving full voice to his romantic faith in the English spirit, re-attuned to the atmosphere of wartime, Priestley sang the praises of the people, declaring that since the Blitz had begun the 'fog and whispering figures' of the early months of the conflict were disappearing and 'through the fading mists there emerge the simple, kindly, humorous, brave faces of the ordinary British folk.' A people charged with a momentous task: 'On them, on us, on all of you listening to me now, there rests the responsibility of manning this last great defence of our liberal civilisation.' Posterity would again judge them kindly, for whatever the 'past follies' or 'weaknesses', 'here and now, as the spirit of the people rises to meet the challenge, I believe that it will find no flaw in the sense, courage and endurance of those people.'[23]

Priestley returned again and again to the virtues of the ordinary people who he believed had now found themselves. A year on from the start of the war he recalled how on the outbreak of war the previous September, he had travelled to London to broadcast the first chapter of *Let the People Sing*. He told listeners that whilst no-one at that point realized that Britain would soon stand alone against the Nazis, 'there was something that wasn't unforeseen', for he had 'already written it down, and it has all come gloriously true'; namely that 'the true heroes and heroines of this war, whose patience and good humour stand like a rock above the dark morass of treachery, cowardice and panic, are the ordinary British folk.' Again stressing the close relationship that had developed between broadcaster and audience, he told them 'talk about giving courage and confidence – you've given me more than I could ever give you; not only courage and confidence in the outcome of this war, but also faith in what we can all achieve after this war.'[24]

In total war, the dividing line between civilian and military no longer held, and the people, now 'soldier–civilians' had discovered a common strength and purpose.[25] And London, the city which the Yorkshireman had never really liked, currently lay at the heart of this resolve. 'A lot of us, especially if we are from the North' he announced had thought Londoners 'too gullible, easily pleased, too soft'. Yet they had been proved wrong, and he admitted having 'come to love London', for the tragic beauty of fire-lit nightscape; 'the other night, when a few fires were burning so fiercely, that half the sky was aglow, and the tall terraces around Portland Place were like pink palaces in the Arabian nights, I saw the Dome and Cross of St. Paul's, silhouetted in sharpest black against the red flames and orange fumes'. And from 'the roaring centre of this battlefield' had sprung forth 'the strangest army the world has ever seen, an army in drab civilian clothes, doing quite ordinary things, an army of all shapes and sizes and ages of folk, but nevertheless a real army, upon whose continuing high and defiant spirit the world's future now depends.'[26]

The need to use the war as a stepping stone to a more radical future was repeated with equal vigour. Using both metaphor and more literal arguments Priestley sought to provide an ideology and purpose for this awakened army. On 14 July 1940, for example, he described a recent visit to wartime Margate, where he found the trappings of war on the outskirts but a largely deserted seafront. Gone were the 'hundreds of thousands of holiday-makers, of entertainers and hawkers, and boatmen', he told listeners, 'as if an evil magician had whisked everybody way'. In its place was an atmosphere 'unreal and spectral', largely silent with little activity where even an 'elderly postman on a bicycle may have been real or yet another apparition'. Recalling a visit to Margate 10 years earlier he asked 'had that been a dream? - or was this strange silent afternoon a dream? It seemed impossible they could both be real.' Had the evil magician 'muttered an enchanted phrase' and conjured up a wind 'from Hell' that had 'blown away' the old Margate? Continuing in this surreal vein, Priestley told listeners that if a 'better' magician offered him the chance to go back to the Margate of a year ago, he would 'want no such miracle'. Instead he would ask the magician to 'move our minds and hearts towards steadfast courage and faith and hope' in the knowledge that something better lay in the future. Reiterating this point in more direct terms, he continued:

> I say to all of you who are listening, for in your common will there is an even mightier magician: This Margate I saw was saddening and hateful; but its new silence and desolation should be thought of as a bridge leading us to a better Margate in a better England, in a nobler world. We're not fighting to restore the past; it was the past that brought us to this heavy hour; but we *are* fighting to rid ourselves and the world of the evil encumbrance of these Nazis so that we can plan and create a nobler future for all our species.[27]

The following week Priestley provided a more straightforward version of this message. After describing a frustrating meeting with an 'official', he explained that 'there are two ways of looking at this war'. The first, the 'official' line, was that the war was 'a terrible interruption' and that once the Nazis were defeated the nation could 'go back to where we started from, the day before the war was declared'. From Priestley's standpoint, however, this wasn't an option as there wasn't 'real peace' even before the conflict. 'If you go back to the sort of world that produces Hitlers and Mussolinis, then no sooner have you got rid of one lot of Hitlers and Mussolinis then another lot will pop up somewhere, and there'll be more wars'. Moreover, this must be a world that prioritizes creativity rather than power, and favours community over property.

Making a clear, socialist point, Priestley argued 'property is that old-fashioned way of thinking of a country as a thing, and a collection of things on that thing, all owned by certain people and constituting property, ' as opposed to seeing the nation as 'a living society, and considering the welfare of that society, the community itself, as the first test'.[28] In support of this, he cited the example of a house nearby to where he lived which stood empty, as its owner had gone to America. He argued that 'according to the property view' it was acceptable to 'fight to protect this absentee owner's property'. However from the 'community view this is all wrong', and the house should be used for billeting or similar.[29] And he believed that the tide was moving in the direction of this 'community view' due to the 'huge collective effort' involved in prosecuting the war. 'We're all in the same boat' he told them, and 'that boat can serve not only as our defence against Nazi aggression, but as an ark in which we can finally land in a better world'. Building on this theme he suggested 'I tell you, there is stirring in us now, a desire which could soon become a controlled but passionate determination to remodel and recreate this life of ours, to make a glorious beginning of a new world order'.[30]

Priestley also related this argument to the betrayal of expectations that had occurred after the last war (an argument that he had presented so forcibly in *Rain Upon Godshill*.) Writing of the commitment and bravery of a young bomber pilot and his wife, Priestley asked how the nation would repay their sacrifices. Recalling 1918, he told listeners 'I will tell you what we did for such young men and their young wives at the end of the last war. We did nothing-except let them take their chance in a world in which every gangster and trickster and stupid insensitive fool or rogue was let loose to do his damnedest.' After this war, Priestley argued the nation had a responsibility to prepare 'a world really fit for their kind'. He also suggested that the servicemen themselves had been introduced to co-operation during the conflict, and they would find it hard to return to old competitive ways. He cited the letter of a correspondent in support of this. The latter told him that his son, now serving in the RAF, had been a salesman before the war, but now having experienced the 'give' rather than 'get' of the RAF, he could never go back to 'that life that I call the survival of the slickest'.[31]

The theme of community and co-operation versus property and competition became more focused in the final postscripts. On Sunday 22 September, having praised the role of women during the war, and pointed out the male role in both 'high finance and big business', and the Fascist regimes, Priestley criticized certain middle class women 'with any amount of room to spare' were reluctant to take in evacuees.[32] This was part of the pre-war world, he suggested, 'a world of cold narrow minds, of greed, privilege and love of power', when the war was about putting 'an end once and for all to that world, and to bring into existence an order of society in which nobody will have far too many rooms in a house and nobody have far too few.'[33]

Two weeks later he returned to this subject, when discussing the way hotels in pleasant rural and semi-rural areas were filled with the better off, who had fled from the effects of the war. Priestley noted that he had not seen many poorer families from 'badly bombed areas' put in 'nice, quiet rooms in pretty places where they might quickly recover from recent shocks'. Indeed some of them had 'been regarded as a nuisance'. Priestley suggested that this discrepancy suggested that 'for all our grand, vague talk we are at present floundering between two stools', one of which was 'our old acquaintance labelled "Every man for himself, and the devil take the hindmost", which can't really represent us or else why should young men. . ..tear up and down the sky in their Spitfires to protect us, or why should our whole community pledge itself to fight until Europe is freed.' He continued, summoning up all his radical fire, 'the other stool, on which millions are already perched without knowing it, has some lettering round it that hints that free men could combine, without losing what's essential to their free development, to see that each gives according to his ability, and receives according to his need.' He suggested

this was a statement that might have come from the merest and mildest sermon, used to shock our fathers and grandfathers, but we-who've seen a thousand things that would have shocked them still more, who've seen all hell let loose because men refuse to think properly and feel decently, are now being hammered into sterner stuff, and may even consider, before we've done, letting Sunday's sentiments spill over into Monday's arrangements, and acting out a mild sermon or two; and so prove that not only when we say we'll fight, we'll fight–which we have already done to the great astonishment of the Nazi leaders– but also that what we say we are fighting for is the very thing for which we are fighting; that here, at least, is no mere propaganda but the blazing truth of the mind and heart.[34]

This was, quite literally, fighting talk, and the 'each gives according' statement was drawn from Marx, although Priestley cleverly illustrates its link to the radical Christian thought of his youth. And it was in this sense that it was meant, as Priestley was no communist and the broader argument, with its emphasis upon 'free development' and the 'blazing truth of mind and heart', was classic Priestley radicalism. This, as we have seen, involved taking an everyday incident as a starting point, before jumping to an idealistic vision of the possibility of national and international change, and even a change in human nature.

We must remember that Priestley was trying to enthuse and encourage an audience suffering the consequences of total war. This was not the place to present detailed blue prints for social change. Indeed he told listeners in one broadcast that critics who told him to provide more detailed plans for change were 'clean forgetting, of course, that my job is here to provide a seven-minute postscript...not to give a four-hour lecture on all possible political, economic, and social developments.'[35] However, if we recall Priestley's writing from before the war, he was always more comfortable with the grand romantic statement, than the detailed analysis of ideas – something which he would try to address, but not really overcome in his writings during the remainder of the war.

It should also be added that the passion of the later postscripts might have been influenced by concern that the popular mood was beginning to dissolve. Although Priestley cited tiredness and the strain of broadcasting as a reason for curtailing his broadcasts, he also explained in the final postscript of 20 October 1940 that they had shared the 'high mood' of summer as the nation resisted the Nazis, but that they 'were now entering a new period', and that they needed a new 'postscripter', someone 'who feels the same exultation about this period that I did about the earlier one'. He went on, 'the high generous mood, so far as it affects our destinies here, is vanishing with the leaves. It as if the poets had gone and the politicians were coming back.'[36] In plainer language he told A.D. Peters the following month that 'the Tories are hardening again' and 'public morale is going down with a bang'.[37]

By the time the first, and main, series of postscripts finished, they had proved to be 'something of a national sensation'. They attracted a remarkable share of the audience, averaging 31 percent of the adult population. Nor was this simply passive listening, with 'bulging postbags' of mail arriving at the BBC. The press were similarly supportive early on with even the *Daily Mail* singing Priestley's praises.[38] Friends, fellow writers and political figures also wrote to convey their regard for the 'postscripts' and 'Britain speaks' broadcasts. Storm Jameson, for example wrote in June 1940 that 'these broadcasts are the best, far and away the best, the most heartening, the most English of any that are being given.'[39] In a similar vein, Lord Kennet also wrote 'thank God that all I love in my land is still alive, that its survival is certain, proved by your voice and its splendid utterance.'[40] Ernest Bevin, Minister of Labour, thanked Priestley for an overseas broadcast telling him 'No one can do this more effectively than you',[41] whilst Edward Davison commented on a more personal note that hearing one of Priestley's talks left him 'with tears' in his eyes.[42] A less emotional response came from George Bernard Shaw who, in typically idiosyncratic style, told Priestley that 'the broadcasts are a fearful waste of your time, but they are very enjoyable.'[43]

The popularity of the postscripts continued, although Priestley's forays into politics led somewhat inevitably to a rising tide of criticism from those on the political right, and unease amongst some in the BBC. Former Chairman of the Conservative Party, Lord Davison and Colonel Scorgie of the Ministry of Information were two prominent critics who complained about the political messages in the 'postscripts', and the BBC Director of Talks, Sir Richard Maconachie questioned whether Priestley's popularity was healthy, citing the example of the populist Father Coughlin in the United States.[44]

Always sensitive to criticism, Priestley used the postscripts to answer such complaints. In the final broadcast, adding to his reasons for withdrawing from the series, he complained 'stupid persons have frequently accused me in public of – I use their own words – taking advantage of my position to bring party politics into my talks.' He claimed this was 'ironic' he was 'not a member of any political party', nor did he have any close connections with any party, whereas 'it is obvious that these critics of mine are members of a political party'. He continued 'it's not I, but they, who put party before country', and all he had asked for was the war effort to be 'really democratic.'[45] His frustration with those in authority was confirmed in a private letter to Hugh Walpole, whom he told 'I seem to be out of touch with everybody but the great British Public for weeks and weeks.'[46]

Priestley's broadcasts were bound to be controversial. The very thing that made him popular with the audience, including his empathy, passion and down-to-earth radicalism, were always going to lead him, in the tense wartime atmosphere, to ruffle political feathers; after all that was what he had been doing for much of the 1930s. This should hardly have surprised anyone at the BBC, or in the Conservative party. Similarly, given Priestley's critique of those in authority, and his profound dislike of the Tories, he could hardly expect anything but retaliation on their part, particularly as his broadcasts exposed the ongoing struggle between, in his words, the values of the 'community view' and 'property view'.

Nor was Priestley quite as non-partisan as he suggested. He was not a member of any political party in 1940/1941, but he was to become involved in the 1941 Committee and later, briefly, Commonwealth, and his politics had always over- lapped with the Labour Party. Indeed writing to Harold Laski in December 1940, he complained that the Tories were playing the 'old game' at the BBC 'i.e. pretend- ing that everything on their side is non-political and not tendentious, but that anything on *our* (my italics) side must be barred because it is political and tenden- tious.' He continued, 'as a broadcaster I cannot help feeling in the position of a man who has powerful official enemies, but no official friends, and here I blame the Labour members, whose point of view I have put over.'[47]

Given Priestley's anger at the Tories and their influence upon, and within, the BBC, it was hardly surprising that that there was renewed discord, when seeking to restore the popular touch to the 'postscripts', the BBC asked him to return to the series in January 1941.[48] These broadcasts were again popular with listeners, but they encouraged further attacks from those on the right, and even brought a complaint from Churchill, before coming to an end amidst much acrimony after eight 'postscripts'.[49] Priestley claimed that he 'was asked to stop . . .although listen- ing figures had gone soaring up' because 'I offended too many influential reac- tionaries'.[50] Similarly he told Walpole that he was told to end the broadcasts 'with much inartistic lying on the part of Duff Cooper and the BBC'. He added that he had refused their offer of further broadcasts on the overseas service due to the 'damned impudence' of wanting him 'to say to the Americans, Germans, Swedes, anybody, what I am not allowed to say to the English'.[51]

Looking back on the postscripts over 20 years later, Priestley still held to this position, recalling being 'taken off the air' and receiving two letters 'one was from the Ministry of Information, telling me that the BBC was responsible for the deci- sion to take me off the air, and the other was from the BBC, saying that a directive had come from the Ministry of Information to end my broadcasts.'[52] It appears that the final decision was actually taken by Minister of Information, Duff Coo- per, although it's not clear whether Churchill played any role in the process.[53]

The postscripts also ended amidst an ongoing dispute between Priestley, the BBC and Duff Cooper over exactly how many broadcasts he was expected to give, with some at the BBC, who found Priestley 'difficult', being less supportive about con- tinuing the broadcasts.[54] This point has been taken up by the historian Sian Nicho- las, who has suggested that Priestley was arrogant in his dealings with the BBC, threatened the organization's desire for 'impartiality' and 'anonymity', and through his frequent appearances on radio, represented a disquieting 'monopolization of "prime time"' broadcasting – something that was 'unprecedented in peace or war'. He was guilty she concludes of 'a bad case of microphonitis'.[55]

The title of the paper was taken from a quote about Priestley, made by Harold Nicolson in October 1940, describing him as a 'Sly Demagogue'.[56] It is true, that

Priestley could be arrogant, believing as he did that he was the voice of the English people, and that he could be awkward and over-sensitive. However, the last two factors were hardly unusual traits amongst artists and intellectuals who came into contact with the BBC, and those were hardly relaxing times. Priestley was sometimes working 18-hour days on various war-related projects in difficult circumstances, and attempting to live, like other Londoners, amidst the blitz.[57] The latter was illustrated in the starkest terms for Priestley when, on 16 September 1940, he narrowly avoided being killed when his room at the Langham Hotel was hit by a bomb.[58]

There may also have been less tolerance of Priestley because he was an outsider. His ordinary Yorkshire roots would have sat uneasily with an overwhelmingly public school educated, southern, upper middle-class elite at the BBC (it was this ordinariness of course which struck a chord with the public). There was also the fact that Priestley was seen as a popular writer, rather than an intellectual heavyweight. This certainly went for Duff Cooper at the Ministry of Information, who Nicholas quotes, describing Priestley as 'a second rate novelist who got conceited by his broadcasting success.'[59] And of course his passionate and forthright style, and his radical views were, as suggested above, hardly unexpected, but they nevertheless affected his treatment at the BBC. Writing of his longer relationship with the BBC, Priestley suggested that complaints in the press, 'questions in the House', and 'angry telephone calls from retired admirals' made him seem 'like trouble' to BBC administrators. He argued the idea that he was 'difficult' was 'entirely false, for if I undertook a thirteen-minute talk, that is what I gave, and I was punctual and reasonably keen and sober.'[60] This didn't quite answer the allegation of 'difficulty', but it revealed his belief that he was always professional in his work practices.

It should also be remembered that it was the BBC who twice asked Priestley to take over the postscripts, which filled a short slot after the Sunday evening news. Although Priestley had his own plans and ideas about broadcasting, and spoke on the overseas service (again, at the BBC's request) he was more comfortable with the written word - hardly a case of dominating prime time, or 'microphonitis'. Nor was Nicolson's characterization of Priestley as a 'Sly Demagogue' very helpful. Priestley may have been many things, but sly was hardly one of them. He was not furtive, nor was he good at concealing his intentions; in fact he was quite the opposite of this, often shooting from the hip. Furthermore his passionate, democratic Englishness hardly equated to the demagogic anti-semitism of the likes of a Father Coughlin, and in terms of values, he had more in common with another American, Franklin Roosevelt.[61] In truth, Priestley ran against the grain of the BBC and their middle class vision of 'impartiality'. He also, more significantly, angered powerful figures in authority who were unhappy about a radical voice reaching such a wide audience.

Although Priestley later played down the significance of the 'postscripts', it is clear from his anger at being removed that he believed his broadcasts were having an impact on listeners.[62] Radio was a useful medium at a time when progressives were keen to seize the initiative in debates about the conduct of the war, and the shape of the post war nation. Pamphlets and tracts advocating social change sold well in this period,[63] and Priestley was already chairing a progressive grouping, the '1941 Committee'. This had come into being after the radical Liberal MP, Sir Richard Acland, inspired by one of Priestley's summer 1940 broadcasts, met with the author to discuss the political situation. This led, in December 1940, to the creation of a grouping that became the '1941 Committee', which attracted various liberal and left wing figures, including editor of the *New Statesman* Kingsley Martin, the *News Chronicle* correspondent Vernon Bartlett M. P., J. L. Hodson and the economist Thomas Balogh. The committee met at the home of the radical publisher of *Picture Post*, Edward Hulton, who also provided initial funding for the group.[64] Priestley described the committee as a 'research and propaganda organisation' that issued statements on 'various war problems'.[65] By the end of April 1941, Priestley was in full swing on his own contribution to the debate working on a pamphlet 'Out of the People' which gave him the opportunity to put some flesh on the bones of the arguments put forward in the 'postscripts'.[66]

Priestley was not an organization man or a political animal though, either by nature or profession, and with the pressure of other commitments building up, including, despite his May comments about not working for the BBC, weekly broadcasts on the overseas service, he was, by the end of the year, beginning to lose interest in the 1941 Committee.[67] Matters were also complicated by Priestley's relationship with the idealistic aristocrat Acland. The latter had become a socialist in 1936, a year after being elected as MP for Barnstable, and a committed Christian in 1940. He outlined his radical political philosophy in *Unser Kampf* (1940), and formed the Forward March movement with his acolytes. Intent on practising what he preached, he was also in the process of handing over his estate to the National Trust (a task completed in early 1943).[68]

Acland was a vigorous and charismatic leader who believed that community ownership and a more moral order were a genuine possibility, and to this end, he favoured social change during the war and was open to challenging the existing parties at by-elections. In contrast, the more pragmatic Priestley was more of a gradualist, believing significant change would only be possible when the war was finished, and also preferring a strategy seeking to influence rather than challenge the Labour Party.[69]

Despite Priestley's misgivings, both men were involved in the creation of a new political organization in the summer of 1942. Amidst public doubts about the conduct for the war, culminating in the fall of Tobruk on 21 June 1942, independent candidates inflicted a number of by-election defeats on the Conservatives. Seats were lost to independent candidates at Grantham in March, Rugby and Wallassey in April, and Maldon (won by Tom Driberg) in June. Acland's Forward March movement supported the independent candidate George Reakes, at Wallasey, and both Acland and Priestley were signatories to a subsequent radical 'Nine Point Manifesto' for use at further by-elections. Priestley, Acland and other members of the 1941 Committee were also active in support of Driberg. In July 1942, keen to seize the political initiative at this juncture, the Forward March Movement and the 1941 Committee merged to create the new political party Commonwealth, with Priestley as President.[70]

Commonwealth had some success at by-elections, starting with Eddisbury in Cheshire in April 1943, and at its peak it had 300 branches, 15,000 members (20% of whom were in the forces) and three MPs. It was very much Acland's party however, and Priestley departed in the autumn of 1942. Commonwealth offered an idealistic vision of common ownership, and democratic, open governance, and threw itself behind the Beveridge Report. It drew its support from the young, professional middle classes, and was strongest in suburban areas around London and Merseyside, weak in working class Labour areas.[71]

Commonwealth's interest in the middle class, and the potential of salaried middle class managers, was to become a facet of progressive thinking more generally, and of course echoed Priestley's prioritisation of the middle class as an agent of change. And despite his departure from Commonwealth he remained in contact with Acland, and wrote an introduction to his political programme *How It Can Be Done* (1943). 'I agree with most his conclusions' Priestley wrote, although 'both his temperament and his approach are different from mine'. He added 'he is much more of an Old Testament character, just striding in from the wilderness....whereas I am a more easy-going and modern type, an author compelled to protest because he is sick of living in a blood spattered ruin of a world.' Priestley urged readers to engage with Acland's argument, and where they found shortcomings to come up with something better of their own. [72]

One wonders whether this was quite the introduction Acland had in mind, particularly as Priestley also managed, in defending Acland from the charge of being 'woolly', to describe him as 'intolerant, fanatical, tactless, humourless, too impatient...anything but "woolly"'.[73] It was testimony to Acland's broad shoulders that he allowed it to appear. Priestley also wrote the pamphlet *Here are Your Answers* (1944) for the Commonwealth Popular Library.

Priestley's retreat from direct political involvement saw no let up in his commitment to the war effort. He still travelled and spoke across the country, wrote at every opportunity, and continued broadcasting at the BBC and other media work – all of which occurred amidst a disrupted and complicated domestic life.[74] For the rest of the war, he continued to push the themes that emerged during the postscripts, trying desperately to fan the embers of the popular spirit that he had celebrated in his broadcasts during the summer of 1940. The pivotal importance of the people, the fact that the war marked a watershed in recent history, and the need to move towards a new, more democratic future – all figured large in his arguments, alongside the more radical edge that had made an appearance during the later postscripts. *Out of the People*, written at the height of his involvement with the 1941 Committee represented the fullest attempt at expressing these views. It also reached a large audience, having sold 41,000 copies by 1942.[75]

Out of the People updated many of the arguments made in *Rain Upon Godshill*, and offered a detailed vision of Priestley's liberal socialism in the context of war. As with the postscripts, it offered an almost mystical celebration of the people, and their ability to make their own future, citing Walt Whitman in support, and his suggestion that 'everything comes out of the people' – a point Priestley reiterated throughout the 127 pages of the pamphlet. The war had sharpened his misgivings about using class as a defining social factor, with Priestley arguing that 'we are all the people so long as we are willing to consider ourselves the people'.[76]

The crisis of the war had emphasized people's common humanity, and only those who continued to think in terms of class and pursue special interests were outside the ranks of the people; and indeed, might 'be lucky if they are not included among the enemies of the people'.[77] What tied the people together, he argued, was a 'social conscience' that bound the individual to their community.[78] Returning to a theme in his writing during the 1930s he argued, that the people were not to be confused with the 'masses', a designation which was part of the process of dehumanising the people, and justifying their subjugation. This reached its peak with Hitler who 'thinks and acts always in terms of the masses and never for a moment in terms of the people', but was also common amongst communists, and even the 'new conservatism', which 'is already flirting with these newer notions of masters and masses'.[79] In Britain, talk of 'classes' had represented a nostalgic ruralist façade, which covered up economic differences within the nation, the right's push for centralized power, and presented an unrealistic image of Britain to the world. The war, however, had shattered this façade, and shown the real England, which was 'democratic-industrial England, which never saw a row of footmen in its life and does not want to see one'. Instead it wanted to see 'a reasonable chance of security and a healthy civilised existence' for all.[80]

Reprising an argument from the later postscripts, Priestley argued forcefully that the 'free, creative spirit' of the summer of 1940 needed to be nourished in order to allow the people to bring about change. Unfortunately, Priestley argued, there were 'missed chances' in 1940, and there was a danger that having awoken from the slumber of the 1930s, 'they must not go to sleep again' for 'if they should slip back once more into the passive mood, they may lose their very souls'.[81] There was no going back he argued, as it was the decay of the interwar years that had created the current situation. The choice was between a 'real democracy' or a 'kind of fascism',[82] and for democracy to work people needed to be active and involved. This, Priestley argued, was the key ingredient of a democratic state, rather than a gradual evolution to democracy, or a rising standard of living underpinning democratic practices. 'Let it be admitted, once and for all', he argued, 'that you cannot have democratic government long, cannot make a democracy function properly, if you have an apathetic and passive people.'[83]

In order to construct this 'real democracy' the people would need to overcome three principal 'obstacles', which were 'produced by our own time' and made worse by the war.[84] These were the 'decay of religious belief', which encouraged the dehumanization of people, the 'organisation of authority in the modern world' which allowed Governments to dominate and control their people via both force and control of mass communication (this included a swipe at the Government's control of the BBC), and the finally 'the development of large-scale industry'.[85] Echoing *English Journey*, Priestley suggested that although this had narrowed differences in wealth, it had created a small group of specialists who controlled production and a 'great mass of ordinary people who are inside the machine'.[86] Moreover, summoning up his dislike of popular culture, he suggested this 'robot-like existence' left people open to 'passive' undemanding cultural pastimes, like Hollywood, the 'cheap press' and radio, that made them go 'soft'. He concluded 'soon, all too soon, they are only so much wet clay in the hands of the dangerous men who think of themselves as masters and of the people as mere masses'.[87]

Priestley argued that these 'obstacles' were products of the modern world, and that they were less advanced in Britain than elsewhere, and that the war presented an opportunity to remove them.[88] A sense of religious feeling remained in Britain, granting greater respect to the individual,[89] and although the centralizing forces of the state were strong, there were countervailing forces outside the control of the state. These included, despite his misgivings about them, the trade unions who not only wielded considerable power, but also gave strength and encouragement to the industrial worker, preventing them from turning into mindless 'tiny cogs in a vast machine'.[90]

Priestley also cited the co-operative society, professional, educational and cultural associations, where people met freely and exchanged ideas outside the control of the state. In addition, the war had seen the emergence of new voluntary associations like the Home Guard, Observer's Corp and ARP, which encouraged a sense of 'shared responsibilities'. These organizations were made from the 'real citizens', not masses, and represented the 'true democratic spirit'.[91] With these advantages, Priestley suggested that reform should begin 'at home' as a prelude to European and world reform.[92] Britain would act as beacon to the rest of Europe because its people 'aroused wonder and admiration throughout the world' and 'if these were the people who found a way out. . ..who proved that democracy was not ending but just beginning, then people everywhere would take heart and try to order their own affairs in the same fashion'.[93]

These reforms would include changing the very nature of politics. Priestley attacked what he saw as the poor quality of contemporary politicians, who came to power in the 1930s, who pursued their own careers rather than the national interest and indulged in 'intrigue and bad rhetoric'.[94] Priestley argued that much of what went for politics was actually 'simply problems of effective organisation', and could be done by the large number of suitably qualified women and men with organizational skills. The other 25% would be undertaken by the 'true statesmen... not simply the leading politician...there should live in him something of the poet, the sage, the prophet' and 'he should reflect and then act greatly'.[95] Politics would also be different in structure, starting at a local level, and rebuilt, from the bottom by the now politicized people. 'Actually, many of the activities that public-spirited defence workers have been engaged in recently, settling local feeding, billeting, health and fire-fighting problems, belong to the new politics'.[96] The agency of the people came together in the 'community', a term like the people which had an almost mystical significance for Priestley: 'the community consists of living persons...some of us would declare that the community is something more than the sum of the people in it...(it) might have a sort of mind or soul of its own.' Moreover it was the lynchpin of a democratic system: 'that is why democracy, which insists upon the individual worth of persons has never denied but has always affirmed the value of the community'.[97] Priestley attacked those who linked the state and democracy, and the Fascists who believed the state *was* the community. Instead it was 'an instrument, a machine' which the 'democratic community can make good use of'. [98]

Priestley's state (the 'organisation of the community') would take charge of large and important organizations, natural monopolies like power, water and transport and economic interests that became too powerful. 'The treasury should be the only big capitalist in the community' and would be responsible for all 'banking, financing, money-lending'. This would enable the economy to be run in the interests of the community and the quality of life, rather than the 'profit motive'.[99] A regulated private sector would remain, in part because Priestley feared that too dramatic a change in the economic order might precipitate a more authoritarian system. This was an important point, as it related both to his belief that change must not be imposed from the top-down and must come from a more gradual change of 'atmosphere and values'.[100] The press would also remain private hands, although it would be subject to monitoring by a non-state board of control. The state would also be barred 'wherever originality, variety and flexibility' were 'essential', as in the arts and culture, and from what he hoped would be a burgeoning area of associational life where the new politics would take root.[101]

Priestley was well aware that his 'vital democracy' was not attainable in full during the war, however he did believe that moves towards a more democratic society might 'enlarge and vitalise our war effort'. He continued that 'so long as it could be proved that there would be popular support for certain immediate reforms, the war is the worst possible excuse for not bringing about those reforms.'[102] In the appendix to the pamphlet, he set out with a broad brush stroke the changes that he thought were attainable during, and then after the war, suggestions made bearing in mind that 'we are not fond of change for the sake of change'.[103] With regard to the former, he suggested that rationing should be applied so as to give 'everybody a basic standard, and no more than that', a national wages policy should give 'equal pay for equal work', family allowances and 'modification of income tax for families' would also be used to bring about greater equity. The state would requisition any underused buildings for the war effort, and there would be greater planning in industry and agriculture. The banking industry, transport, fuel and power would be 'taken over by the community as soon as possible', and the Ministry of Information should be reorganized as part of a drive to establish a proper political debate within the nation.[104] The changes after the war would include community control of 'essential utilities and services', with a National Banking Corporation overseeing the financial sector, a 'basic minimum standard of living', and the new community values prevalent in social and economic decision-making.[105]

As suggested in the body of the pamphlet, 'private enterprise' would continue, although now in a change of argument, not for the fear of too dramatic a change, but because it allowed 'more experiment, flexibility, and efficiency'.[106] Land would be taken into public ownership, and then let out to farmers. Far from undermining this sector, Priestley sang the praises of agriculture as 'healthy for democracy', both because younger people valued country life, but also because it played an important role in sustaining family, village and the 'provincial or regional community', part of the 'network of associations' which were key to Priestley's view of a reorganized society. Taking the argument further, he suggested that these groups gave 'richness and depth to the life of the individual, and toughness and resilience to the fabric of life itself', which were lacking in 'so many vast urban areas'.[107]

This argument was interesting as it seemed to shift the emphasis towards rural and suburban England as a guarantor of the democratic impulse. Yet in the main pamphlet Priestley had described the 'real' nation as being 'democratic-industrial England', going on to suggest that the war had put an end 'once and for all' to the 'stupid and dangerous notion that this England, which does the work, is only a sort of dirty annexe to some other and more important England' – the 'other' England, of course, being the loathed Tory country house England, with 'the villagers touching their caps'.[108] Priestley's argument involved a totally different pattern of ownership in these areas, with the public control of the land, however it would also use the pre-existing 'network of associations' which had been 'beginning to disintegrate' in the pre-war world.[109] This however left open the extent to which these associations were riddled with the social distinction that Priestley abhorred in rural society. Unlike the urban workers who never wanted to see a

footman, wasn't it in the village and rural community that more traditional relationships required the touching of caps? The tension in this argument illustrates
Priestley's somewhat contradictory relationship with modernity. For Priestley, the
urban areas were both the working heart of the nation that had bravely backed the
war-effort, as well as the cutting edge of the modernizing process. On one hand,
as he had suggested in *English Journey,* this had acted as a democratizing force,
however as he put it in the pamphlet, it also led to the 'flavourless, sapless, root-
less'[110] mass experience that Priestley was so suspicious of. Rural England was in
his eyes the home of the Tory squires, but could still be imagined as an authentic
democratic community of characters like those he celebrated in the postscript of
16 June 1940.

Out of the People was written quickly, at a tense time, which no doubt encouraged Priestley's tendency to write about large social and political issues, without
really engaging in the detail. The pamphlet was long, and presented a passionate
and admirable case for democracy and the agency of ordinary people. However,
it didn't take the reader much further than the arguments of the postscripts, and
in particular failed to explain how the energy of the people, which he had already
admitted was dissipating, could lead to substantial change within the nation. To
be fair, Priestley argued that it was important to establish the 'right atmosphere
and ideas', in other words the 'Why', after which the setting up of the machinery
of reform, the 'How', would be 'easy'.[111] However, this didn't address the need for a
more coherent strategy and effective organization to get to the point where there
could be reform, even if then such reform would be 'easy' (somewhat unlikely
given proposals like state ownership of land). Priestley was well aware of the
power of conservative interests within the nation, and had witnessed first hand
the way they operated; yet he implies that the power of (his) good ideas, and a
broad and unfocused popular will would overcome any such opposition. There is
also the issue of the extent to which Priestley's designation of the people remained
problematic, collapsing social differences into an unrealistic shared narrative.
Something which was perhaps reinforced by Priestley's tendency to sometimes
single out at for special focus in the pamphlet his potential 'grand people'– the no
longer quiescent middle class of the inter war years. [112]

Priestley was one of many voices urging reform via the printed word, and not
alone in presenting an imaginative if imperfect case. In many ways his approach
coincided with that of George Orwell, whose *The Lion and the Unicorn* (1940) represented the latter's clearest statement on national identity and radicalism. Orwell,
who died in January 1950, would later be eulogized by post war intellectuals and
radicals, who saw him as one of a relatively rare breed – a genuine English radical
intellectual. This was in stark contrast to Priestley who not only attracted much
less attention, but as we have seen, suffered under Woolf's 'tradesman of letters'
and similar jibes, implying a lack of intelligence and intellectual rigour. Both men

offered a damning critique of the 1930s, something they had previously explored in fiction. Indeed Orwell's *Coming up for Air* (1939) echoed many of Priestley's concerns with its picture of a characterless, mass culture poised on the verge of a dark and bloody war. If there was none of the redemptive quality apparent in Priestley's work, let alone the exuberance of *Let the People Sing* published that same year, similar themes appeared, like tacky American milk bars, poor quality beer, a degraded countryside, an attack on 'sham countrified stuff' created in its place, returned servicemen let down at the end of the last war, and totalitarian forces at work in the world.[113] As the central character, Bowling discovered, there was no 'coming up for air', because there 'isn't any'.[114]. And many of Priestley's characters would have agreed that 'the old life we're used to is being sawn off at the roots'.[115]

Of course, unlike Priestley, Orwell was initially opposed to the war against fascism, believing that it would merely lead to a further instalment in the imperialist quarrel, a position he only changed once the war had got underway.[116] However by the time he wrote *The Lion and the Unicorn* (1941) he was convinced of the need to oppose the totalitarian machine of the Nazis, the revolutionary potential presented by the war, and vigorously attacked those on the left who clung to his previously held position of opposing the war.[117] Like Priestley, Orwell believed the war had shown once and for all the 'utter rottenness of private capitalism' and the need for a new, planned economy.[118]

England had been a badly run, class ridden society: 'a family with the wrong members in control' whose financial self-interest had not only failed domestically, but prevented them from confronting fascism earlier in the 1930s.[119] The experience of the war had convinced people of the need for change, and Orwell argued that an 'English revolution' from below was already in progress. This was not a movement of the left or right, but of 'multitudes of unlabelled people who have grasped...that something is wrong'. Orwell cited, as examples of this, *Picture Post*, *Cavalcade*, leading articles in the *Evening Standard* and 'Priestley's broadcasts'. [120] This revolution would set free the 'native genius of the English people' and allow them to move towards an English version of socialism.[121] Orwell was much more emphatic than Priestley in his belief that the revolution and prosecution of the war were interchangeable – 'either we turn this war into a revolutionary war...or we lose it', [122] but both men shared a belief in a unifying Englishness that could contain all of those outside the elite, including the middle classes.[123]

In some ways, Orwell's remarkable analysis of England in the first section of the pamphlet offered a less romantic and darker, more complex version of Englishness than Priestley. It would be difficult to see Priestley, for example, taking the hanging judge as representative symbol of the contradictions within the nation.[124] However, a lingering affection shone through the description of an English exceptionalism based on a disappearing 'private liberty', 'gentleness', a suspicion of authority and a belief in 'justice, liberty and objective truth', albeit overseen by an incompetent ruling class who showed 'an infallible instinct for doing the wrong thing'.[125] Furthermore, despite being 'the most class-ridden country under the sun', England had 'an emotional unity…a tendency of nearly all of its inhabitants to feel alike and act together in moments of crisis'.[126]

Orwell was a more committed socialist than Priestley, and this could be seen in the language he used. Whereas Priestley uses 'socialism' and 'revolution' comparatively rarely, these terms are central in Orwell's writing. Similarly, the 'state' makes a more regular appearance than its occasional, qualified appearance in *Out of the People*. However, the language is in some ways misleading as Orwell's actual programme was more pragmatic than the language might suggest. Nationalisation, limitation of incomes, educational reform (including abolition of the public schools), and reform of imperial relations were all proposed, but suggested with an awareness of the difficulties involved in bringing about reform.[127] Some of these policies 'could be carried out immediately' but others would take much longer and 'even then would not be perfectly achieved'. He added 'it is always the direction that counts'.[128]

Whilst the vision of nationalization seemed more complete than in Priestley's mixed economy, Orwell did suggest that 'certain kinds of petty trading, and even the small – scale ownership of land' would see no interference from the state.[129] Moreover, Orwell's state was not a monolithic, dictatorial force associated with the Stalinism both men opposed. Orwell believed that greater equality in the distribution of power and wealth would ensure that it remained under the control of the people, meaning that for 'the common people' the state would be 'themselves'.[130]

There would also be room, within the democratic culture, for the practice of religion, and indeed echoing Priestley, the post-revolution nation would 'retain a vague reference for the Christian moral code, and from time to time' be seen as "a Christian country"'.[131] The latter point related to Orwell's argument that revolutions must reflect the context in which they occur, and this revolution, made by an English Socialist movement 'will still bear all over it the unmistakeable marks of our own civilization', which would allow inconsistencies including possibly the monarchy and 'anachronisms and loose ends everywhere'.[132] Once again this pragmatism, and respect for English idiosyncrasies, as opposed to revolutionary blue prints, was very similar to the position taken by Priestley.

That is not to say, however, that the two men held to identical positions. Orwell's embrace of socialism amounted to more than a use of socialist language, and was reflected in a longstanding concern about the operation and consequences of Empire. Whereas Priestley mentioned the Empire at times in his writing, it was a central theme for Orwell, and played a significant role in *The Lion and the Unicorn* where he depicted a nation where the working class didn't know that the Empire 'exists', whilst the incompetent ruling class profited from it. [133] Furthermore, by the 1930s there had been 'a general weakening of imperialism' and the war presented an opportunity for reform, which helped explain why three of the points in his six point programme dealt with imperial issues and foreign policy.[134] Orwell also had less faith in the voluntary associations like the Home Guard, who were to play such a vital role in paving the way into Priestley's new England.[135] Even clearer, however, was the belief that there would be a confrontation over the shift in power from the ruling elite to the people, as opposed to Priestley's assumption of an easier transition. 'There will be a bitter political struggle' he wrote 'and there will be unconscious and half-conscious sabotage everywhere', although the people would prevail, because 'patriotism is finally stronger than class hatred'.[136]

Nor was the struggle necessarily going to be peaceful: 'It may be necessary to use violence' he suggested, citing the example of a possible pro-fascist rebellion in India.[137] Moreover, domestically the new regime would 'shoot traitors' after a 'solemn trial' and 'crush any open revolt promptly and cruelly'.[138] Bernard Crick describes this statement as a sign of Orwell's 'republican rather than liberal frame of mind', and the fact that this suppression would not interfere with free speech as sign of the egalitarian and libertarian lines within his thought.[139] It was also clinical, and contained more than an element of revolutionary posturing, undercutting the more pragmatic and democratic arguments in the pamphlet. Priestley may have underestimated the barriers across the path to a new order, but he would not have been so careless in suggesting actions that would soon corrupt the democratic and positive side of this English revolution. And indeed Orwell, given his experiences in Spain, and his belief in the unifying force of Englishness, should probably have known better.

Aside from the flirtation with a suggestion of violence, the argument presented in the pamphlet was not without its tensions. Orwell arguably overestimated the immediate significance that the state ownership of industry and land would have on the country, suggesting that 'from the moment' this was done people would become aware of their collective strength in the form of the state, and be re-committed to the war effort. Furthermore, 'on the day' that formal nationalization occurs 'the dominance of a single class will be broken'.[140] Whilst the latter point might be true in its most literal sense, the broader case was both over-optimistic and sat uneasily with Orwell's perceptive arguments about the cultural context in which change occurred. The need for what Priestley described as 'the right atmosphere', and the peculiarities of Englishness, which Orwell was otherwise so sensitive to, suggested that the transformation of hearts and minds would not be an automatic response to structural change.

There was also the issue of Englishness itself. Much like the complications in Priestley's definition of the people, the logic of Orwell's depiction of a class-ridden nation ran against the grain of a unifying national identity for those outside the elite. An 'emotional unity' may have been possible during times of stress like the

Blitz, but in a nation where class operated in both economic and cultural terms a strong, coherent and radical unity would be more problematic. In particular, given the limited footholds socialism had made in the previous sixty year, the prospects of a patriotic socialism were especially doubtful. Indeed Priestley, whose writing usually made frequent references to England and Englishness, was not convinced of its ability to provide a binding force in the context of the War, preferring the concept of the people. To believe that nationalism was 'a unifying idea' was 'a mistake', he argued in the *New York Times* in 1942, continuing 'it no longer has the necessary driving force.' Instead there was a need to think Internationally – 'the United Nations must be more than the united nations'.[141]

Orwell's vision of radical England could also shade into a more romantic celebration of the English spirit. After quoting Shakespeare on the final page he suggests that the 'heirs of Nelson and Cromwell...are in the fields and the streets, in the factories and the armed forces, in the four-ale bar and the suburban back garden' and that they will find themselves in their English revolution. Through overcoming the 'ghosts' who keep them down they will bring 'the real England to the surface.' Orwell concluded 'we must add to our heritage or lose it, we must grow greater or grow less, we must go backward or forward. I believe in England, and I believe we shall go forward.'[142] The last statement could have as easily have come from the mouth of Churchill.[143]

By 1944 Orwell admitted that in the early years of the war he had overestimated the extent of the social changes caused by the war.[144] However, he was not alone in believing he had made this error, and this and other shortcomings were part and parcel of trying to construct a radical programme in the midst of a total war. Like Priestley, Orwell was trying to wrestle control of the arguments from the 'ghosts' of the ruling elite, seeking to empower ordinary people and establish a more democratic future. They were clearly both on the same side, but Priestley's inclination towards liberalism and Orwell's socialism proved a source of difference between the two. It is also apparent that, despite its drawbacks, *The Lion and the Unicorn* is a better piece of writing, making several perceptive observations, not least in its awareness of the colonial dimension to British life, whereas *Out of the People* is more passionate, also perceptive, but generally less incisive. Both, however, made important contributions to wartime debates on the relationship between the state and people, and the frequently rocky path to a modern radical national identity. Their ideas would help shape the post war concensus, but it was only Orwell who would gain widespread respect as a radical English intellectual.

Out of the People marked Priestley's longest written political intervention during the war, and the arguments presented within it, drawing as they did from his writing during the 1930s and the postscripts, remained largely consistent for the remainder of the conflict; as did his unshakeable belief that he could help provide the spark and vision needed to restart the march to a brighter future. As he put it in a characteristic 1943 article, 'grim purpose' had 'replaced the sudden romantic enthusiasm of 1940' and a desire for change was still abroad. The trouble was that 'many of these folks may not be good at expressing their own ideas...but they know when somebody comes close to what they are thinking and feeling'. The clear implication was ever familiar - that Priestley and his kind were to be the people's tribunes.[145]

Priestley continued to use his writing to try and provide the spark to re-ignite the public mood. Of the novels, the most substantial, *Daylight on Saturday* (1943) revealed both the difficulties faced by workers in the war-industries, and repeated the by now familiar political message.[146] Work at the Elmdown Aircraft Company factory in the south midlands is hard and repetitive, with the workforce arriving at dawn and departing in the evening, and only ever seeing 'daylight on Saturday'.[147] Key characters suffer from damaging personal problems, including Elkrick, an assistant manager, who has made it up from the shopfloor, but whose violent temper and lasciviousness it is suggested is in part related to the psychological problems of his wife.[148] There was also the Womens' Welfare Officer, Jean Shipton, involved in a disastrous relationship with an older, married man and Bolton, who works on the factory floor and whose emotions are frozen after losing his family in an air raid.[149]

Added to these characters are the representative political types. Blandford, a Cambridge-educated Tory assistant manager, who looks forward to a corporate fascist order where 'there'll be no more silly chatter about democracy', and his cousin, Lord Blixen, a minor Tory Minister who presents himself as a country gentleman, but whose money and influence came through politics and marriage.[150] Priestley's dislike of the Tories, and his resentment at their role in his removal from the postscripts is again given voice, when he describes how the latter believed that any 'anti-Tory talk' should be 'condemned as political', whereas 'pro-Tory talk' was 'common sense or obvious decent Patriotism', allowing him to 'denounce with a clear conscience, some of the Labour fellows and one or two of those popular wordspinners at the BBC for being political in wartime.'[151]

There is also a decent Communist who has been hoodwinked by propaganda, and a more aggressive 'bitter' Marxist who argues that any problems within the factory are related to the faults of the management.[152] Priestley also finds room for a character reminiscent of Jess Oakroyd who is an 'old fashioned radical' mistrusted by both right and left alike, and adrift amongst the culture of the younger generation.[153] Even the mistrust of officialdom is given voice, with an unflattering picture of relations between the factory and the Ministry of Aircraft Production, epitomized by the visit of two inspectors, one of whom had been dismissed from the factory before the war, and the other an academic with no insight into the lives of those working on the production line.[154]

The central character represented Priestley's (and Acland, Orwell et al) image of the middle class technician who was now closer to the skilled working class than his social 'superiors', in other words, one of the people. James Cheviot, general manager of Elmdown was 'at home' in the 'new world of engineering and organising', moreover although some might suggest he was part of 'tomorrow's ruling class', his lifestyle ('a little villa not far away', a wife and two grown up children, and moderate tastes), and his own belief that despite his power 'there was not any great difference between himself and any other man in the factory', meant that he was closer to 'any of the shop-stewards' than the Board of Directors.[155] Cheviot is the most competent, and controlled character in the novel, often exercising a wise, paternalistic judgement, and realizing that he has a responsibility to act for the good of society to help avoid the mistakes of the past. 'I'll be an engineer *and* a politician' he tells the willing listener Sammy, adding 'and I know a few others who will too.' [156]

The sombre environment of the factory is also reflected in the mood of the workforce who lack both enthusiasm and energy. There are frequent references in this regard to how the mood has changed since the Blitz. One woman worker complains that production has slowed because of the 'state of the war', and the 'dummies' that had come to work in the factory in recent months. 'They ought to have been with us in 1940 when we were working until we were ready to drop and sirens going every hour or two.'[157] This mood is also related to Priestley's familiar line on the longer-term problems with English life, voiced by the upper middle-class Freda Pinnel, who is working on the shop floor, who tells one of the inspectors that ordinary workers lack energy because 'nobody tries to make them really enthusiastic'. The problem was, she suggested, that 'they've mostly had a dreary life' and that they 'still feel dreary'. She concluded 'I've been thinking lately that, for all our talk, this is just a dreary country. Perhaps it's been safe and respectable too long.'[158] In a similar vein, Cheviot suggested that 'some say the English are lazy. They're not though. They soon get bored, that's all.' The ruling elite did nothing about this because, echoing Priestley's public statements, 'they don't know when the people are getting bored, because they don't know anything about the people.'[159]

Inevitably given Priestley's intention of boosting morale, and the broader liberal intelligence behind his work, the personal and political mood is changed by several events. Firstly, visiting ENSA performers bring 'an air of release and instant happiness' to the workforce, followed later in the book by the welcome news (conveyed by Cheviot) that the Eighth Army were making significant advances.[160] Finally, Elkrick, suspended for his assault on a female worker, sacrifices his own life to save another from being killed in the 'big machine'.[161] By the end of the book even the proto-fascist Blandford had shifted to a position that was more sympathetic to the workforce, and was 'beginning to understand that this job was something more than settling a deskload of technical production problems.'[162] The final word however went to Cheviot, who was recommitted to his place among the people: 'he knew in spirit he must never leave them and their kind', and realized his leadership responsibilities in this regard.[163] 'There would be no cosy settling down for him now, no easy acceptance of bribe or pension from the moneyed interests, no leaving it all to Lord Blixen, no comfortable pretence that the people must naturally live on the other side of the high wall. There was', he concluded, 'a mountain of a job to be done for and with these people.'[164]

The optimistic realism of *Daylight on a Saturday* gave way to a more ambitious, symbolic version of Priestley's message in the most famous of the wartime plays, *They Came to a City* (1943). A straight political parable, this placed nine socially representative characters outside the walls of a mysterious city. None of the characters know how they arrived at this scene, but all enter the city when at the end of the first act, the gates open. The second act presents their contrasting responses to their experiences in the city; a utopian community embodying Priestley's belief in community, democracy and social justice. As one of the central characters, the stoker Joe Dinmore puts it, 'a city full of healthy people, and busy people, and happy people. A really civilised city.'[165] Some characters reject the city out of hand, and prefer to throw themselves back into their former lives. Predictably these characters were part of the reactionary elite who Priestley considered to be outside the ranks of the people: The upper class Lady Loxfield, the 'self-indulgent' landed gentleman, Sir George Gedney, the unpleasant financier Cudworth (not even allowed a Christian name) and the fussy housewife from Leamington Spa, Mrs. Stritton.[166] The latter is a particularly unsympathetic, one-dimensional character who is emotionally mired in a world of suburban values, and willing to manipulate her husband who wants to stay in the city. Her attempt at arguing against her husband's open-minded response to the day, leads to an inarticulate exchange including her suggestion that the people of the city were 'silly' and 'common'. Her husband's defiant suggestion that to the contrary 'they're alive', and his motion at re-entering to the city alone is foreshortened by his wife's tears, and the reluctant decision to stay with her.[167]

A still more significant discussion occurs between Joe Dinmore and the waitress Alice Foster, who have fallen in love with each other and the city. Joe however returns to the gate, where he is joined at the last moment by a reluctant Alice. Representing Priestley's vision of social responsibility, Joe tells Alice that he has to return to the real world to spread the message about what they have discovered. 'Somebody's got to go back and tell the truth about it' he tells her, before acknowledging that it will not be an easy task. [168] However he continues assuring her that there will be 'hope' and 'every time we find a spark of hope in anybody we'll blow it into a blaze', eventually drawing together 'millions of us-yes armies and armies of us-enough to build ten thousand new cities.'[169]

Joe and Alice's decision is significant as it represented not only an unselfish desire to spread a progressive message, but it revealed how Priestley still saw a leadership role for committed and energetic working class figures, performing a slightly different role to the middle class technicians celebrated in other works.

Priestley kept up the political arguments across various written forms,[170] remaining concerned in the latter stages of the war with the immediate prospects for the post war world, with particular regard to the returning servicemen. The novel *Three Men in New Suits* (1945) addressed this issue directly, providing a now familiar range of characters, both progressive and reactionary. The book was not one of his best by any means, although its message about the solidarity through shared experiences of the ex-servicemen, and the difficulties they encountered when returning home was coherent and fitted with Priestley's longstanding concerns. Priestley later admitted that the book was not meant 'to make a lasting contribution to the art of fiction', and was 'deliberately polemical'.[171]

He would also explore this theme in a more effective manner in the pamphlet, *Letter to a Returning Serviceman*, published at the time of the 1945 General Election. This was an appeal to an imaginary character, Robert, calling on him and his fellow soldiers to avoid the mistakes that Priestley's generation made in 1918. The arguments against free-market Toryism, and for a democratic socialist society, were wrapped within an appeal for active citizenship and social responsibility. 'We cannot be indifferent any longer' he argued, telling the fictional Robert that 'when you come back, be a real citizen and not a hermit in a bungalow'.[172]

Whilst writing such political interventions, the realization that the war was drawing, in a military sense, to a successful close allowed Priestley to also devote his attention to less polemical writing. His work as a propagandist clearly did him little harm, as he was able to write one of his best plays, *An Inspector Calls* in only one week in the winter of 1944–1945,[173] followed by what was arguably his finest novel *Bright Day* written toward the end of the war, although published in 1946.[174] It is also clear that in this period, although *Letter to a Returning Serviceman* and other works continued the campaign to bolster the public groundswell for reform, he was becoming disillusioned by what he saw as the lack of success to this end. In a letter to the Davisons in October 1944, he admitted that 'there is far more cynicism and self-seeking than there was in the dangerous days of 1940 and 41'. Repeating a regular theme from his published writing he argued that the British 'react magnificently to a crisis', but the successful progress in the war had made them 'lazy-minded and indifferent again'. What was needed, he suggested, was to make the issue of peace and the post war order 'a great crisis'. On a slightly more optimistic note, he told the Davisons that although the right were seeking a return to pre-war values, there would be 'a definite split between Right and Left', which was 'healthy', and based upon a 'swing throughout the country to the left'. Moreover people were now 'more politically-minded' and the country was 'more advanced' intellectually and artistically than in 1939. However, returning to his more downbeat assessment he argued that this move to the left did not mean that 'Labour had more enthusiastic followers' and that people were 'nothing like sufficiently educated in politics yet'.[175]

Priestley's comments are interesting as they underline a nagging sense of doubt about the future, implicit and sometimes explicit in his writing since the autumn of 1940.[176] Priestley's wartime vision had placed a heavy emphasis upon the agency of the people, and the consequent move to a more democratic and egalitarian society. Time and again he had celebrated and encouraged the people, urging them to become active citizens and carry the spirit forward from the Blitz. Radio postscripts, journalism, pamphlets, novels, plays were all dedicated to this end, yet as the war drew to a close, Priestley, who saw himself as the people's tribune, clearly felt that the people had not come far enough.

Of course, as a committed radical, Priestley swallowed his doubts and threw himself into the 1945 election campaign, speaking and writing on behalf of the Labour Party. One such article appeared in *Reynolds News* with parallel articles by Priestley and Herbert Morrison, under the heading 'two famous men urge you to vote for a people's victory'. Priestley's appeal ended with the call to 'help people to take their heads out of the sand and vote Left'.[177] Rather bizarrely, Priestley also ran as an independent candidate for the Cambridge University seat. It is unclear why someone who was uncomfortable with the cut and thrust of party politics, was not a particularly good team player, was an avowed enemy of Conservatism, and had little good to say about the University or city, should have thrown his hat into the ring for such a seat. Inevitably he was soundly defeated, coming a dismal third with 5,745 votes. The Conservative victor won with 71,641.[178]

So Priestley had to swallow defeat as radicals across the country celebrated the victory of the Labour Government. As we have seen, however, he already had mixed feelings about the potential for change, and it would not be long before Priestley's disillusionment hardened in both private and public. In truth, Priestley was always destined to be disillusioned, as much like the Jess Oakroyd's and Hope Allerton's before the war, there never were going to be enough Joe Dinmores or James Cheviots to build a New England. As we saw in the inter-war period, Priestley constructed a positive, democratic view of the people and their agency, which submerged class differences, and romanticized their potential. The early stages of the war encouraged Priestley to believe that his people were capable of fulfilling their destiny. However, as he himself was well aware, a crisis was one thing, the drag of wartime quite another, and it was here that he arguably misread the people and circumstances he claimed to understand.

The people's responses to the war were never going to be one-dimensional, or clear-cut. Later historians would tussle over the significance of the war, some arguing that the war produced a unified, radical nation, others more recently concluding that indifference and division may have been more characteristic of the period, whilst others still have argued for a more subtle and complex picture of change.[179] Of relevance in this regard, Hinton has proposed a nuanced picture where hopes were raised, before being tempered by the historical memory, particularly concerning 1918 (something that Priestley himself referred to in various publications). People were more active and involved, but also cautious about change, because, quoting Mass Observation, 'they have developed, through disappointments, a protective device for guarding against further disappointment.'[180] Priestley, the pragmatic Yorkshireman, tribune of the people, spokesperson for a decent, democratic England was well aware that people were 'more politically minded' and should have realized that their caution and hesitation was not necessarily down to a lack of understanding, but on the contrary, a commonsense understanding that the world often worked against their interests, and that constructing a new post war order would be no easy task.

4

The Disillusioning of Mr. Priestley

In 1953, J. B. Priestley told readers of the *New Statesman* that the 'The English People should have a good life',[1] a statement that included an element of desperation, as he believed that this good life was slipping further from view in the years following 1945. Priestley's wartime doubts about the saliency of the post-war world, and its ability to deliver a decent quality of life for the British people, hardened in the years that followed, as he became progressively more disillusioned with the rise of the mass society, the Cold War and the pattern of domestic politics. This coincided with personal and professional troubles that contributed to Priestley's disgruntlement and sense of isolation – of being a 'voice in the wilderness', as he put it. Of course Priestley had, to some extent, always seen himself in this light, and his work continued to present a clear, cutting edge, including a number of important interventions in social and political debates, most notably over nuclear disarmament.

In May 1946, Priestley wrote to Natalie Davison expressing optimism about the year ahead, despite having experienced a 'protracted convalescence' from pneumonia. He told her, 'I have written what I think is my best novel', referring to the newly published *Bright Day*, as well as mentioning that three plays were 'ready for production'.[2] *Bright Day* became one of Priestley's most respected novels, striking a chord with many in his own generation, as well as those that followed, and remaining one of the author's favourites.[3] Priestley admitted that the book was partly autobiographical, particularly in the central character, Gregory Dawson's work in the Yorkshire wool industry and later in Hollywood, and the palpable sense of loss with which he viewed the pre-1914 world.[4] In this and other ways, the book reflects a number of themes that were to prevail in Priestley's writings in the post-war period, not least the issue of 'nostalgia'.

The novel starts with Dawson staying at the Royal Ocean Hotel in Cornwall, trying to complete the screenplay for a Hollywood movie, 'The Lady Hits Back'. The script and the film are mainstream, but Dawson and others involved in the project have included a 'private message' that tells the audience 'to expect nothing from a world such as this but the worst, imploring them not to be fooled again by anybody',[5] a sentiment that captured Dawson's feelings of alienation from Hollywood and life, more generally. Dawson meets two new guests, a Lord and Lady Harndean, the latter of whom he thinks he recognizes. It is only when the hotel's musical trio play the slow movement of Schubert's B Flat Major Trio that he experiences a Proustian recall of 'Bruddersford' (Bradford) over 30 years earlier. Lost in thought – 'I was far away, deep in a lost world and a lost time' – he places the Harndeans as none other than Malcolm and Eleanor Nixey who had arrived at exactly the same point in the music at a party held by the Alingtons in 1914. The Nixeys and the Alingtons were to play a central role in a series of events, ultimately ending in tragedy.[6]

The book contains some of Priestley's best fictional writing, not least in the powerful emotional recall of Bruddersford. In this sense, the novel seems to represent a deep nostalgia for Bradford and the Edwardian world, more generally – something that has contributed to the idea that Priestley increasingly embraced a nostalgic Englishness. However, while the book does present a tremendous sense of loss and contains an array of criticisms of the 'modern' world, its ultimate message is about the futility of living in the past and the need to embrace (albeit critically) the present. Many of the criticisms also echo those of Priestley's pre-war work, with an emphasis on the importance of community, free-thinking individuals and a lively popular culture.

From the outset, Dawson is not seeking residence in the past and believes that he needs to 'go back, so to speak, before I could take another step forward'[7] – an interplay between past and present that is reflected in the way the story moves backwards and forwards between 1946 and 1912–14. The mining of the past also takes a considerable toll. When the film star Elizabeth Earle, who is to appear in 'The Lady Hits Back' and who is romantically linked with Dawson, arrives at the hotel, she tells Dawson that he seems different. He replies that 'I'm a thousand years older. When I'm not working on the script, I spend my time thinking of my distant past'.[8]

And this past was not only distant but also painful to recall because it was a 'lost arcadia',[9] destroyed by World War I. Several of the key characters later die in the conflict, and the coming of war casts an increasing shadow on the world he describes. Dawson even suggests that there may be a metaphysical element at work here, with Jock Barniston's mysterious and, in some ways, mystical presence being explained by the fact that 'perhaps he already knew…that before the next four years were out, that body which he had put on like an overcoat to wear among us would be so much bleeding meat in a sandbag'.[10] In a similar vein, Dawson speculates whether journalist Ben Kerry, whose affair with Eleanor Nixey and betrayal of Eva Alington had such serious consequences, may have been influenced by the 'dark of his unconscious' where 'there was already a whisper that time was running out fast'. Mystical or not, Dawson's anger is straight Priestley, as he describes how Kerry, along with other members of the 'Bruddersford "Pals" Battalions', was 'smashed into the chalk' of the Somme one morning in 1916. 'And then some people, politicians and editors and the like, were surprised and pained afterwards to discover that places like Bruddersford used to be short of clever, lively young men', Dawson notes, angrily adding that 'They ought to have looked in the chalk and among the sandbags'.[11]

Dawson's anger and sense of loss give his memories of pre-war Bruddersford a particular poignancy: 'I am certain these people lived in a world, in an atmosphere that I have never discovered again since 1914'.[12] Bruddersford is presented as a thriving, creative community where people were friendly and sociable and where they 'never dreamt of living that boxed-up lonely life which left so many house-wives on edge during the 1930s'.[13] People read widely, ate well, drank in good pubs and attended concerts, music hall and variety shows. Dawson recalled the latter with particular fondness, contrasting it with his own experiences in Hollywood, where actors received 'ten times' the salaries of the music hall performers but did not 'possess one-tenth of the talent. Thus we progress', he continued, suggesting that 'I see now that in those noisy smoky halls, with their brassy orchestras, their plush and tarnished gilt, their crudely coloured spotlights raying down from the gallery, we were basking in the brilliant Indian Summer of popular art'. And this was not the mass-produced art of Hollywood but 'a unique folk art that sprang out of the gusto and irony, the sense of pathos and the illimitable humour of the English industrial people, braving it out in their mills and foundries and dingy crowded towns'.[14]

This was pure Priestley and became a stronger motif in his post-war work, illustrating his belief in the authenticity of local 'real' culture as opposed to mass-produced, commodified culture. Dawson's unease at working in Hollywood and the way it catered for 'passive mobs of film goers'[15] reflected Priestley's own mis-givings in this regard and comes across at several points in the novel. This culmi-nated in his decision at the end of the novel to turn his back on Hollywood and work with a trade-union-financed film project.[16]

The dislike of commercialized culture also extended to music. The string trio only played Schubert's B Flat Major Trio after Dawson chided them for playing popular songs by Kern and others,[17] while back in 1913, the Nixeys' party had 'a fatman at the piano rattling out ragtime'. The Nixeys are clearly a disruptive force, from outside Bruddersford (London), and the ragtime acts as a disturbing soundtrack to the party where Dawson witnesses Eleanor and Ben's attraction to each other.[18]

Dawson's Bruddersford and its localized sense of community was not, however, an isolated community. The wool trade meant that 'Bruddersford men went all over the world',[19] and this environment helped produce a range of interesting and free-thinking characters, such as Dawson's Uncle Miles, who had some 'mysteri-ous' role in the wool trade, which allowed him to watch Yorkshire play at Lords, holiday in the Dales and take part in a range of cultural pursuits. Dawson suggests that the textile trade was 'able to support hundreds of these independent lucky fellows'.[20] There were also strong characters, who on one level could be 'bellow-ing and blustering' but on another 'sensitive' and 'aware of other people's feel-ings'. Dawson was thinking of the seller Joe Ackworth in this regard, an intelligent, independent man he respected a great deal.[21] Nor did the textile trade necessar-ily produce irreconcilable class divisions. Socialist councillor Fred Knott praises manager John Alington as 'a grand chap...he runs the business and doesn't let it run him', before continuing that 'socialism's coming...there's no stopping it'.[22] Knott was a radical socialist and therefore liked more for his character than his politics. He also represented an 'earlier and more innocent phase of the Labour Movement, when it was still uncorrupted by power, not yet embittered by the thought of lost leaders, still lit by the sunrise of simple and noble aspirations'.[23]

A more reformist radicalism had a wider resonance and was intrinsically linked to the nature of the community. Thus, Dawson's Uncle Miles along with many others 'held strong, progressive views', and Jock Barniston had 'made the finest speech the town had ever remembered hearing' during a local strike.[24] This politics of community rather than class reflected Priestley's views, and the novel captures the extent to which by 1946 he was already becoming disillusioned with the way politics were functioning and who had power. Dawson notes that the 'party machinery had grown too elaborate' and also the success of the Nixeys 'who had always lacked something essential and vital' and had seemed extraordinary in 1913 but now, as Lord and Lady Harndean, seemed ordinary because there were so many like them in important positions 'because what had once been a tiny fifth column was now a settled and familiar army of occupation'.[25] When unable to sleep one evening, Dawson comes up with a story that ends with a revolution that puts 'thousand of Very Important Personages, officials, prominent executives' into long-term cold storage.[26]

Dawson's emotional re-engagement with his past is in many ways nostalgic, but the novel also makes clear the limits of nostalgia and the need to live in, and try to change, the present. This is illustrated by Dawson's relationship with the Alingtons, which is central to the novel. After first glimpsing the family, includ-ing the three attractive daughters (Eva, Bridget and Joan), on a tram, Dawson is drawn into their lives, not least because they offer excitement and sense of family that he lacks.[27] However, appearances are deceptive, and as the novel progresses, the family are revealed as troubled and ultimately destructive. John Alington is a decent man but also weak and indecisive. Joe Ackworth implies as much when, on resigning from the firm, he leaves Dawson with the impres-sion that he blames Alington for not standing up to London when Nixey was imposed on them. Significantly, Dawson remembers this as he is thinking about the appeasement of the Nazis. Alington also collapses after Eva's funeral, allow-ing the firm to come under the control of Nixey and the equally unpleasant cashier, Croxton.[28]

Eva's death also provides a revealing twist at the end of the novel. Eva seemingly falls accidentally to her death from Pikeley Scar after learning of Ben Kerry's betrayal.[29] However, Dawson's understanding of this event and his nostalgic memories of the three daughters are gradually revealed as illusions. He recalls an unsatisfactory meeting with Joan in 1919, who tells him that Eva committed suicide.[30] Then meeting with Bridget in 1946, he discovers that she is unrecognizable from the lively, pretty woman of 1913 – 'I felt the flame and fire I remembered had burnt out long ago and had left behind some toughened metallic deposit' – she tells him that Joan died 10 years earlier after becoming 'unbalanced'.[31] She calls Joan's account of Eva's suicide 'rubbish' before claiming that Dawson not only 'never understood what Joan was really like' but also did not 'really understand any of us'. She tells him that they used to laugh at his romantic view of the family and that 'he never saw us as we really were'.[32] Their meeting ends with Bridget refusing to admit the importance of the past and Dawson left to deal with the shattering of his memory of the Alingtons. His journey into the past had been hard and unsuccessful: 'I had gone back to my youth, to the Alingtons and Bruddersford on some daft treasure-hunt that I'd never really understood and had come back empty-handed...I was dead'.[33]

The final resolution, in a slightly forced happy ending, sees Dawson accept the role in the production of British films and, in the process, realize that he cannot live in the past. Mrs. Childs, who is involved in the project, tells him that the trade unions were 'worried about the kind of films people saw' and wanted to make films that 'show how real people behaved in a real world'.[34] The energy of the young people working on the project makes Dawson feel 'alive again', although still confused.[35] He then discovers that Mrs. Childs is in fact Laura Blackshaw, who at age 10 had been at the fateful picnic on Pikeley Scar. Laura effectively leads Dawson out of his preoccupation with the past and into a concern with the present. She tells Dawson that he 'must stop going back' and that 'life goes on...the worst thing to do is to turn your face away and hold yourself rigid and not let life go flowing through you'.[36] Laura is talking from experience, as her husband had died 10 years before, but she also reveals a secret that she has kept to herself about that 'dreadful Sunday', which dramatically alters the memory of that day. She tells Dawson that she saw Joan push Eva off the ledge after an argument, a confession that shatters her own poise. The tables now turned sees a more confident Dawson comforting Laura, telling her to 'blast the Alingtons' and 'march on'. Dawson is now through the barrier of his disillusionment, and having revisited his Bruddersford past, he is now convinced that he can get his life moving again by engaging with the world as it is. In doing so, he hopes that he might even find it the 'same rich warm world' of his youth.[37]

Priestley later admitted that this ending forced the novel 'out of its natural key and tone', and this is certainly true.[38] However, the ending is useful if we see the novel as a reflection of Priestley's ideas. The importance of his youth in making him who he was, but the limits of nostalgia, and the need for active citizenship to challenge the encroaching mass order had appeared earlier in Priestley's work, but *Bright Day* suggests the parameters for the following years, as Priestley, like Dawson, grappled with the rapid changes of the post-war world. However, like any artist, Priestley's ideas were influenced by his personal and professional circumstances, and the optimism of his 1946 letter to Natalie Davison proved hard to maintain in the years that followed.

The reception of his work played an important role in this process. *An Inspector Calls* has become one of Priestley's most performed and best-known plays; however, Priestley suggested that it was 'sourly noticed' by critics when it opened at the Old Vic, London, in October 1946 and it ran for less than 50 performances. The play had an interesting history to that point, having been written in a week in the winter of 1944, but due to the war, it was unable to find a theatre in London, and it was first performed in a translated version in Moscow in summer 1945.[39] Indeed, with critics tending to line up along political fault lines when the play opened in London, Priestley lamented that although written in London, it was never appreciated there and 'succeeded almost everywhere else', including Germany where there were 1,600 performances.[40]

Priestley did achieve a successful run of 422 performances with *The Linden Tree*, a powerful, if more conventional, play, which opened at the Duchess Theatre, London, in August 1947. The play is deftly written and attracted a good response. Laurence Olivier, for example, told Priestley that the final scene was 'the finest thing you have ever done'.[41] However, other than a popular but not critical success with the 'mediocre' *The Scandalous Affair of Mr. Kettle and Mrs. Moon* in 1956, Priestley was not to experience genuine success again until 1963 with his adaption of Iris Murdoch's *A Severed Head*, which, as Braine points out, is not the 'same thing' as a play written from the writer's own imagination.[42]

Priestley felt his work was undervalued and blamed this, among other things, on the changing economics, management and increasing role of fashion in theatre land. *Home Is Tomorrow* opened in late autumn 1948, and Priestley suggested that his associates thought it was one of his best (an opinion subsequent writers have not shared), but it turned out to be 'a thumping flop'. The critics were to blame according to Priestley, as their comments 'seemed to us completely idiotic, as if (they) had gone to the wrong theatre'.[43] The economics of post-war theatre was illustrated when *A Summer Day's Dream* opened in 1949, which received better reviews but pulled up short because of the expense of putting the play on. Priestley lamented in the introduction to the collected edition of his plays how costs had risen and without a subsidy the 'author-director-team theatre' was under threat, with London theatre increasingly under the control of acquisitive businessmen more interested in profits than quality plays, alongside the tendency to prioritize star performances rather than the play itself.[44]

From the end of the 1940s, Priestley also suffered from the inevitable generational shift as younger writers like Beckett and Osborne came through with new ideas, accentuated by their need to interpret a more complicated and contingent post-war world. By contrast, Priestley's work was often seen as traditional and naturalistic, with commentators missing his more experimental side: something not helped by the uneven quality of his output in this period.[45] In 1950, Priestley attacked the younger critics as 'a strange epicene type' who only praised what was fashionable and had a great influence on the box office. 'These boys are my despair', he told Davison, 'a bloody nuisance'.[46] After the disappointing failure of *Dragon's Mouth* and the difficulty putting on *The White Countess*, both of which were co-authored with Jacquetta Hawkes, Priestley complained that 'nothing is happening. I seem to have reached a point of absolute stagnation. . .in theatrical production'.[47]

Priestley's perception that he was not receiving a fair hearing in the theatre caused problems with his agent, A.D. Peters. Priestley and Peters had often had frank exchanges of views, but a particular seriousness emerged in the early 1950s as Priestley encountered problems with his plays. In 1951, the two did not see eye-to-eye over suggested revisions to the play *The High Blue Door*. Priestley was hurt by criticism of the new draft, including the suggestion that it 'lacks sympathy'. Disagreeing with this criticism, he asked Peters whether 'a horrible thought must be faced – that I am losing some sort essential gift for the theatre'. Reflecting on the dip in his fortune in recent years, he added, 'I badly need help now for my theatre work', but he denied that this had anything to do with the quality of his work. There had 'been no real falling off in my plays during these last years', he wrote, and 'I put more stuff into my serious plays than Anouilh, Fry, Tennessee Williams or any of the fashionable dramatists, it seems to me'. He continued:

> Deep down I am a hurt or now a little numbed by the antagonism or indifference to me in the theatre. On the amount and variety of work done, and in the world appeal it has had, I can reasonably count myself as the most important living English playwright; but nobody writes sympathetically about my work, no managers or actors ask for my plays, nobody seems to care a damn if I never write another play.

Priestley told Peters that he had 'probably heard this before' but that it was 'rather more serious now'. He wanted Peters to tell him whether he was 'about through with the theatre' or 'again as a friend, as my agent' to advise him and get his plays to the 'right managements and actors'. Clearly implying that Peters had not been supporting his work adequately, he told him, 'I don't want to feel that I'm lifting a dead weight from the floor, that I must not only write the plays but also plan all the moves to bring them on the stage...but want to feel that you...are with me all the way'.[48]

Peters responded to Priestley the following day telling that 'I know very well how you felt and have felt for some time...you have been passing through a bad phase', suggesting that his plays needed to be less forced and more natural and 'in tune'. He also alluded to Priestley's 'private worries' perhaps having affected his ability to write plays and told him that he had been working hard and 'behaving as if you were the most important client I have'.[49] The situation did not improve, and Peters withdrew as Priestley's theatrical agent in November 1953, although he remained in place for his other work. Priestley complained that he had 'certainly done nothing for me for some years – I did the *White Countess* job myself – and I wish he had told me earlier instead of simply not doing the job'.[50] Priestley moved to a new theatrical agent, Peggy Ramsay, but it had little effect on his fortunes in the world of theatre.[51]

Priestley's disillusionment with theatre was not compensated for by his work in other areas, where although experiencing more success, he was still subject to criticism. A return to the world of film saw him produce a screenplay for *Last Holiday* (1950) starring Alec Guinness, which, while popular with audiences, again received a mixed press.[52] He also produced a libretto for an opera *The Olympians*, composed by his Hampstead neighbour Arthur Bliss. The performances at Covent Garden in September 1949 were not a success, and the opera was not performed again until 1972.[53]

Nor was his fiction an unalloyed success. Priestley dismissed *Jenny Villiers* (1947) himself, but the mixed reception for the more significant *Festival at Farbridge* (1951) caused him more disappointment.[54] Priestley wrote the large comic novel between April and November 1950, at a terrific pace (260,000 words).[55] It was intended as 'a good natured satire' using the Festival of Britain as its subject, something that Priestley later regretted as he thought the Festival was 'a stupendous thing' with its emphasis upon the importance of the arts in the community.[56] The book sold well in Britain and became a Book Society choice for May 1951, and Priestley told Davison the following month that it had sold nearly 100,000 copies and that he was receiving 'enthusiastic letters all the time'. The United States was a different case, however, and Priestley thought that it was 'not to the ordinary American taste'.[57]

Ten years later, Priestley wrote with regret that 'its reception disappointed me as that of no other novel of mine has done'. The 'popular dailies' did not like the book because they did not like the Festival for political reasons, and intellectuals disliked his 'high spirits'.[58] *Festival at Farbridge* was a well-written comic novel, which offered a panoramic view of post-war Britain, with great characterization and genuine instances of humorous writing. However, it was also long and conventional, and its 'high spirits' were never going to please everyone in the more edgy terrain of the early 1950s. Besides, Priestley may have overstated the case, as the reviews were not quite as bad as he suggested, and even in the United States, they were not uniformly hostile.[59] The same could not be said for *The Magicians* (1954), his next novel. Priestley bridled at the suggestion that the book should be altered for the US market, and disappointed by the mixed reviews at home, he told Davison that the press treated him so badly 'you would think I was a public criminal'.[60]

A.D. Peters' mention of 'private matters' referred to the complicated conclusion of Priestley's marriage to Jane and his eventual marriage to Jacquetta Hawkes in 1953. These events have been described at length elsewhere but suffice to say the breakdown of the marriage was a long and protracted process, with Priestley conducting an affair with Hawkes from 1947. It also came to the attention of the wider public when the divorce judge granting the Decree Nisi on grounds of adultery to Jacquetta's husband, Christopher Hawkes, launched into a strong admonition of Priestley and his behaviour, including describing the latter as 'mean and cunning', which was then picked up by the press.[61] Priestley was hurt by this and blamed the publicity-seeking nature of the judge concerned. However, the incident did little to benefit his public image or his own impression of the faults of the press.[62]

Although the break-up created numerous financial and emotional problems, it coincided with other issues, including psychiatric problems suffered by the couple's daughter Mary. However, Priestley's affair and then marriage to Hawkes ultimately provided Priestley with a strong and fulfilling relationship. Ironically, Hawkes had been dismissive of Priestley before she got to know him, but the two formed a strong bond after meeting during and after a UNESCO trip to Mexico in late 1947. Hawkes was intelligent, charismatic and adventurous. Her father was a Nobel Prize winner, and she had graduated with a first from Cambridge and was an accomplished anthropologist and writer, publishing the highly regarded *A Land* in 1951. She co-authored plays with Priestley as well as the important travelogue *Journey Down a Rainbow* (1955) and was not only his companion but also his intellectual equal.[63]

Priestley's concerns about his personal finances were exacerbated by the divorce. He wrote to Mary in August 1953 that he was 'not really very well off' and that in contrast Jane, with her marriage (to ornithologist David Bannerman), was in a much better position. Rather disingenuously he suggested that he was not 'grumbling' but that he had 'tried to be generous' over the divorce settlement but had 'come out of the sticky end of it all, landed with all the tax worries, a farm I never wanted etc'. This at a time, he suggested that he had 'a reasonable desire not to work as hard as I used to'.[64] Undoubtedly, the divorce cost Priestley, and it also coincided with the downturn in his theatrical fortunes; however, Priestley was already a practiced moaner about money, and particularly taxation, and his sense of grievance grew with the passing years.

Priestley was still well off and held property in the Isle of Wight and London, but his concerns about income could be quite trivial. In 1953, he tried to let his apartments in Albany, Piccadilly, for three weeks during the coronation. He asked Natalie Davison to arrange this in the United States, so that the payment could be kept in dollars probably via American Express cheques, which he could use when he travelled abroad. In this way, he would avoid paying tax. He mooted the not-inconsiderable rent of more than $1,000 but suggested that they should wait on naming the price so that they might 'get all the traffic can bear'.[65] The plan came to nothing, however, as there were no replies to the adverts in the *New Yorker*, and then to make matters worse, the secretary of the Albany apartments, a Captain Adams, whom Priestley claimed 'hated him', made it clear that he could not sub-let his flats under the tenancy agreement. 'He is quite right', Priestley admitted, adding 'but of course I could have got round that if he hadn't spotted the adver-tisement'. This meant the plan was 'quite definitely off'.[66]

The correspondence also illustrated another interesting aspect of Priestley's life at this time. He told Natalie that the apartments would include the services of three servants, which would mean that Priestley and his son Tom would have to stay in a hotel for those three weeks as they could not go to Brook Hill on the Isle of Wight 'without the staff'. [67] Maybe not that unusual for the time, if you were part of the wealthy middle class, but nevertheless, it showed how far Priestley was living in a different world to many of the people he sought to connect with and represent in his work.

Bright Day had captured the extent to which Priestley was frustrated by the failure of politics to deliver on the promise of the early war years. As the 1940s passed into the 1950s, Priestley's criticism of the Labour Government became more frequent, and his politics shifted further to the centre. Priestley remained good at outlining a vision of what might be, but arguably he was not as effective at understanding the constraints under which the Labour Government was forced to operate or the practicalities of politics. Priestley's ideas remained relatively con-sistent with his lines of thought before and during the war, namely, his opposition to 'big', alienating institutions (private or public), an emphasis upon the quality and creativity of British life and the idea that the middle class (including artists and intellectuals) should be the driving force towards a new society. This con-tained a criticism of bankers and financiers and the unfettered free market, and in this regard, it was in tune with elements of Labour thinking. However, the use of 'big' government proved a key point of difference.

In his foreword to a biography of Francis Jowett published in 1946, Priestley lamented the fact that Jowett had not lived to see Labour's victory the previous year, which he suggested recalled some of the 'enthusiasm and breadth of appeal' of the pre-1914 Labour Movement. He suggested that it was a victory that was based not on working-class agency but on the 'swing' of middle-class voters, whose 'continued support and essential skill' were essential to the successful prosecution of politics.[68] In the same year, he told his readers, 'I like this government', but he argued that Labour must embrace new ideas and think creatively ('we want a creative community not an almshouse').[69] However, by September 1946, he was complaining to Davison in his private correspondence that the 'chief trouble' of the Labour Government was that it was 'so unimaginative', lacking any real spirit. [70]

The Linden Tree, produced in 1947, while not concerned with party politics, contained a stark picture of the need to struggle for individuality and creativity in the face of the onward march of machines. Interestingly, the play was not an exercise in nostalgia, and the central character Professor Linden resists those urging him to retire and preferred to do battle to build a better world side-by-side with some of the enthusiastic young people he has met. There are echoes here of *They Came to a City*, and although Linden is forced to accept partial retirement, he maintains enough to 'make mischief' and challenge the machines. The machine encompassed education, the civil service and the trade union in this instance, and it was the latter that marked an obvious difference with Labour and with the ending of *Bright Day*, where Dawson works on a trade union funded project. However, as we have seen, Priestley had always been critical of trade unions, seeing them as large, impersonal and often self-interested organizations, and this became sharper as time went on. In the *New Statesmen* in 1948, he included trade union leaders as part of the 'tweedledee and tweedledum' society, which saw a powerful elite, regardless of party or ideology, dominating the Cold War world. This argument had, as we shall discuss later, an international component, as the tweedles could be 'American soap manufacturers, Communist Party bosses' as well as the aforementioned trade union leaders. 'Real democracy', he told his readers, 'is disappearing from the earth'.[71]

Priestley's argument inevitably led to a clash with Labour, not least when he stressed his view that there was little difference between the parties or ideological systems. This occurred most publicly after Priestley published an article entitled 'The Truth about Democracy', in the *Sunday Pictorial* in January 1949. Reiterating the argument made in *The Secret Dream* and the *New Statesman*,[72] Priestley attacked the way Britain, Russia and the United States all claimed they represented true democracy, yet they were all 'moving away from democracy as fast as they can go' as 'in the larger states the few people who have power tend to have more and more power and the rest of us who never had much now find ourselves with less. The area of lives under our control is shrinking rapidly'. He continued, in classic Priestley mode, 'it is a fact that at the age of nineteen I had more control over my life than I have now thirty five years later', before dropping the controversial lines, 'and it is my belief that if we had a Tory Government instead of a Labour one, or imported American big business men or Russian commissars into Whitehall the result would be much the same'.[73]

Taking aim at the centrepiece of Labour's social programme, Priestley argued that while liberals were denied airtime in the United States, and in Russia 'political bosses' decided what artists should produce, in Britain similarly, 'politicians and senior civil servants are beginning to decide how the rest of us shall live'. In this context, he cited the example of the National Health Service that 'may or may not be a good scheme, but it is in my opinion fundamentally undemocratic just because it turns the private relationship between doctor and patient into official business. You take your pills by permission of the Minister of Health'. The article concluded arguing that insecurity and bewilderment might mean that the 'urban masses' do not want 'responsibility' and they might accept large organizations, and power concentrated in these, and consequently the 'independent, alert citizen, jealous of his rights is probably disappearing'. The 'democratic way' was consequently 'vanishing', and Priestley suggested, 'let us stop this idiot squabbling about which of us really has the thing we do not want. Let us find some terms that mean something, and if we *must* quarrel...then let us quarrel about what we are gaining and not what we are losing'.[74]

A quarrel was duly what Priestley got, when Michael Foot penned an immediate response in an editorial for *Tribune*, entitled 'The Futility of Mr. Priestley'. Acknowledging Priestley's reputation, including his ability to interpret 'the moods of the British public', which during the war led him to be 'hailed as a prophet of the New Britain', he asked why he now 'devotes his talents to the dissemination of a despairing cynicism'. Foot suggested that Priestley had become the most famous of a number of intellectuals who had turned sceptic about Labour's attempt at transforming Britain, making him 'the High Priest of the new defeatist cult'. Foot challenged Priestley's idea of a retreat from democracy, suggesting there were differences between the United States and Soviet Union, with the latter being much more repressive than the former. In Britain, Foot agreed with Priestley that 'bigness is an enemy', but he argued that Priestley had not looked carefully at what had been going on, not least the move towards 'industrial democracy' showed 'that most socialists are awake to the problem'.[75]

Foot focused, in more detail, on Priestley's criticism of the National Health Service, disputing the latter's claim about the new relationship between doctors and patients was now 'official', suggesting instead that 'something quite different had happened. It was the cash relationship between the doctor and the patient which has been changed, and the consequence is that many poor people will be able to afford treatment who could not afford it before, while the doctor need not distinguish between his patients because one of them has a fat purse and the other no purse at all'. Cutting to the heart of Priestley's argument, Foot argued that 'nothing so democratic perhaps was ever previously attempted in this country'. Moreover, the creation of the Nation Health Service was only one part of a more general democratization in housing and other areas, leaving Foot to suggest that 'a huge productive effort has been made' despite facing serious obstacles. He went on, 'criticisms there are in plenty, but who is there who will fail to recognise that that the democracy of Britain has been more active, vigilant and effective in the past three years than at any time in rest of the century?' Priestley's failure to concur with this view, and his emphasis upon the retreat from democracy, led Foot to conclude, 'such is the nihilism of the intellectual who will not deign to join the strivings of the common people'.[76]

Foot's words clearly stung Priestley, not least the allegation that he had lost touch with ordinary people, and he replied a few days later, professing shock at the tone of the *Tribune* article. 'This description of me as a despairing cynic', he wrote, 'is so fascinatingly wrong that I haven't the heart to denounce it'. He argued that the article illustrated the problem with the current debate, with the 'thundering soapbox on party lines', instead of the 'constructive thought in an atmosphere of tolerance' that was needed at such a difficult time. Priestley also returned to the theme of 'Health', writing 'when I am not feeling well, I like to send for our family doctor, who is our friend as well as our physician'. He continued, 'I am well aware of the fact that a great many people cannot afford to do this but I take the view that unlike Mr. Bevan and Mr. Foot of course, this is what they would like to do too. And I want us to try and create the kind of society in which everybody can behave like this, in which the dustman has his doctor just as the Prime Minister has his doctor, both of them in their private capacities as responsible citizens'. This would be 'a democracy', he argued, which they 'should try for the sake of the "common people" whose cause I am wildly accused of abandoning'. Denying this was the case, he argued that he 'was doing what I have always tried to do – namely taking my stand on their interests'.[77]

Priestley had a valid point that he 'was not a politician' and that he had defended Labour in the past and had every right to criticize if things were 'going off the rails'.[78] However, this cut both ways, and politicians had an equal right to reply to such criticisms. Priestley's original article was polemical and designed to draw a response, and he should not have been surprised when *Tribune* returned fire with additional force, as Priestley was attacking the very heart of their project. Priestley was also a little slippery in his reply, stressing a more 'constructive' approach than in his original downbeat 'democracy is vanishing' line. His argument about Health provision was also rather shaky, shrinking the delivery of health down to his personal experience as a wealthy middle-class citizen of his relationship with the family doctor. Foot was right to pull Priestley up on this and point out the fact that the issue was about money and access, and Priestley's reply not only failed to answer this but also described what Labour were trying to achieve – a doctor for every citizen. It is not clear what he was trying to say here, and what this exchange really reveals is Priestley's suspicion of large organizations and a powerful state.

Attracting the opprobrium of *Tribune* contributed to Priestley's feelings of alienation from party politics, not least because they coincided with his professional and personal problems. Priestley increasingly felt on the outside, a position which he later saw as being placed in an intellectual wilderness. This was an identity partly based on creeping personal and political disillusionment, but it also contained an element of satisfaction that suited Priestley's own personality and an acceptance that a writer should, to some extent, stand outside conventional politics. In March 1949, Priestley told Peters, amid a more general complaint of everyone being against him, that 'I did a hell of a lot to help Labour into power (I addressed more big meetings at the General Election than anybody except the top four Labour men), and got precious little thanks for that'.[79] Six months later, Priestley made a similar point to Davison, linking politics and his professional problems. He wrote, 'people like me will soon out with everybody. The Tories hate my guts; Labour is ungrateful and suspicious with types like me; and the Communists may at any moment denounce me as a fascist hyena; the highbrows think I'm a low brow; the low brows think I'm a high brow. I'm too experimental for the commercial theatre, and not silly enough for the avant garde'.[80]

However, despite his sense of being an outsider and his misgivings about Labour's appreciation of his past efforts, Priestley continued campaigning for Labour and remained on good terms with key Labour figures. He contributed to an appeal to women to vote Labour in the 1950 election, telling them that he 'hoped that women voters especially will not allow themselves to be influenced by the deliberate campaign of unpatriotic slander being carried in certain sections of the press'. This appeal to vote Labour and 'keep out the Tories' started, unlike other contributors, with the rather lukewarm suggestion that Priestley 'was not in agreement with everything' the Government had done, 'or many of the things it wants to do'; however, it suggested that he remembered what the country was like before the war and that the Tories had not 'learnt anything since then'.[81]

In January 1950, he told Davison that he had 'helped to start the election game going by a Labour Party broadcast', which was well received. Making clear his support for Labour, he told his friend, 'it may be rather a bitter election but I think Labour will win again', warning him that if that did not happen, 'then we are in for a very bad time, and our misfortunes will not help the rest of the world in general'.[82] Prime Minister Clement Attlee wrote to Priestley the following day to thank him for the 'excellent' broadcast about which he had 'heard many appreciative comments'.[83] Harold Laski did likewise, and Priestley also remained in communication with Minsters on other issues, including an appeal addressed to Herbert Morrison to consider Arthur Bliss for an honour. Morrison replied, addressing the letter to 'My dear Jack', telling him that while it was obviously too late for the New Year's honours, it would be considered for a later date.[84] Atlee again wrote to Priestley in April 1951 to thank him for sending a copy of *Festival at Farbridge*.[85]

Labour of course achieved a narrow victory in the 1950 election, but Priestley's disillusionment with the party hardened in the next few years. His enthusiasm for the 'Festival of Britain' has already been noted, but while he celebrated an 'English tradition' he could 'applaud' and criticized those who said it could not be afforded, it did not restore his faith in Labour or the belief that the nation was back on course.[86] *Festival at Farbridge* illustrated this point well, showing a country in desperate need of an injection of humour, vibrancy and life. As Laura Casey remarks early in the novel, 'what's wrong with us now is that we don't *feel* enough. There isn't enough richness and joy and glory in our lives. We are all living a thin flat sort of existence. And don't think it's anything to do with money and taxes and rations and Conservative and Labour', she added, 'because it isn't, though I'm not pretending those things don't matter'.[87]

This was not a new message, and Priestley had been calling since the 1930s for greater vitality in British Life, and the depiction of Labour and Conservative as part of the same ruling elite 'Tweedles' had been apparent in his writing for several years – hence his argument with Foot. However, in 1951, there is a more dramatic break. In a significant letter to Davison, he commented on Labour's divisions, which might lead to an election and a Conservative victory. Somewhat surprisingly he wrote, 'this does not worry me', suggesting that he was more concerned that 'Tory blunders' might lead to a swing to the 'hard left'. He told Davison that 'although I am still anti-Tory, I am becoming dubious about the psychological aspect of much of what Labour does'. Returning to his concern for the middle classes, he added that there was 'too much emphasis upon drab security, too much equalisation of a rather dreary kind, too few incentives for people to work hard and plan their futures'. He continued that 'the poor old middle classes (who on the whole are the most useful people we have, in and out of working hours) are ignored by both parties, for the Tories think about the rich and Labour about the Trade Union workers'. His solution was 'a strong revival of the Liberal Party', which was currently a 'miserable rump'.[88]

Three months later, in August 1951, Priestley told Davison that he was hoping to be out of the country in October, as he wanted to miss a possible General Election (which duly took place on 25 October and delivered a Tory majority of 17). 'I would prefer to dodge it as I don't want to do any speaking', he wrote, as 'on the whole I hope the Tories get in this time – not because I like the Tories but because either they might pull the country together or make such a mess of it that Labour would return with a much bigger majority than at present'. He added, 'there is a certain staleness about the present atmosphere that is not good'. [89]

In the same letter, Priestley also made some interesting comments about his relationship, as a writer, with politics. He told Davison that he was 'temporarily bored to death with political talk and world problems' and that he had done his fair share of 'battling' in politics 'where even your political friends dislike you if you're an author'. He suggested that there was a 'real danger in authors beginning to think and act like politicians', something which was apparent in 'Kremlin kind' communism, where 'authors are told to toe the line but never invited to decide what the line should be'.[90] Priestley clearly felt that he had been getting too close to politics and that he now wanted a degree of distance.

Priestley did not become a Conservative supporter, rather his disillusionment with Labour and a belief that the two main parties had moved closer together left him more pragmatic about party politics. His longstanding dislike of Tory politics coupled with the way Conservative figures criticized his supposed bias made such an outcome an unlikely occurrence. The argument over the postscripts was the most obvious example of what Priestley's sense of grievance was in this regard, but this was not an isolated incident. Indeed less than a year before Priestley penned the above letter to Davison, he had been embroiled in a disagreement with Tory MP, Patricia Hornsby Smith, over alleged party political bias in his work commissioned by the BBC.[91]

Priestley blew pragmatically lukewarm and mostly cold over the Conservatives in office. In January 1952, he told Davison that the 'atmosphere here is not good. The Tories can think of nothing but cutting public expenditure, raising the bank rate and shortly, I imagine, increasing taxes'. The latter being one of Priestley's bugbears, he added that the 'people need to be shown a way out' from 'apathy or chicanery', which was too present. 'I am not happy about us', he added.[92] The following month he complained that the 'Tory "cuts" have no glimmer or imagination: there is not a glimpse of any really creative action: and I despair of them'.[93] However, by April 1953, he told Davison that 'I am not fond of our Tories, as you know, but truth compels me to say they behave more sensibly than Labour did in its final years', although he criticized their support of the atom bomb.[94] Commenting the morning after the 1955 election, which gave Macmillan a 54-seat majority, Priestley wrote that they had spent the previous night at an election party given by the Conservative *Daily Telegraph* and that the result was 'in the present circumstances probably all for the best' as the Tory majority was small enough to make them 'move carefully' rather than swinging to the 'far Right'. Illustrating his disillusionment with Labour, he said that Labour 'deserved defeat because it is barren of ideas, as I have been pointing out for some time'. He added, 'the truth is, that almost all that Labour (as distinct from revolutionary socialism) wanted had been achieved'.[95]

Underlying Priestley's disillusion with Labour, and party politics, was an abandonment of his belief in socialism. Of course, as we have seen, Priestley was never a conventional socialist and had always believed in community rather than large organizations. Liberalism was also an important part of his world-view, and by the early 1950s, it was stronger than his allegiance to socialism. Complaining in 1952 about the 'Beaverbrook Press' always describing his plays as left wing propaganda, he wrote that it was ironic as 'I no longer believe in Socialism and that the Socialist-Capitalist duel is really out of date and the whole thing calls for fresh thinking instead of wrangling about dead issues'.[96] Priestley's contribution to this 'fresh thinking', which moved beyond party politics, was put forward in a series of articles published in the *New Statesman*, the first of which was called 'Thoughts in the Wilderness', which later became the title for the collected articles that were published in 1957.

Priestley began writing the articles in September 1953, but he was not sure 'how long they'll last' as 'they attack almost everything the *New Statesman* stands for'.[97] Priestley need not have worried, however, as *Thoughts in the Wilderness* contained articles through to 1957. Priestley clearly enjoyed being a polemicist, and the articles were intelligent and provocative, with Priestley even claiming rather excitedly while writing them that 'I am and now shall remain an anarchist'. [98] In the introduction to the collected edition, Priestley argued that the articles were important because, although he noted in a self-deprecating manner that an English poet had suggested that he had 'a second-rate mind' (something that Priestley conceded, although not without noting that the same was true of the poet), he had 'two assets' that were of value. The first of these was 'some sort of intuitive insight into what English people in general are thinking and feeling, a glimpse of the national mood of the moment'. He suggested that this explained the appeal of his postscripts, and 'when it was working', as he claimed it did in some of the articles collected in the book, he could 'be a jump ahead of the politicians, leader-writers and assorted pundits'. He claimed his other asset was that fact that he had his own mind, 'nobody has hired it; no hidden plan of campaign guides it', and returning to his view of himself as the spokesman for the English people, 'what it chiefly desires, even more than applause is that English people should have a good life'.[99]

Priestley clearly felt he still had his finger on the national pulse, and the articles, while not so much 'fresh thinking', restated and developed his arguments over a number of areas, some of which he had been discussing since before the war. The 'wilderness' was an important idea, as Priestley saw himself as being 'out' with both Right and Left, both of whom presented an outdated form of politics.[100] The articles depicted a modern world dominated by big organizations and structures and 'block thinking', producing a consequent alienation and lack of creativity – 'men are in despair', he argued.[101] Priestley again returned to the issue of the state in these considerations, pointing out rightly that even when a 'left propagandist', he had mistrusted the powerful state.

Now, echoing claims made in earlier writing, he claimed that both parties were 'state parties', even though one claimed it was not, and the public had become 'subservient to the idea of the state', turning citizens into unthinking beings.[102] The Welfare State attracted criticism, because the role of the state in welfare was 'creating a dim passivity',[103] and Priestley even questioned spending so much on state education, while not creating a vibrant world outside school. He contrasted his own Bradford youth where he learnt more outside than inside school when 'the state was not investing a penny in me'.[104]

Mass culture was always near the top of Priestley's agenda, and in the *New Statesman* articles, he saw it as being instrumental in the alienation of modern life in the Cold War era. Priestley argued that books and quality journalism had declined, replaced by mass communication via television, radio and the popular press. Priestley had, of course, been making similar points since the 1930s, but he argued that the situation was now even worse. Compared to the localized culture where people had been on the 'fringes of real culture', which he claimed had existed in the early twentieth century, mass culture was manufactured and unoriginal. 'To succeed in mass communications you must flatter the customer and never disturb him'. Talented people were no longer interested in 'elevating the masses' but instead 'catering to all their whims, prejudices, and idiocies'. In this post-war world, 'everything must be made smooth and easy. No effort must be required. History must be falsified, science distorted, religion sentimentalised, human relations hopelessly over-simplified so that nobody is challenged, disturbed, asked to reflect or feel deeply'. High art was no better, often setting out to be 'anti-mass culture', but instead producing 'thin, sterile' work. 'Thus in BBC terms', he argued, 'the Third Programme is as bad in its way as the Light Programme...thrillers written in American slang are sad bosh, but so are "experimental" novels...the arts are so precious, fancy and fenced-off' that ordinary people had lost interest. [105]

Priestley had always seen culture in political terms, and he argued forcibly that mass culture was a politically conservative force that helped destroy what was left of the vibrant wartime spirit. He conceded that 'many of us were too optimistic' during the war and 'did not realise then how easily mass culture, with its immense resources of publicity, could defeat us. We were like a man with a woodcut trying to compete with a four-colour poster thirty feet by ten'.[106] This was a powerful image that captured Priestley's ability to make his point in an accessible and emotionally powerful way.

And matters were made worse by the fact that mass culture was also playing a role in undermining Priestley's chosen agents for change, the middle classes. He told readers that middle classes who were 'overworked, worried and on the edge of a ditch' were his chosen audience.[107] However, the 'new' middle class of the post-war world was losing its radical edge and sense of social responsibility, replacing it instead with a desire for security and an acceptance of the 'any shoddy cheapjack set of values'. He continued, 'so more and more we find ourselves amongst either the simple or the cynical, the manipulators and the manipulated'.[108]

Thoughts in the Wilderness covered an array of subjects, including Priestley's scepticism about science and rationalism and 'neat sets of beliefs and opinions', believing that it may be 'that men need some form of religion', albeit not in its orthodox form.[109] Priestley's interest in metaphysics also led him to discuss his theories on Time, claim the significance of Jung, and to consider the problems facing the world in terms of Eros, Yin (feminine) and Logos, Yang (masculine), suggesting there was too much of the latter and not enough of the former.[110] The articles also examined the question of 'Americanisation' and the Cold War and atomic threat, both of which will be discussed later.

However, for all the breadth and energy on display, Priestley was still short on solutions, other than calling for a more vibrant cultural life and greater engagement in a new (undefined) politics. It was also unclear quite how Priestley had an 'intuitive insight' into the feelings of the English people, as the articles were different to the postscripts that spoke to a nation sharing the common experience of war. Instead, these articles were written in by a self-confessed voice in the 'wilderness' and spoke mainly to the middle class in a changing and more diverse nation. Despite these shortcomings, it must not be forgotten, as he had pointed out, that he was a writer not a politician, and it is the artists' role to think in the abstract and big ideas rather than draw up detailed policy plans. Priestley clearly impressed many readers and other public figures, including Malcolm Muggeridge who told him how much he liked Priestley's argument in the first of his articles, saying he held very similar views himself.[111] Hugh Gaitskell also told Priestley that he liked the *New Statesman* articles, particularly his views on the impact of television.[112]

Priestley's disillusionment with Labour, and broader party politics, and his concern about the deteriorating quality of life in Britain were often considered within the context of the Cold War. As we have seen, Priestley was no 'Little-Englander', and from his youth in cosmopolitan Bradford, he had been interested in the wider world, and this had been cemented by the global nature of World War II. The messy end of the latter conflict and its segueing into the Cold War were matters of great interest to Priestley, and as a consequence, Cold War issues were directly and indirectly considered in much of his work. And, as in domestic politics, Priestley was sceptical of the approach taken by those in power, being particularly critical of anti-communism and anti-Sovietism, believing that no one side had a monopoly of right and wrong. He also had deep misgivings about the way the world was dividing into two oppositional blocs, not least because he believed Britain still had an important, independent role to play on the international stage. In some ways, his views coincided with the 'Third Way' of Bevan and others in Labour; however, he was more independent and idealistic in his approach to the Cold War. [113]

Priestley's views on Russia were influenced by a visit he made in the autumn of 1945, after receiving an invitation from the Soviet 'Society for Cultural Relations with Foreign Countries'. Priestley's account of the trip was published in the *Sunday Express* in November and December 1945 and was then reprinted as a pamphlet, *Russian Journey*, the following year. He described a country still reeling from the massive disruption and dislocation of war, but one that showed energy and resilience and was considerably freer than he had been led to believe, including 'strolling around by ourselves' in Moscow, unbothered by secret police or anyone else. [114]

He was very well received, finding himself to be 'one of the most popular authors' in the country, with crowds bursting through the doors of a large hall in Moscow so they could hear him speak. [115] This helped inform his view that Soviet cultural life was much richer than many in the West thought. This included freedom of worship, which Priestley observed in Leningrad.[116] Priestley also felt that he connected with the ordinary Russian people, particularly 'Young Russia', and he appreciated their sociability with food and drink and their knowledge of English and Britain. [117] Describing the end of the journey, he wrote, 'the last we saw of Russia was the sight of their friendly faces...They welcomed us as friends; they said good-bye to us as friends: and, come what may, we shall remain their friends. Wouldn't you?'[118]

In the final article in the series, which Priestley described as the 'most important', he discussed the way his visit had informed his view of the relationship between 'The Russians and Ourselves'. He argued that a lack of communication and propaganda on both sides had led to a misunderstanding between Russia and the West. 'In many important matters', he wrote, 'as, for example, in our conception of what is and what is not democracy – we and the Russians are simply at cross-purposes, and could do with more frank discussions'. He went on to challenge the West's view of an aggressive, expansive Soviet Union. Pointing out the destruction caused by the Nazi's attack on the country, he argued that the Soviets wanted 'security' and that 'in the same situation we should want exactly the same thing'. He continued, 'I say that the USSR is not fundamentally an aggressive power, hungry for more territory (it has enough and to spare) but a war-weary and still fearful power, insisting on security, while it heals its deep wounds'.[119] He hammered the point home by questioning the longstanding hostility towards the Russian regime and returning to the theme of 'friendship'. 'I declare emphatically that what the Russians want is not power or glory or some of the outside world's possessions but friendship, real solid friendship' and that 'years ago we made a terrible blunder, for which we have all paid heavily, by refusing to encourage them and help them, by even attacking them in force'. This hand of friendship should be made in spite of the repressive elements in the Soviet Union, as underneath the 'steely front' of Marxism, the Russian people exhibited a collective sense of 'fraternity', and a more positive interaction, including 'friendly criticism', would 'enrich both our lives and theirs, for we have much to teach, and much to learn'.[120]

Priestley's views not only ran against the grain of the strengthening anti-Sovietism of the Cold War years, but his writing sought to counteract the barrage of anti-communist writing – something that in part explains his sympathetic portrayal of Russia. This position somewhat inevitably led to further suggestions that he was a communist or communist sympathizer. Any cursory reading of Priestley's work from the 1940s and 50s, much like that of the 1930s, made such a suggestion bizarre – his independent streak, and dislike of the state, being the most obvious reasons – but such was the climate of the times that even George Orwell included him in his infamous list of 'crypto communists'. Orwell produced the list for the Foreign Office's secretive 'Information Research Unit' on 4 May 1949, and in it, he suggested that Priestley 'appears to have changed latterly' and was a 'strong sympathiser' who 'possibly has some kind of organisational tie-up'. Orwell went further and speculated that Priestley probably made 'huge sums of money in the USSR' and that he was 'very anti-USA'. However, two question marks at the end of the comments did mean there was some doubt about these assertions.[121]

A communist he was not, and it is interesting that in the final article on Russia, Priestley mentions the oppressive side of the Soviet regime, yet barely mentions it in the earlier articles describing the visit. His depiction of the latitude given to writers was somewhat contradictory, suggesting that on one hand they 'cannot publicly produce work that violently disagrees with Soviet policy', yet on the other 'they certainly do not feel themselves to be fettered in any way, and are more inclined to pity than envy their colleagues in capitalist countries'.[122]

The 'capitalist countries' may not have had the moral superiority they believed they had, and indeed the West had its own ways of stifling artists, including the anti-communist crusade that was at its strongest in the United States, and silenced dissenting and different voices, as did the market that prioritized commercial, mainstream and mainly white, middle class and male work over that of other groups. However, this was not on the same scale as Soviet intervention in the arts, and Priestley had only to look more carefully at the problems experienced by artists like Dmitri Shostakovich to see the fear, threats and forced compromises that Soviet artists were forced to work under.[123]

However, Priestley's views on engagement rather than demonization of the Soviets and the argument that security rather than aggression was at the heart of their interaction with the West were on better foundations. The Cold War may have seen a widening gulf and increasing polarization between the Soviets and the West, but a substantial minority at the time saw this as mistaken, something that had been backed up by revisionist historians. [124]And Priestley remained consistent in his views, maintaining a trenchant critique of the Cold War, arguing, as we have already seen in his spat with Michael Foot, that all sides could learn from each other.

This was linked to his argument that there was a growing gap between leaders and led and that his English 'people' had more in common with the Russians he met in 1945 than they did with the powerful elites who dominated the country.

Priestley made his views explicit in his 1946 pamphlet, *The Secret Dream: An essay on Britain, America and Russia*, developed from radio broadcasts, which suggested that having defeated fascism, the three powers needed to share ideas with each other, with the British representing liberty, the United States equality and the Russians fraternity. In these terms, Britain's dream of 'liberty' was currently in abeyance, in accord with Priestley's argument about a lack of vitality and imagination in British life. However, it could be revitalized by the American sense of equality and enterprise, while also learning from the Russian a sense of collectivity.[125]

The United States was seen as economically and politically powerful, but it had seen its dream of equality falter, with corruption, inequality and a trivialization of culture coming to the fore. The celebration of the American Revolution had become a myth and acted as a barrier against further change, meaning the United States might move 'towards a kind of Fascist economy'. The United States, he argued, could reignite their interest in equality by learning about 'collective living' from Russia and liberty from Britain. [126]

The Russians were treated more generously, with fraternity seen as being held back by a repressiveness caused largely by Western criticism: 'The Russian dilemma arises from the fact that the revolution was not welcomed by the outside world, but was continuously and bitterly attacked, and so had to mask and amour itself and turn the country into a national fortress'. The experience of war presented a new opportunity and with the British idea of liberty and the American's equality, Russia might widen 'the narrow entrances, pulling down the high walls, and declaring the fortress and open city'.[127] Learning from each other, the three powers could 'create together a broad highway for a world civilization, which should know the blue air of liberty and the twinkling and glowing white and red stars of Equality and Fraternity'.[128]

The pamphlet notably placed Britain on an equal footing with Russia and the United States and this continued in later articles, including the depiction of a shared, interchangeable elite suggested in the *New Statesman* and *Sunday Pictorial* in 1948-49. Priestley's sharp criticism of the United States had drawn Foot's ire, but Priestley was concerned about American influence. Thus, in September 1946, he blamed the Americans for pushing the anti-Soviet line, despite the fact that the Russians 'wanted war about as much as I want ten rounds with Joe Louis'. [129] He wrote to Jane from Mexico in November 1947 that he would 'have a good try to prevent UNESCO from becoming an instrument of American propaganda'.[130]

He also discovered that his criticism of the United States and his attempt at understanding Russia were not reciprocal on the latter's part and also left him caught between two stools. 'I have recently been having a little dust-up with the Russians and some of the Communists here as I have refused to support those phony 'Peace conferences and appeals', he wrote in June 1950'.[131] Two months later, an angry Priestley asked Davison, 'did I tell you I have been denounced in Moscow as a war-monger? All because I have refused to have anything to do with these impudent 'Peace conferences' and have pointed out that the Kremlin has done everything possible to avoid creating a genuinely peaceful world'. He then complained about the Americans assuming anti-communism and 'Americanism' are the same thing, suggesting that 'sometimes it looks as if we must choose between Russian Communism and Americanism'. He told Davison, 'we prefer the latter, of course; but what a hell of a dilemma to be in'. He added pointedly, 'It is ironical too that post-war Britain, so often denounced and libelled by American journalists, should be the country with the fewest communists'.[132]

Priestley made the same point about being forced to choose between two unpleasant alternatives in the *Thoughts in the Wilderness* articles where, using his Eros/Logos analogy, he argued that both the United States and Russia were too Logos (masculine), and he 'did not want either of these Yang-heavy societies, which are less harmonious, less civilised, less capable of providing the deeper satisfactions than the smaller and older communities' they were oppressing. 'We should form a neutral block', he wrote, with a 'banner of Eros...which had not yet been completely banished from Western Europe'.[133]

A more critical line on Russia also reinforced Priestley's disillusionment with political leadership across the board. He repeated his established argument about politicians and their bureaucrats having more in common with each other than the 'ordinary, sensible citizen', but also argued that far from sharing the best ideas from each other, as he had argued in *The Secret Dream*, political elites were becoming repressively similar. The Russians, he argued, 'in whose lives politics are the cancer, have set the pace for our world. If the Reds have leaders fifty feet tall, then we anti-Reds must have giant leaders too, ten feet this year, twenty feet the next; and all the time for the rest of us the barbed wire rises and more and more gates are slammed in our faces'.[134]

In the same volume, returning to the theme of Dawson's dream in *Bright Day*, where world leaders were put into long-term cold shortage, Priestley imagined a 'Hesperides Conference' attended by political and military leaders, where, by the fifth day, everyone had fallen into a light coma. Far from collapsing in the absence of the political elite, the world becomes happier, more creative and peaceful and wonderfully bereft of the dialogue of recrimination that passed for politics.

For the first time for many years no important speeches were made, denouncing the West from the East, the East from the West. No new crusade against communism was mentioned. World Revolution was placed in cold storage. Neither God nor the historic destiny of mankind was loudly proclaimed an ally. No threats, no jeers, were exchanged ......
Millions of people who had been weighed down with feelings of fear, hate, horror and guilt now found themselves in a different world. At last they could breathe freely. They began to make sensible long-term plans for the future.

Comically, this utopia is threatened by a Spanish doctor who injects an antidote into 'one Chief-of-Staff, One Under-Secretary for Foreign Affairs and one economic adviser'. In less than an hour, the three 'were beginning to make angry speeches or to demand secretaries to attend so that they could dictate aggressive memos'. When the Spanish doctor offers to come back with more antidotes and to treat the whole conference, he is led away, and the article ends with him being addressed by the doctors monitoring the sleeping conference. 'What was their decision?' Priestley asked, finishing with 'No prizes for the best reply'. [135]

The Cold War also provided the subject for some of Priestley's fictional writing. The unsuccessful play *Home Is Tomorrow* (1948) was influenced by Priestley's experience at the UNESCO conference and explored the problems of internationalism in a period of power politics and ruthless commercial self-interest. The play sees the United Nations Underdeveloped Treaty Organisation (UNUTO) who are helping the small South Caribbean Island, Corabana, emerge from colonial rule but are being undermined by Pan American Alloys who want to control the island for its supplies of Beryllium (which can be used in atomic production). Britain and the United States connive in this process, and even UNUTO is presented in an ambivalent way as providing education and order, but also a bland uniformity. [136]

Home Is Tomorrow was followed by the more effective and successful drama, *Summer Day's Dream* (1949). [137] Priestley played down the political nature of the play, arguing instead that it was 'a fantastic comedy' in which 'certain values come up for discussion'. [138] However, the play is more forthright than Priestley suggested, offering an alternative, localized utopia where, following an atomic war, the Dawlish family have rediscovered a balanced and satisfying life amid the rural setting of the South Downs. Set in the year 1975, the play tells how three visitors, Franklyn Heimar representing American big business, Irina Shetova representing Soviet Communism and Dr. Bahru representing Scientific rationalism, arrive in the area to test whether the chalk on the downs can be used in the manufacture of 'a new synthetic substance'. [139] Bahru's conclusion that it can be used opens the way for the potential destruction of the Dawlish's rural idyll, with the removal of the chalk, and the construction of an industrial plant and supporting town. [140]

The play presents a debate over the fate of Dawlish's utopia and a learning process for the three outsiders who discover the simple beauty of life in the unspoilt

Sussex downland as opposed to their modern, fast moving industrial world. Romance makes an appearance in the relationship between Irina and Dawlish's grandson Chris, and the reverence for nature connects with a debate between rationalism and mysticism. In the end, heart rather than head wins, even for the particularly hard-headed Heimar, when the visitors decide not to pursue their interest in the area. As the visitors are on the verge of leaving, all changed by their visit, Dawlish thanks them, adding 'and God be with you'. When his daughter-in-law, the mystical Margaret, chides him for not knowing 'anything about God', Dawlish gives voice to Priestley's philosophy and captures the meaning of the play. 'I never pretended to', he tells her, 'but man is a god-worshipping creature, and if he doesn't choose to worship a mysterious power of goodness and love, then he'll find something else – and something much worse – to adore'. [141]

Dawlish then unravels the three alternatives suggested by his visitors. The state comes first and 'is about as sensible as making a god out of the local gasworks', followed by Heimar's 'business, which asks you to adore dividends and bank balances', and finally, and most damning of all, science, 'which means that a man's mind worships one bit of itself – idiotic! Or the devil himself who can easily masquerade as God'. Bahru counters that there is 'no devil', but Dawlish replies emotionally, 'stupidity and pride, booted and spurred on in power, are the devil – and for sixty years I watched his temples and instruments multiply, until a thousand cities vanished in flame and dust and a hundred million bodies were consumed in agony upon his altar'. [142]

This graphic portrayal of nuclear conflict illustrated Priestley's growing concern about the atomic arms race. He was not alone in these fears, and both artists and their audiences shared a fear of previously unimaginable destruction, which was expressed across the plurality of art forms. [143] For Priestley, as Dawlish's words suggested, nuclear war was the ultimate consequence of the poisonous political developments he was writing about in his journalism. Science, or rather the worship of science and the scientist, was intrinsic to the culture that produced the bomb, the 'devil' acting as god. This had always been a theme for Priestley and remained so. 'You may be feel that pseudo scientific thought about man and the universe, sinking into the popular mind, has done much to create a mood of despair, making men feel homeless exiles, caught in a blind machine', he wrote in 1953, before making the link to the bomb writing about taking 'a sour view of recent contributions of nuclear physics to human progress, and discover in its professors a certain irresponsibility'. This irresponsibility of the scientists concerned underlined that there was a choice here, and the latter could choose to 'make narrower claims and take longer-term views'. [144]

Priestley made a similar point in 1957, when bemoaning a cold he had picked up in Bradford he asked that science 'give me a cold cure before a sputnik'. He also returned to the more manipulative role of science 'as a kind of substitute religion' where scientists 'do not adapt themselves to our desires. We have to adapt our desires to them'. [145]

Priestley's suspicion of the science/nuclear issue had been given further impetus by a visit to the United States in 1954. The visit that was recorded in *Journey Down a Rainbow* (1955) included an account of a tour of Los Alamos by Hawkes.[146] This helped inspire Priestley to make an important intervention in the domestic debate over nuclear disarmament and, in the process, temporarily rediscover some of his faith in dormant English radicalism. This began with an influential article 'Britain and the Nuclear Bombs' published in the *New Statesman* in November 1957, shortly after Aneurin Bevan had announced his turnaround on nuclear disarmament.[147]

Priestley challenged Bevan's decision, systematically attacking the assumptions that lay behind a British deterrent and making a powerful case for unilateral disarmament. He poured scorn on the competitive nature of the nuclear arms race as 'an insane regress of ultimate weapons that are not ultimate', and the idea that they would not be used. 'Why should it be assumed that the men who create and control such monstrous devices *are* in their right minds?. . .three glasses too many of vodka or bourbon-on-the rocks, and the wrong button may be pushed'. Priestley knew that the procedure for launching a nuclear attack was more complicated than this, but the imagery neatly apportioned blame to both the United States and Russia and illustrated the dangerous climate that currently existed. Hammering home this point he wrote, 'combine this stockpiling of nuclear weapons with a crazy competitiveness, boastful confidence in public and a mounting fear in private, and what was unthinkable a few years ago now at the best only seems unlikely and very soon may seem inevitable'. [148]

Criticizing those who approached the nuclear issue with fatalism, Priestley countered that 'the spell can be broken. . .by an immensely decisive gesture, a clear act of will'. This meant 'in plain words: now that Britain has told the world she has the H-bomb, she should announce as early as possible that she has done with it, that she proposes to reject, in all circumstances, nuclear warfare'. This was not an act of 'pacifism' but something that would strengthen Britain's security, because in the arms race, Britain was not a significant player: 'once the table stakes were being raised, the chips piling up, we were out'. The British had been 'fooling ourselves' worried about 'losing our national prestige', when in fact 'we have none in term of power'.[149]

And to make matters worse, this was undermining what Priestley saw as Britain's real contribution to the world. 'We ended the war high in the world's regard and we could have taken over its moral leadership, spoken and acted for what remained of its conscience; but we chose to act otherwise'. Priestley mocked Bevan's suggestion that if Britain disarmed, the world would then be 'polarised' between the two superpowers, arguing that Labour had rejected the idea of a 'Third Force' and had ceded any independence by allowing US bases in East

Anglia. 'We cannot', he wrote, 'at one and the same time be both an independent power, bargaining on equal terms, and a minor ally or satellite'. Instead of this 'nuclear gamble' where Britain had little or no influence, disarmament would set the world an example to contrast the current polarization. Priestley noted that there would be opposition to this move as 'all habit is against it', including allies in NATO and similar organizations and the United States, who would find that the 'unsinkable (but expendable) aircraft carrier would have gone'. This would also affect the 'service chiefs and their staffs' who would have to resign and were just as 'fantastic and unreal' as their 'political and diplomatic colleagues'. Priestley commented with due irony that their 'professional duties' involved 'attending in advance to the next war. Number three in the World Series'. [150]

In contrast to these critics, Priestley argued that 'sensible men and women' were already seeing through some of the arguments for a nuclear deterrent. Using language reminiscent of the postscripts, Priestley concluded

> Our bargaining power is slight; the force of our example might be great. The catastrophic antics of our time have behind them men hag-ridden by fear . . . If we openly challenge this fear, then we might break the wicked spell that all but a few uncertified lunatics desperately wish to see broken, we would could begin to restore the world to sanity and lift this nation from its recent ignominy to it's former grandeur.

This referred, of course, to World War II, when 'alone, we defied Hitler; and alone we can defy this nuclear madness into which the spirit of Hitler seems to have passed, to poison the world'. And this energy and ambition could be rediscovered. 'The British of these times, so frequently hiding their decent, kind face behind masks of sullen apathy or sour, cheap cynicism' wanted more, 'something great and noble in its intention that would make them feel good again. And this might well be a declaration to the world that after a certain date one power able to engage in nuclear warfare will reject the evil thing for ever'.[151]

'Britain and the Bomb' was impassioned, independent, engaged and subjective, and it drew an immediate response and was turned into a fast-selling pamphlet.[152] It joined an intellectual critique of nuclear defence policy with an almost religious moral stance. Kingsley Martin's editorial in the same issue of the *New Statesman* approved enthusiastically of much of what Priestley had written but suggested that the 'trump card' of NATO membership should not be given up so easily.[153] Many *New Statesman* readers had even fewer quibbles and bombarded the paper's offices with messages of support, so many in fact that the paper passed a large number of them on to the Hampstead-based 'National Campaign against Nuclear Weapons Tests', led by Bertrand Russell. The latter was part of a fledgling anti-nuclear movement, and Bevan's speech followed by Priestley's response became the 'final catalyst' for a more effective campaign to kick off. [154]

Following discussions, the Campaign for Nuclear Disarmament (CND) was launched at Central Hall, Westminster on 17 February 1958, addressed by leading radicals including Priestley, A. J. P Taylor, and interestingly Michael Foot. Priestley's speech was as 'spell-binder', and subsequently Priestley and Hawkes threw themselves into the campaign. However, the lack of press coverage of the meeting was a warning sign that many did not share, or were not interested, in the anti-nuclear campaign.[155] Priestley, however, was hopeful, believing that there was 'a steadily rising tide of indignant feeling about the whole nuclear lunacy', and spoke across the country, as well as secured the showing of his nuclear satire *Doomsday for Dyson* on ITV on 10 March 1958.[156] The following year he organized a benefit 'Stars in Their Eyes' at the Royal Festival Hall; however, he was not prepared to join CND marches, unlike Jacquetta, who not only marched but also was often at the front alongside Priestley's friends Canon John and Diana Collins. Jacquetta was also involved in setting up with Diana Collins a women's group within CND, which would travel to the UN and White House as part of its campaigning.[157]

Priestley's spirits were beginning to flag as early as spring 1958 as he found the campaigning was distracting him from writing, and he was also taken aback by the significant opposition they were encountering, including having been the subject of 'smears' and being 'insulted in the press'.[158] In May 1958, he told Davison that the politicians were 'worried' by the campaign, but he lamented that CND was 'almost entirely a middle class movement' because the working class were more interested in watching television.[159] Given Priestley's comments in published articles, this comment was not surprising, but it was nevertheless a somewhat patronizing generalization (not least because both middle- and working-class viewers welcomed television) and illustrated the extent to which Priestley's belief in the 'people' had now collapsed into an unrealistic prioritization of the middle class. It also underlined how unrealistic he had been in his idealistic assessment of the potential re-awakening of the British people. Priestley would continue to work for CND, but with less enthusiasm, not least when disputes opened up over tactics, and he finally resigned when Russell departed in 1962. [160]

Priestley's involvement in CND had brought him into the public eye again and illustrated his radical approach to foreign policy. His hopes of a rejuvenation of wartime radicalism were disappointed though, and this fitted in with a general sense of disillusionment in the years following 1945. Personal and professional problems crowded in, as did his unease at the domestic and international political situations.

Priestley's problematic relationship with Labour was fractured in the early 1950s, and he moved from liberal socialism to a more centrist, liberal position. In many ways, this was inevitable, as Priestley's dislike of large organization, including the state, was always going to be tested when a Labour Government actually held office and attempted to rebuild the country after the war. Priestley's willingness to challenge assumptions and call the powerful to account was valuable and often perceptive, and as an artist, Priestley was often trying to create a debate and make people think. In this, he was successful, but there was also an element of exaggeration, not least in his celebration of the middle class, and dismissal of the working class, at a time when popular culture and affluence were shifting class boundaries. Priestley had found the spread of the mass society problematic from the 1930s, and by the 1950s, he was more willing to see its negative consequences than anything more democratic. His relationship with the mass society and the United States was intertwined and would provide further evidence of the strengths and weaknesses of his approach to the post-war world.

5

Priestley, Admass and the United States

In November 1954, J. B. Priestley and Jacquetta Hawkes embarked on a month-long trip to the United States to research a book that would contrast the 'earliest men' of the South West with life in contemporary Texas. Planned as alternate chapters, possibly in the form of letters (a format that was partly adopted), the two writers received the necessary advance they sought from their publishers and embarked on their voyage of discovery. [1] Unsurprisingly perhaps, Priestley found his task harder going, complaining from the Baker Hotel in Dallas, on 12 November 1954, about 'heavy rich oil hospitality (very boring)' and that he was worried about whether he would find enough material for the book in the Texan cities, in contrast with Hawkes who was engaged in 'a much pleasanter' and fulfilling journey in rural New Mexico.[2] However, two weeks later, the couple met in Sante Fe, and Priestley believed that they both 'had a promising amount of stuff' in note form and they were 'busy working out the form and general plan of our book'.[3] The book was written over the following months and was published in September 1955 under the title, *Journey Down a Rainbow*. While not selling particularly well, it attracted a number of good reviews and marked an important, and in some ways visionary, intervention in the debate on the post-war mass society. It also reignited longstanding accusations of anti-Americanism on Priestley's part and underlined his difficult relations with members of the American fourth estate.

The book was a clever mix of travel writing, social observation and personal and philosophical comment. In the preface, written by Priestley, he made it clear that this was not just another volume by European writers visiting the United States and, moreover, that 'the proper time for such books has gone'. This was because 'we are already in another age, when America mostly pays the piper and calls for most of the tunes. There is no longer any point in leaving Leicester Square and Coventry Street in order to describe Broadway, which merely has more electric light, newer Hollywood films, larger cafeterias'. Reiterating this point, Priestley argued that 'English readers have not to be conducted across the Atlantic now to observe the American style of urban life; it can be discovered in the nearest town. It is now the great invader'.[4]

Explaining the basis for the comparison between the older community structures in New Mexico and the most modern in Texas, Priestley reiterated the relevance of choosing the latter that represented 'the social and cultural pattern of the mid-twentieth century', which were currently 'only dimly seen in many English and West European cities'. Interestingly, Priestley mentions the fact that it was impossible to pass through any American town without 'seeing the crimson-and-gilt facade of a Woolworth's store' and that the largest of these was in Houston, Texas.[5] This is significant, as Priestley had of course used Woolworths as a symbol of modern mass society 22 years earlier in *English Journey*.[6] The preface defended the book's concentration on issues such as popular leisure and culture as opposed to 'official' sources and statistics, suggesting that the United States was best understood by looking at people 'when they are spending the money they have earned, when they are feeling easy and relaxed'. This approach explains much about the book's significance and its affinity to later approaches in academia that stressed studying society from ordinary people's experience.[7]

The book covered a variety of themes, most prominently the issue of the mass society. Both authors were consistently critical of the modern Texan experience, and Priestley coined the phrase 'Admass', which he introduces a third of the way through the book, to describe what he was experiencing. Admass was 'the whole system of an increasing productivity, plus inflation, plus a rising standard of material living, plus high pressure advertising and salesmanship, plus mass communications, plus cultural democracy and the creation of the mass mind, the mass man'. The Communist Bloc also had its own counterpart, 'Propmass' with 'official propaganda taking the place of advertising', which tallied with Priestley's views that were expressed in other media in this period. Admass had held most Americans in thrall 'for the last thirty years', although there were 'some fine rebels' against this system. Britain and 'most' of Western Europe had been under its spell since the war. Priestley's description of life under Admass was withering. He acknowledged that the system was better than starving and being unemployed; however, he added, 'that is all that can be said in favour of it', before describing the rest as 'a swindle. You think everything is opening out when in fact it is narrowing and closing in on you. Finally you have to be half-witted or half-drunk all the time to endure it'.[8]

Priestley's kingdoms within the 'empire' included 'Nomadmass', which was based around the car, the trailer parks, bill boards, motels, drive-in movies and related elements of car culture, including pensioners and others forever on the move travelling through these areas. 'Hashadmass' was where everything was 'turned into one tasteless hash', a post-modern mixing of styles and themes. Priestley likened it to 'one of those Hollywood studio' lots 'that contain town halls, churches, mansions, saloons, all without interiors' done in the style of 'New York, London, Paris, Shanghai and Tombstone, Arizona circa 1885'. These were meant to be filmed in the background, whereas people were expected to live in hashadmass, which is an existence robbed of character and essence. Finally, 'Luxad' was built on the wealth from hashadmass, where the wealthy are 'unpaid actors in character parts - Men of Distinction, Gracious Living Hostess, member of Casual Living younger set etc.'[9]

These terms were deployed occasionally for the remainder of the book, but it was the umbrella term, Admass, that would pass into more general usage in the years to come. However, the book offered more than such general theories. Hawkes explored Native American ceremonies, ancient settlements and the way Native American culture co-existed uneasily with contemporary culture (including tourism). She also marvelled at Native American goods, as when seeing a pueblo pot, she recalled 'becoming more excited as I discover how all these things can annihilate all the expensive machine products of the age', while a basket maker's sash made from dog hair made all the items for sale in a Fifth Avenue store in New York pale into insignificance. [10]

Hawkes admired the resilience of the Pueblos and hoped that they would be able to resist the incursion of mainstream United States. She also came into contact with what she described as 'refugees from the American Way of Life' who were in rebellion against mainstream American values.[11] Many of them gathered in Sante Fe and were artists, anthropologists, historians and 'cranks', a large number of whom were engaged in working with the local Indians. [12] Hawkes admired their opposition to Admass but noted that Priestley probably would not. 'They are individuals flying their own colours...members of the resistance', she wrote, whose ideas were spreading to other parts of the country.[13]

Hawkes also visited Los Alamos while she was in the vicinity, discovering a dull, regulated one-industry town that was not as frightening as she had expected. She wrote, 'as we passed the colossal dark drum of the Black Mesa I wished Los Alamos had been built on its summit, then we'd have the devil's stronghold without disguise', before considering whether the residents felt any guilt about the work many of them carried out. [14] The visit helped encourage the anti-nuclear beliefs of both Hawkes and Priestley, and the Cold War is ever present in the book. A red cap porter might, Priestley mischievously believed, be an FBI agent, while a fancy dress competition at the 'Allied Arts Costume Ball' was won by a group who were all joined together. They took the title 'chain reaction'.[15]

Priestley kept coming into contact with the anti-communist campaign, which was still strong in the United States, although Joe McCarthy was compromised after the 'Army-McCarthy' hearings and was censured by his Senate colleagues on 2 December 1954.[16] Priestley noted the anti-communist 'drivel' in Texan newspapers, including letters from readers who believed that Alger Hiss had given China to the 'Reds' as a gift and that 'war was to be avoided by threatening with total destruction everybody who did not agree with the folks in Sweetwater, Eagle Pass, or Brownswater'. [17] On meeting a vehement anti-communist who saw 'Reds everywhere, Red plots in everything', he suggested that in a political culture dominated by Admass, where people were 'anxious for complete security without reference to ideas', such a man could take advantage of the 'frustration' people felt and 'stampede crowds into lunatic action'. Moreover, this could happen on a larger scale where backed by oil money and using television, 'God only knows what kind of a crackpot but dangerous thing could soon be let loose in these parts'.[18] Priestley no doubt had the wayward Senator for Wisconsin in mind as an example of this. Priestley's opposition to anti-communism in American Foreign Policy had been made patently clear in other publications, but as *Journey Down a Rainbow* showed, he was equally critical of US domestic anti-communism. Indeed his views on this matter led in June 1955 to a bitter spat with Rebecca West, when he attacked what he saw as her sympathetic approach to US anti-communism.[19]

Priestley was also concerned with gender relations under Admass, mocking suggestions that American women had everything and that a 'matriarchy' was in operation. Anything but, he argued, with masculine values dominating and women left frustrated, or via the sex industry, objectified. Priestley suggested that American women were 'haunted by a feeling of inferiority',[20] and after describing a meeting with a 17-year-old girl with big expectations of what life might hold, he wrote angrily, 'they expect too much. They get in the end, too little. The glittering treachery of an Admass life'.[21] This view was reinforced by a car journey with a married mother, in her early thirties, who he had met at the University in Dallas. She took him on a tour of a 'stretch of Nomadmass' on the outskirts of the city, but on the return, her mood darkened and she said to Priestley, 'Tell me – what's wrong with all this?' [22] This was the same message that Betty Friedan would bring to the attention of the world 8 years later when she discussed 'the problem that has no name' in the *Feminine Mystique* (Frieden). Frieden was shocked at the way American women's concerns had been ignored, and it is interesting that Priestley is talking about this issue in 1955.[23]

The book's assault on Admass was captured particularly well in two chapters dealing with commercialized leisure. The first of these looked at a College football game at Fort Worth, which Priestley described with a mixture of bemusement and criticism. Priestley of course had a strong interest in sport, having written about British football occasionally in the past. [24] However, he was taken aback to discover an overblown spectacle that exaggerated the significance of the event and was more concerned with cheerleaders, marching bands and mascots than the sport, a noisy PA providing the icing on the cake. He saw 'nothing wrong' with the actual mechanics of the match itself but felt that the atmosphere accompanying the game was 'no longer that of vigorous young males enjoying themselves and giving plea-sure to their fellow students, but a perfervid atmosphere of huge crowds, big money, false standards, hysterical publicity'. He continued, 'what was good, and probably remained good, was buried under a mountain of rubbish; over-organisation on one level, hysteria on another. Even at play, Admass was at work'.[25]

Admass was present not only in the event itself but also in the journey to the stadium, where Priestley mocked the over-reliance on the most obvious symbol of post-war affluence, the car. Part of his journey was undertaken on a bus that was, he noted, 'now the preserve of black Americans and other disadvantaged sections of the community'. Having been picked up at the bus terminal by a college professor and his daughter, Priestley listened to their intent discussions about where to park, noting wryly that the spread of car ownership made travel and parking at public events a major issue. 'It was not for me, without a car, an irresponsible rider in buses', he wrote with due irony, 'to suggest that the terrible stadium-parking problem might be banished by our walking the half-mile there'. [26] Keeping silent, he considered what would happen when the sons and daughters of the current car owners themselves became drivers, and as traffic increased, new roads, car parks, traffic signals and 'traffic experts' would be needed, leading to 'nervous breakdowns and ulcerated stomachs'. Casting his eye across the Atlantic, he noted that only 'a lack of means' stopped Europeans from creating the same problems and that they were 'worrying day and night how to catch up with this lunatic progress'.[27] Priestley would of course later see his fears come true.

If car culture was one of the most obvious manifestations of Admass, then so was television, the importance of which Priestley noted on several occasions and most obviously in a chapter that described his attendance at the inauguration of a new television channel – channel 13, KTRK in Houston. 'Whatever else this age may be', he wrote, 'it is the age of television', before attacking the superficiality and manipulative hysteria surrounding the event and television more generally.[28] This was Priestley writing at his polemical best, pondering whether the event would be of public importance or rather a sign 'we are drawing nearer to collective idiocy'.[29]

There was never much doubt which side Priestley would come down on, and he gently mocked the crowds with tickets, the 'Admass swarms' without and the tense self-importance within the auditorium. The event involved live transmitted performances from the stage and other recorded events from a studio, the latter of which could be seen on monitors in the auditorium. Priestley had witnessed at first hand preparations for live performance in the theatre and other venues, but this had not prepared him for what he witnessed. 'The host of technicians passed from a frenzy of activity into a frozen agony of anticipation. Earphones were adjusted, watches stared at, hands raised to give the signal at the exact fraction of a second: all as if a hydrogen bomb was about to be exploded'. This was all done so that 'the idle-minded shall not be kept waiting...for their trivial entertainment'. [30]

The entertainers live on stage did little to raise his spirits, including 'an accomplished torch singer whose torch burned without heat', joyless dancers and a mezzo-soprano from the Metropolitan Opera who, Priestley claimed, 'wasted a magnificent voice and years of training on popular rubbish'. Priestley's dislike of mass culture led to a sharpening of his critique, as he argued 'that there is something almost vindictive about this aspect of cultural democracy: it bribes such fine singers to leave the opera houses, to desert the genuine culture that nourished them, so they may serve whatever brand of treacle the mob currently prefers'. Hammering home this point, Priestley argued that under Admass, the crowd were 'no longer asked to make some effort to get out of its armchairs', and culture that might have enlightened their lives was 'delivered down to that level'.[31] In other words, this was 'dumbing down'.

The only performer who impressed Priestley was a ventriloquist who he found genuinely engaging and funny, not least because it brought music hall to mind. He commented, 'if only a constant stream of such humorous magic found its way through channel 13!' [32] Such magic was missing in the material transmitted from the studio, which involved performers whose shows had been scheduled for the KTRK-TV, welcoming the new channel. Priestley considered these 'the dullest dogs who ever reached a TV studio', and he was similarly unimpressed by the chairman of the station who concluded the proceedings. The evening ended with Priestley overindulging in shrimps and whisky, as he tried to outmanoeuvre a troublesome guest at the after-show party.[33]

In the penultimate chapter of the book 'Night Reverie at the Shamrock', Priestley recalled a solitary night in Houston, in a characteristically personal and downbeat tone, which drew together some of his feelings about his travels in the world of Admass. Describing how he no longer felt he could travel alone, he suggested that the solitary traveller actually sees more, despite loneliness, and, as a result, they get closer to the truth. However, loneliness and occasional depression, with no one to talk him out of it, may also encourage a loss of perspective. The observations that followed were made in this light, as Priestley downed three whisky on the rocks and took an almost nightmarish view of the city from his hotel window, the grandiose hotel publicity brochure, and humorously considered press cuttings about the disastrous overblown opening of the hotel in 1949. This was an 'Age of Anxiety', Admass 'at work and play', where real values had been submerged beneath hype and cynical manipulation via the media.[34] 'There was a time when stupid people had to make an effort to understand and enjoy what was in print', Priestley wrote, reiterating a theme elsewhere in the book, 'but now every foolish or dangerous prejudice, every gaping idiocy is carefully catered for, endlessly flattered'. Looking at the traffic and skyscrapers of Houston, Priestley felt that he was 'homeless for ever, at the wrong planet'.[35] Towards the end of the chapter, he comments chillingly, 'having disinherited ourselves, we have to keep on inventing new ways of forgetting what we once had and who we were'.[36]

This was powerful stuff, and the immediacy of the writing made the readers feel that they were in the hotel room with the author, rather than reading the carefully written memoir of an emotional night. In the process, it allowed Priestley to underline the true horror he felt at the Admass order. Priestley was of course a well-known critic of the mass order and its social, cultural and political consequences and had been attacking the effects of this in Britain since the 1930s; however, the book, through its American and transnational angle, presented a new dimension to his work.

Its criticism of the American mass society was shared with a number of significant US commentators, who were becoming increasingly vocal as the 1950s progressed. The sociologist David Riesman and others had published *The Lonely Crowd* in 1950, which had suggested that post-war affluence had seen a move from 'inner-directed' to 'other-directed' in the younger, wealthier sections of the American population. 'Other-directed' people acted in accordance with values taken from their peers and the mass media, resulting in conformity and a loss of independence and character.[37] C. Wright Mills put forward a similar argument in *White Collar* (1951), which argued that under the weight of a growing bureaucracy, middle Americans had lost their independence and were increasingly alienated from the workplace. Mills' later book, *The Power Elite* (1956), argued that an interchangeable, group-conscious elite dominated politics, the military and the economy, which tallied in many ways with Priestley's depiction from the late 1940s of an aloof bureaucratic elite holding sway both not only in Britain but also in other Cold War powers.[38]

Priestley, of course, also shared the American critics' concern about the viability of the middle classes, the group who he had seen as the main architects of change, and by the mid-1950s, other American critics were joining the fray on the issue of middle-class alienation. These included William Whyte, an editor of *Fortune* magazine, who wrote the influential and best-selling book *The Organization Man* in 1956. This argued in a similar vein to Riesman and Wright Mills that middle-class workers were drawing their values from the organizations they worked for, replacing earlier commitments to the protestant work ethic and other sources of identity, including religion and class.[39] Whyte's critique encompassed suburbia, which he saw as reflecting the rootlessness and mobility of the modern organization man. As he put it, 'Suburbia is the ultimate expression of the interchangeability so sought by the Organization'.[40] The American suburbs were growing dramatically in these years, and other writers including John Keats and Lewis Mumford shared Whyte's belief that suburbia marked a shift towards conformity and a loss of American individualism.[41]

J. K. Galbraith also attacked the economic values at the heart of the mass society in his important, groundbreaking and still relevant analysis, *The Affluent Society* (1958). Galbraith argued that the mass society had created an imbalance between an expanding consumer culture based on growing private wealth on one hand and poorly funded public services and infrastructure on the other. Advertising played a key role in this process, shaping consumption against a public sector that lacked even political support in some quarters. Galbraith was an accomplished writer and carefully pointed out the way that greater private wealth placed more demands on the public service, commenting, 'the family which takes its mauve and cerise, air conditioned, power steered and power-braked automobile out on a tour passes through cities that are badly paved, made hideous by litter, blighted buildings, billboards and posts for wires that should have long since been put underground. They pass into a countryside that has been largely rendered invisible by commercial art.'[42] Or in Priestley's words, they were passing through 'Nomadmass'.

American artists also dealt with the suffocating nature of the mass society and the pressure this placed on individuals, whether it was the other-directed Willy Loman in Arthur Miller's *Death of a Salesman* (1949), Harry 'Rabbit' Angstrom left running away at the end of Updike's *Rabbit Run* (1960), Sal Paradise and Dean Moriarty fleeing convention in their quest for spontaneity and authenticity in *On the Road* (1957), or Holden Caulfield sorting out the real from the 'phony' in *Catcher in the Rye* (1951).[43] The visual counterpart of this was Jackson Pollock's controversial drip paintings, and in music, it was the nervous genius of Charlie Parker, while in Hollywood, 'Invasion of the Body Snatchers' used science fiction to explore the corrosive pressure to conform. [44]

All of these works, and others, illustrated a profound unease about an America in mid-century that was coming to terms with the shock of World War II, the reality of the atomic bomb, the consequences of McCarthy's hunt for communists and unparalleled affluence. Priestley's depiction of Admass fits perfectly into this cultural context, and it is a shame that it did not sell more at the time or have the same long-lasting impact of some of the other works on this subject.

However, for all its strengths, *Journey Down a Rainbow* also arguably shared some of the faults of other social criticism from this time. Intellectuals have often had a problematic relationship with popular culture, or the mass society itself, whether from an elitist standpoint or a Marxist view, the latter often associated with the Frankfurt School, that saw the popular culture as a product of ruling-class manipulation. The American critics had their counterparts in England who, alongside Priestley, made similar arguments, frequently adding an element of anti-Americanism to their views. Priestley's prioritizing of 'real' culture over commercial culture was a common thread, as was his depiction of a degraded popular culture where 'every gaping idiocy is carefully catered for'. Television was often seen as the prime example of this for many in Britain and the United States.[45] Priestley's damning account of the opening of KTRK-TV was representative of a lot of intellectual opinion at that time, and indeed Newt Minnow, Kennedy's appointee to chair the Federal Communications Committee, famously talked about commercial television offering 'a cultural wasteland' when he addressed the National Association of Broadcasters in 1961. A year later, the Pilkington

Committee reported on television in the United Kingdom, concluding that it would 'worsen the moral climate'. The latter committee included the prominent critic Richard Hoggart, whose path-breaking study, *The Uses of Literacy* (1957), took a similar approach to Priestley and other British dissenters.[46]

Television's sins were compounded by what was seen as its link with the other 'enemy within' in the 1950s: the teenager. Post-war affluence and the growth of a more adaptable popular culture, most notably in the shape of rock and roll but also including film, television and literature, dramatically widened the generation gap, creating misunderstanding on one level and, with the help of a sensationalist mass media, fears of delinquency on another. The American sociologist Herbert Gans suggested that the 'cultural differences' between the generations 'precipitated an undeclared and subconscious war between them'. [47] Priestley made only occasional comments on teenagers, but he illustrated Gans' point well, suggesting, in his whisky-fuelled night at the Shamrock, that there were 'millions of youngsters who, so far as traditional human values are concerned, especially those expressed in religion, philosophy, art, might as well have arrived here from another planet'.[48]

The intellectual attack on the mass society of the 1950s, while in many ways justified, also lacked subtlety and an awareness of complexity within popular culture. Television could be poor, and historians have pointed out the significant role advertising and sponsorship had on programmes in the United States. However, there were exceptions, including Ed Murrow's 'See It Now' and pioneering sitcoms such as 'I Love Lucy'. [49] In Britain, advertising was less prominent, arriving with the launch of ITV in September 1955, which led to a chorus of derision from intellectuals. However, the BBC under Hugh Carleton Greene adapted well to the changing terrain of the mid to late 1950s, producing quality television, as on occasions did ITV. Similarly, teenage expression and difference did not equate to rebellion or mass delinquency, and even the suburbs were not as conformist as Whyte and others suggested. [50] The greater social turbulence of the 1960s suggested that conformity did not have such an iron grip on ordinary people as the critics of the 1950s suggested. Popular culture could be commodified, but it could also be considerably more vibrant than was often suggested. After all, to take three examples, the 1950s also saw the birth of rock and roll, the dramatic development of modern Jazz and the emergence of the previously mentioned Beat generation, all of which would later be seen as significant, vital movements that cast a shadow over popular culture in the succeeding decades.

Priestley was constantly dismissive of popular music, 'popular rubbish' as he put it, when describing the mezzo-soprano at the opening of KTRK-TV; however, his views on television itself were subtler, or perhaps more contradictory, than *Journey Down a Rainbow* might have suggested – not least because his approach to television in the latter was deliberately polemical. Like other writers, Priestley worried about the effect television would have on both books and theatre. Mentioning his own frustrations with theatre at this time, he wrote to his daughter Mary in October 1954, complaining that he had 'practically given up on Theatre', which was 'hopeless', and that 'television is affecting it badly, especially in the provinces'.[51] However, in spite of this, he also embraced what might be described as a critical engagement with the medium.

Television offered work, presenting the opportunity to raise the standard of what was on offer, to add a stronger cultural component and to even promote his own literary work. He told Davison in March 1955 that he was writing a weekly programme 'about the way people talk and behave', for which he was 'being very well paid – for the BBC'. He added that he was involved in the programmes 'partly to familiarise myself with the medium and partly to help my books and plays'. Television, he added, 'steals the limelight from everything else here, more I think than with you'.[52] The latter comment seems rather strange given Priestley's experiences in the United States the previous year and the fact that the BBC was, at this point, the only organization making television programmes. The programme 'You Know What People Are' eventually numbered six episodes, the first of which was shown on 1 June 1955 and the final one was broadcast on 6 July 1955. Priestley acted as the host, discussing the way people talk and behave, with actors then illustrating the point in dramatized scenes, a format which the author worried dismissively might 'be a bit above the head of our bigger t.v. public'.[53]

The following year, Priestley was involved in a fortnightly 15-minute programme on books, which he hoped would promote literature.[54] The experience did not meet his expectations however, and he complained that he was 'a bit disgruntled' as 'nobody either in the BBC or the book trade has sent me one single word of thanks for what was a stiff little job, not badly done'.[55] Priestley also succeeded in getting a number of television plays produced, both on the BBC and on the newly established ITV. Interviewed by *The Radio Times* about 'The Stone Faces' in late 1957, he was asked about working in the medium, to which he responded that 'after twenty-five years in the theatre, I find the change stimulating. In my stage-plays, for instance, I've always been a great one-set man. I should think I know as much as anybody living about the problems of getting half a dozen characters in and out of two doors and the french windows! Television is flexible, allowing more sets, and with them a different lot of technical problems'. He went on to suggest that television has the advantage of allowing the viewer to 'almost see an actor think', whereas in theatre, actors had to 'project' in 'some huge barn of a theatre'. Adding that television was already on its way to building up 'a repertory of really worthwhile, original' programmes, he concluded, somewhat surprisingly, that television 'offers the dramatist a worldwide market. In fact, as a playwright, all other things being equal, I must say I would prefer to be writing for television than for the theatre'.[56]

Priestley's positive appraisal of television was obviously influenced by the journal he was being interviewed for and the fact that he was promoting his own play. However, his correspondence reveals that he was feeling similarly positive in private. Following the successful broadcast of a TV play 'Now Let Him Go' in September 1957, which was shown as part of the 'Armchair Theatre' series for ABC on the ITV network, he told Davison that the play, while not well produced, received 'splendid' reviews in the press 'rather to my surprise'. He went on, 'I find the flexible medium fascinating after so many years grappling with the stiffness of the Theatre', and he was pleased he had more opportunities to do similar work in future. 'Financially it's not very rewarding at the moment', he wrote, 'but TV is coming along so fast there will soon be a big market for good TV pieces'.[57]

Priestley's involvement with ITV was interesting, given the general antipathy intellectuals felt towards commercial television. However, Priestley gave a qualified welcome to the new channel principally because 'it is competition and breaks the BBC monopoly'. He assured Davison that unlike in the United States, the advertisers would not be directly involved in the programmes or be allowed 'to interrupt them' to any great extent.[58] Clearly, Priestley's dislike of large organizations and his own earlier run-ins with the BBC establishment predisposed him to give the new channel a chance, despite his misgivings about the commercialization apparent in popular culture.

By December 1957, Priestley was still involved in good quality television programmes, but he now usually worked with recorded shows that were more straightforward than series such as 'You Know What People Are'. He told Davison that 'I insist upon doing everything on film now, which cuts down the sweat and agony of studio transmission'. He was currently making 'Lost City' for the BBC, a television essay concerning his return to Bradford.[59] The latter film was shown in October 1958 and was generally well reviewed, although it was not without its critics in Bradford. Priestley clearly enjoyed making it, encouraging further optimism about television. 'We don't do too badly with TV here', he told Davison, 'especially on Sundays'.[60] And of course, Priestley was also able to get his anti-nuclear play, 'Doomsday for Dyson', screened in March 1958 by Granada, a station that pioneered quality commercial programming. Priestley described the play as a 'thick, hot slab of antinuclear propaganda', something not missed by the critics.[61] As we have already seen, Priestley was beginning to have doubts about the saliency of the CND campaign by early summer 1958, and despite having 'Doomsday for Dyson' shown, he remained critical of the impact of television, seeing it as part of the depoliticizing current within mass culture. Complaining about the lack of support for CND, he claimed that the movement was middle class, 'because the working class just look at Television and hope for the best'.[62]

The last comment was interesting in a number of ways, not least because it revealed a patronizing view of the 'working class'. After all, television was taken into homes across the country, and CND was embraced en masse by neither working-class nor middle-class Britain (a division that was fraying anyway). However, the quote also underlines Priestley's problem with the Admass society and the role of television within it. On a theoretical level, Priestley made it clear that television was part of a mass media that played to the lowest common denominator and, as we have seen, that it was also a politically conservative force. However, at the same time, he was not a critic who interpreted popular culture from afar, from the windows of an ivory tower, and he was pragmatic enough to take the opportunity for work and to engage with the medium and try and shape its impact, and this tells us something about Priestley's approach to popular culture in general.

He could be dismissive and over-generalize when his writing took a polemical turn, but as his work in this period showed, Admass was not based on an elitist dismissal of the popular. Priestley had suffered enough himself at the hands of the 'high brows', and as he put it in the New Statesman, 'Our society, already looking inhuman in some of its aspects, cannot be restored to a full humanity by a small artificial anti-popular culture any more than it can by the mechanical antics of mass amusement.'[63] For Priestley, it was about what constituted the 'popular'. He may be 'a man with a woodcut trying to compete with a four-colour poster thirty feet by ten',[64] but he believed that 'real' popular culture, as he called it, was made by ordinary people and produced in local communities or individual imaginations, not a popular culture that could be manipulated by executives in large multinational corporations.

However, Priestley's own work for television and the other mass media hinted that mass culture was not a simply commodified 'product', and Priestley admitted as much during his polemical attack on the KTRK-TV, with his appreciation of the ventriloquist, Wences, who reminded him of the energy of music hall. Similarly, in the New Statesman, he also acknowledged the humour of Hancock, Wisdom and other television comedians, although not without suggesting that they had risen too quickly and needed sharper material.[65] Despite the mass medium, genuine art could emerge, including work that attacked the mass society, and at his most optimistic, he realized that there was a demand for 'good t.v. pieces'. Of course, on many occasions, popular culture did not scale anywhere near these heights, and the less optimistic Priestley was in good company when he took a more critical approach. However, the occasional shoots of a vibrant art breaking the surface through the structures of the mass media, some of which evaded Priestley's glance, owed their existence in large part to those (including Priestley himself) who had taken a critical but nevertheless engaged approach to the mass media from the 1930s.

Journey Down a Rainbow's attack on what it described as Admass inevitably ruffled feathers. There were criticisms of Priestley's behaviour during the researching of the book and, more significantly, allegations of anti-Americanism once it was published. These were not new problems for Priestley, as his often complex relationship with the United States had been punctuated by similar disagreements in the past. Accusations surfaced in the Texan press, especially in Houston, that Priestley had been 'antagonistic' and critical of Texan society. Priestley denied any such thing and was angry when Davison brought the complaints up in a letter. 'I leant over backward to be nice to everybody', he complained, and 'tried to keep clear of the press because I know of old what they can do'. He accused the press of exaggerating minor incidents and that a Houston paper published a 'fake' interview. 'The trouble is', he suggested, 'there are people in America, chiefly connected with the press, who for various reasons are always out to "down" the visiting Englishman, no matter how hard he tries'. He suggested that it was a particular problem for English writers.[66]

Priestley received support from the *Dallas News*, although the paper took the line of defending Priestley's right to be critical rather than denying any such thing had happened. Noting that 'Houston seemed to agree with a line attributed to Ogden Nash: "Mr. J.B. Priestley is simply beastly"', the Dallas paper chose to demur, suggesting that 'Priestley was not simply critical. Dallas found him memorable too. He was invariably outspoken, he had the British touch of malice that can be both ingratiating and infuriating, and he was obviously a man of first-class brains'. Detailing Priestley's alleged criticisms, including about food, Texan men and highways, it concluded that 'there is a hard core indestructible in this artist' and that instead of trying to please, currying favour, he made honest criticisms and 'did not betray himself'.[67]

Recriminations drifted on into 1956, and Priestley again protested total innocence to Davison after criticism in the *Saturday Review of Literature*. Claiming that the author, 'Rogers', 'will try to monopolise you, and if he doesn't succeed, he'll turn nasty', Priestley told Davison that 'I want to assure you, as seriously as I know how, that there is no truth in these suggestions that I behaved boorishly...it is absolute nonsense'. He added wryly, 'there have been times in America when I have been fairly riotous but on this Texas trip I was careful from the first to behave as well as I know how'. He suggested that Rogers was angry at him because he only stayed one night in his house and that other Texans, expecting him to be critical, created a 'campaign of slander'. This left Priestley feeling that 'the whole thing leaves a very nasty taste in one's mouth, and I feel I never want to undertake another American trip of this sort. They play to dirty for me'.[68]

Priestley's disillusionment had been deepened by suggestions that *Journey Down a Rainbow* was anti-American. This was apparent in several otherwise generally positive reviews of the book, which both Priestley and Hawkes felt could be explained by a lack of perception from the reviewers. 'We have had many friendly reviews of our book', he wrote, but he was disappointed in the 'low quality' that were 'full of gross inaccuracies and hardly any serious attempt is made to understand what one is up to.'[69] Even some of Priestley and Hawkes' friends seemed convinced that the book was critical of the United States. Priestley told Natalie Davison, 'we can talk about this when we meet, but I do feel you got a completely wrong slant on *Journey Down a Rainbow* in which we did not attack people at all but only a system, against which a great many American are now vigorously protesting'.[70]

Priestley had, by this point, replied to his critics via an article in the *New Statesman* (although his arguments clearly had not convinced Natalie Davison). Tackling this issue head-on, Priestley entitled the piece 'Who Is Anti-American?' He denied reviewers' claims that *Journey Down a Rainbow* was 'yet another attack' on the United States. 'It is nothing of the kind', he argued, making the point that he was attacking the system of Admass, not the United States itself. 'Admass and Admassians are not synonymous with America and the Americans, nor even with Texas and Texans', he argued, supporting this by reiterating the suggestion that 'sharpest' critics of Admass were actually in the United States. In addition, he suggested that although Admass may be at its strongest in the United States, it was spreading and 'post war Britain is one of the most progressive Admass colonies'. He continued, 'we English are more dangerously situated than the Americans because most of us...do not realise we are in any danger'.[71]

The article then explained why the reviews of the book had only contributed to an already established idea that he disliked the United States. As Priestley had frequently claimed, he believed that this was down to the American press who 'after not being able to induce me to say anything rude about their country, have invented offensive remarks, all with a strong American accent, and have conjured them in and out of my mouth'. At 'dinner parties from Long Island to Santa Monica', people had been 'astonished when I have failed to insult everybody within hearing', he added sardonically. This extended, he suggested, to his written work, where essays 'with nothing but humorous exaggeration' were seen as angry and critical. [72]

In the rest of the article, Priestley explained how he visited the United States not only for work purposes but also because he found it interesting and liked it. Pointing out that he had travelled widely in the country and spent more time there than anywhere else outside England (including the Celtic nations), he suggested he had 'a growing affection for the real America' (that word 'real' again) and that explained a tendency to sometimes 'criticise and grumble'. This genuine interest and knowledge contrasted with other British visitors who are seen as more friendly to the United States but are really 'whoring after American wealth and power'. Repeating the argument made by the *Dallas Times*, Priestley suggested that 'the test of friendship does not lie in idle compliments and lip-service but in a close continuing interest and an affectionate concern, which may at times necessitate plain speaking'. Priestley also pointed out that as people 'imagine that the world of political intrigue, newspaper and radio comment, public relations and propaganda, cartoon adventures, is the real world', then criticism of elements of the former is taken as disliking the whole country. This erroneous belief meant that 'if we do not agree with Richard Nixon...then we cannot possibly want to enjoy...the Boston Symphony Orchestra, or the first sight of the desert from the Sante Fe *Chief*. The article ended with an impassioned statement that Admass was 'unworthy' of 'a nation that came out of a noble dream' and that if remembering that dream was anti-American, 'then I am indeed anti-American'.[73]

There was a lot of truth in Priestley's argument, not least that he had an interest in the United States and knew it well, and it was also certainly true that he had longstanding problem with the American press, although the reasons that lay behind the latter were more debatable. Priestley had travelled to and written about the United States since before the war, and he first came face to face with Americans en masse on a troopship to France in World War I, which he later described as like being in the United States 'for the first time'. What he found notable was the lack of distinction between ranks and the atmosphere of 'a river picnic', which 'seemed a hell of a way to sail to war' but had 'a suggestion of something more generous and heart-warming, much closer to the democracy we boasted about on our side'.[74] He began visiting the United States proper from the early 1930s, both for work purposes – to deliver lectures, promote books, oversee theatre productions – and for family holidays. The United States and its social and cultural influences also loomed large in some of his most important writing. Indeed, his first published article in 1919, 'Secrets of the Ragtime King: A Remarkable Interview', was a humorous 'imaginary interview' inspired by seeing the American ragtime trio Hedge Brothers and Jacobsen at the Empire in Bradford.[75]

The United States was at the heart of the volumes of autobiography, *Midnight on the Desert* (1937) and *Rain Upon Godshill* (1939), and it similarly featured in his journalism, travel writing and social criticism, including of course *Journey Down a Rainbow* (1955). A jaundiced view of mass society was also apparent in the lighter, idiosyncratic *Trumpets Over the Sea* (1968), which told the story of the London Symphony Orchestra's participation in the 1967 Daytona Beach arts festival (and is discussed in the next chapter). His novel *Doomsday Men* (1938) was formulated and situated largely in the United States, while the United States and its impact on the wider world were discussed in a variety of works, including his finest, like the social travelogue, *English Journey* (1933), and the novels *Bright Day* (1946) and *Festival at Farbridge* (1951). Of course, as a twentieth-century writer of realist fiction and non-fiction, the United States' cultural and political influence was difficult to ignore. However, there was more than a simple recognition of this in his work, and his published and private writings support his claim that he had knowledge of and an interest in the United States.

One of the notable characteristics of Priestley's writings on the United States from the 1930s onwards was his appreciation of the differences within the United States, which underlined the fact that he did not restrict himself to the geographical limits of the coasts or to the intellectual limits of 'liberal' America. Given his love of the Yorkshire countryside and fine artistic eye, it was not surprising that he was, like many other European visitors, immediately drawn to the sheer scale and haunting beauty of the diverse landscape he discovered. On New England in autumn he wrote, 'I have never seen such woods before. They were a conflagration. Whole counties were on fire...it was like wandering into a burning Eden'.[76] The contrasting landscape of the Grand Canyon summoned a similarly primal reaction, with the weather and landscape combining to create a fantasy landscape: 'one stupendous effect was piled on another; veils of mist and broken rainbows were caught in forests hanging in mid-air; the sunlight far below fell on ruined red cities; and to one hand across the gulf, was a vertical Egypt, and to the other a perpendicular Assyria'. He concluded that the Grand Canyon was 'a sort of landscape Day of Judgement...not a show place, a beauty spot, but a revelation'.[77]

The family came to have a particular regard for the South West, especially the area around Wickenburg, Arizona. Chosen, on the recommendation of John Galsworthy, as a suitable place for his second wife Jane to recuperate from illness, the family liked the clement weather and the outdoor culture of the area, alongside the landscape. 'We ride with cowboys every morning here. The air is the best', he wrote to Davison, 'it really is a grand place'.[78] Tennis, walking and a general outdoor life offered a pleasing contrast to the British winter, made possible by the good weather. 'I think we've only had about two days without brilliant sunshine since I came here', he wrote, 'it really is the most staggering climate'. This suited the children, who 'can roam about just as they like'. 'It's astonishing', he added, 'how the kids who haven't been well pick up here'.[79] The air also contributed to the majesty of the immediate landscape, acting like a 'powerful telescopic lens' that 'magically moulded and coloured' the distant mountains. At sunset, 'things near at hand are dusty green, greyish, brownish, rather drab, but everywhere towards the far horizon rise chunks of colour unbelievably sumptuous'. The night sky was 'spacious' and lit by an array of stars, so beautiful that Shakespeare would have 'gone mad trying to improve upon his "Look, how the floor of heaven is thick inlaid with patines of bright gold!" '[80]

For Priestley, the landscape, in general, and Arizona, in particular, represented a powerful authenticity, ruggedness and beauty on an undreamt of scale that appealed to his romantic inclinations and stood apart from the corrosive elements of modernity that he disliked. He was not alone in this of course, and other British visitors saw the American landscape as a sparsely covered canvas that offered a contrast to the cluttered and transformed British environment – most obviously

D.H. Lawrence, whose embrace of the South West was a celebration of what he saw as its primeval simplicity.[81]

Priestley was also impressed by the way people lived in this environment. The sense of freedom translated into a more general friendliness and lack of social distinction. As Priestley put it in *Midnight on the Desert*:

> Where the older West still lingers, as it does around Wickenburg, where we have stayed, you have a pleasant glimpse of the classless society about which we hear so much now. The equality may be an illusion, but the manners do not hint at any suspicions of inferiority and superiority. To return to England, after a few months of this, is like dropping back into the Feudal system.[82]

Priestley saw this 'classless society' as being rooted in a lack of 'inequalities of income and privilege' where people were 'reasonably sure of themselves, easy in their own mind, not galled by feelings of inferiority and are ready to take others as they find them'. To Priestley, the lack of privilege was important, as both his experience in the army and recent developments in the Soviet Union had suggested that 'privilege', even more than inequality of wealth, was the barrier to a fair and just society. 'What is needed', he argued, 'is a juster distribution of wealth with as little privilege as possible'.[83] The resulting confident, independent citizen – in this case in the American West – was of course an important figure in Priestley's writing throughout his life, standing full-square against the levelling conformity of large organizations and mass society.

Priestley was far too astute to believe that the sense of freedom in Arizona was a deliberate or permanent situation, admitting that it arose due to 'certain local and temporary conditions'.[84] Thus, returning to Wickenburg at the end of 1937, he was already aware of the process of change, the town having 'grown a bit and smartened itself up'; it 'was no longer the scrap of the old wild South-West it had first appeared'.[85] A more dramatic change had occurred when Priestley returned to the area 13 years later. In the interim, Wickenburg had 'grown out of all recognition' and was part of a more commercial South West where eastern money owned many of the ranches and the feel of the Old West had been totally erased. Priestley felt saddened by the experience, remembering the earlier family holidays in the area. Even the weather was poor on his arrival, and Priestley told Davison that he would be moving on to Mexico in the next couple of days.[86]

Alongside the knowledge of Arizona, Priestley was also impressed with other parts of the United States. Much like H.G. Wells, he believed that the United States was at the cutting edge of the modern world, and sometimes he shared the latter's belief that it had the potential to help shape a democratic and collective future.[87] Travelling on the western highways which placed tarmac across deserts and mountains, complete with petrol stations, roadside restaurants and 'little towns passionately claiming your custom', Priestley saw a 'brand-new busy world'. Some of these towns were in the middle of nowhere, miles from any other settlements, but like a 'block from Sunset Boulevard' that had been dropped into the desert, they offered a range of services and lit up the night, as did the air beacons for the aeroplanes that served these communities.[88] The ease of movement and newness suggested to Priestley a 'new way of living' that might herald a 'new civilisation', or 'perhaps another barbaric age', depending on whether the United States understood where it was going.[89]

If the United States was to avoid the latter, it would need to embrace what Priestley saw as the already strong collective elements within American culture. He argued that beneath a language of wasteful individualism, Americans were actually highly conformist, and at its best, this translated into a 'collective action inspired by deep communal feeling' that was in many ways potentially socialist. 'The collective man, the socialist citizen, is not a weird new type', he wrote, 'in almost all but his theories, the average modern American is the collective man'.[90] The collective endeavour was best reflected in the recent engineering achievements of modern America. After seeing the Boulder Dam, Priestley wrote: 'Here in this Western American wilderness, the new man, the man of the future, has done something, and what he has done takes your breath away'. He continued, 'this is the first glimpse of what chemistry and mathematics and engineering and large-scale organisation can accomplish when collective planning unites them. Here is the soul of America under socialism. This is the reply to the old heedless, wasteful individualism'. After describing the dam as a 'work of art', he reiterated his point that 'it is a symbol of the new men, a new world, a new way of life'.[91]

The Boulder Dam was completed under the administration of Franklin Roosevelt, whom Priestley greatly admired.[92] Therefore, it might have been expected that he would see Roosevelt's New Deal as a step in the right direction on the path to this new way of life. However, he was under no illusion that the New Deal offered a complete solution to the United States' problems. Echoing the criticism from the Left, he argued that the New Deal was 'better than the old days' but was still part of a framework that 'no longer fitted the deep instinctive life of the people'.[93] Instead, Priestley envisaged a more radical solution, albeit one that he reluctantly conceded might involve a compromise that 'it is possible that we shall soon have to give up many things dear to us to keep the rest secure' and that 'old landmarks will be missing'. This was not something that he considered lightly, but the world of the mid-1930s and the nature of economic and social development led him to believe that 'I may like persons and distrust mass movements, but we may be in such a dangerous situation that there must be mass movements in order to save persons'.[94]

The second 'may' is interesting in this regard as it suggests a tentativeness about his position, something which is confirmed by his later discussion of his liberal socialist society, which lacked such compromises. His view of the American people as they struggled in the remains of the 'old language' and 'at the beginning of the new' was also less than glowing. 'I felt that if most of them had suddenly transferred to one of the totalitarian states, they would have noticed the lack of comfort long before they would have noticed the loss of liberty', he wrote. This did not seem very promising material for socialist citizens, but Priestley suggested, rather optimistically, that this would come from the pioneer spirit and 'huge impersonal creative forces working through the whole community'.[95]

A similar reaction to this new world occurred 3 years later when, recalling the middle of a tiring lecture tour across the mid-West, he noted that with the newly built, 'handsome, spacious' Tulsa, Oklahoma, you can 'see what America is up to'. He suggested, 'it is a new mixture in a new climate and new landscape; a new civilisation'. Yet, this is again qualified. Tired and depressed by the rigours of his lecture tour, Priestley noted that 'there was no fun left being in America at all. Instead of seeing it as the beginning of some tremendous new civilisation, which I do indeed believe it to be, I would see it as many Europeans do, as something only superficially impressive, youthful and fresh only at a deceptive first glance, already at heart stale and sterile'.[96]

And while the Boulder Dam, and even Tulsa, may have offered a more welcoming vision of the future, albeit with reservations, Priestley was already convinced that the less edifying parts of this new world were closer to the sterility, and even the barbarism, that he so feared. Although as we have seen that he was first and foremost as a 'townsman' who saw urban areas as one of the driving forces for social change, Priestley was uneasy when visiting the larger American cities. This was particularly true of New York, the scale and vibrancy of which initially impressed him but, grated with his sensibilities after the novelty had worn off.[97] On arriving in 1931, he thought the city was 'terrific', but by 1937, he was more cynical: 'on arrival I was exhilarated. . .the city seemed more beautiful than ever', he wrote, 'what more could a man want?' The answer, he suggested, was 'nothing, except to get out of it', as the city was so crowded that it denuded people's humanity and changed 'their internal rhythm'. 'Herd millions of us on to one small island, and keep on herding us until we are piled up in these monstrous layers – and there will be, must be, the devil to pay'. He concluded that he had duly 'paid him' by feeling depressed.[98]

He had a similar disregard for the smaller Los Angeles, which he described as 'merely a place that is a long way from anywhere'. Only at night when the city was lit up did this 'swollen small town' lose 'its air of being determinedly third-rate'. The lack of authenticity and 'sinister suggestion of transience' of Los Angeles were related also to its suburb, Hollywood, where Priestley worked as an occasional script writer.[99] He found the place exciting but also rather empty, and his professional interest was purely financial.[100] Even the older, cultural city of New Orleans failed to impress Priestley, that is, apart from 'a few quaintnesses in the French Quarter and the excellent food in the old restaurants'.[101] San Francisco was one of the few exceptions to this dislike of urban America, as it symbolized a different America from Los Angeles: it was a 'real city with a sparkle and a charm of its own' and reflected the 'large, hearty, devil-may care, romantic America'.[102]

Priestley's reaction to Los Angeles and the suburb of Hollywood was not simply a response to the aesthetics of the environment but was also influenced by his emerging critique of the spread of mass culture beyond America's. He was interested in film as a medium and worked on various films in Britain as well as in Hollywood,[103] but he believed that Europeans made better films.[104] To this end, he wrote screenplays for the British film industry, including 'Sing as We Go' (1934), as well as worked on the documentary 'We Live in Two Worlds' (1937) with John Grierson. Even here, however, his respect was qualified, believing that the documentary makers' claim that they captured real life was essentially wrong. Instead, he argued that they produced a 'very romantic heightening of ordinary life' and that 'for plain truth they cannot compete with the printed word'.[105]

His misgivings about film, more generally, and Hollywood, particularly, concerned the obsession with money and stars and the consequent need to claw profits back from the large potential audience in small-town America. This, he argued, encouraged a tendency to make films that lacked quality and were aimed at 'a not very bright boy or girl of about fifteen' and then shown around the world with a deleterious impact on local cultures, including those of Britain.[106] This explains why he surprised fellow writers by asking for his name to be left off the credits for some of the screenplays he penned and why Gregory Dawson is so disillusioned by his experiences of Hollywood in Bright Day.[107]

Priestley had already written of his concerns about the influence of these films on Britain in the novel Angel Pavement, where the younger characters are nearly all influenced by the surface values they have learned from Hollywood, which affect their ability to deal with everyday life. This was particularly true of the lonely clerk Turgis, who cannot find in real life the amorous dreams he discovers at the movies, leading to potentially catastrophic consequences. On being rejected and laughed at by the flirtatious Lena Golspie, he strangles her in a fit of rage and then leaves the scene, not 'quite real. He was a young man walking in a film'.[108] Of course, Priestley's penchant for happier endings meant that Lena was not in fact dead and Turgis, after a comical attempt at committing suicide, found a more realistic object for his affections in Poppy Sellers. Telling Poppy what had happened, 'it took on a certain romantic colouring...not unlike a good many films that both the narrator and his hearer had admired'. The two depart the novel, appropriately, on the way to the cinema.[109] This critique of cinema was interrelated with the changing nature of mass communications that were at the heart of the mass com-munications, which Priestley would later describe as 'Admass'.

Priestley's concerns about the spread of American values went beyond cinema, and a number of works from the 1930s, including *English Journey*, had thoughtful but ultimately critical references to wider American influences on British social and cultural patterns. At the start of the journey, the Great West Road 'looked very odd... It did not look English. We might have suddenly rolled into California'.[110] By the end of the book, when Priestley ruminates on the different 'Englands' he has seen on his journey, the third of these, if we recall, had its 'birthplace' in the United States and was the modern England of roads and consumer choice, which was 'essentially democratic' but also 'a bit too cheap' and standardized. Even in the early 1930s, the seeds of Admass were planted, with Priestley already lamenting the loss of individuality this represented.

As Priestley suggested in his 'Who Is Anti-American?' article, his troubled relationship with the American press had longer precedents, and this was part of a number of professional and personal problems he encountered in the United States. Priestley blew hot and cold over the United States prior to travelling there in 1931, often viewing the country through the prism of his frustrations with US publishers and critics (often imitating some of the problems he was having at home with the latter two groups). 'Let me now say very frankly that I'm fed up with America just now. One thing after another comes along to annoy me', he wrote in December 1927 to Davison, before citing a series of problems with magazines and his US publisher, Harpers.[111]

Things were little better in 1929 when *The Good Companions* took off in Britain, with Priestley suggesting that Harpers had 'handled the book very stupidly from first to last'. He concluded his letter telling Davison that 'I have no great desire to visit America...and nearly everybody advises me, on the ground that I should loathe it, not to go'.[112] By the end of December, the book was selling 2,000 cop-ies a week in the United States, which was 'better', although it could not match the 50,000 already sold in Britain. Priestley blamed this on American readers and critics: 'I don't expect to be popular with the idiotic American intelligentsia, who seem to me, at this distance, the very silliest people the world has ever seen, entirely without sense or roots'.[113]

Of course, Priestley did visit the United States for the first time in 1931 and dis-covered a more complex and interesting country than he had thought. If anything, however, his frustration with publishers and critics got worse, especially when his plays transferred from London to New York. Although a successful novelist, Priestley often considered himself more a playwright than a novelist, and indeed his more ambitious and experimental work was directed towards the theatre.[114] There was a genuine sense of hurt therefore when his plays, even those that had been a hit in Britain, floundered in New York. After *Eden End* flopped in 1935, he complained that 'the critics were not hostile so much as fantastically incomprehensible'. His disappointment was deepened by the fact that the Americans who had seen the play in London had really liked it.[115]

A similar fate befell *Time and the Conways* in early 1938, lasting only a month and leaving Priestley 'rather bitter' at 'the smart-alecky, Broadway, New Yorker-Time America that doesn't like me'. He added, 'and I don't like it'.[116] *I Have Been Here Before* led to further disappointment after the New York producer and director, Jed Harris, failed to contact Priestley and follow through on his initial enthusiasm for the play, which included a number of accepted revisions.[117] When the play was finally produced later in 1938, Priestley claimed that 'it was taken for a ride by the critics, quite deliberately I gather'.[118] Priestley had already told A.D. Peters in 1936 that 'bad luck seemed to dog' him in the United States.[119]

After the travails of 1938, and his lack of success in both theatre and fiction, he told Davison that 'I can't help feeling rather sour...I feel there is some strange invisible barrier between me and the American mind, though I know – and probably like – the country better than anybody here'.[120] Broadway had also come to represent 'everything I dislike about America', no doubt encouraging a more critical view of the world of theatre, New York and even the commercial side of the United States.[121] Things did not improve after the war, and as Priestley found his star declining in the British theatrical world, his problems in the United States continued.[122]

Priestley felt that some of the negative attention towards his plays was down to the impression in the press that he was anti-American. This dated back to 1931 when having finally made the decision to travel to the United States, he somewhat ironically managed to attract adverse publicity without even having set foot on American soil. The ship he was sailing on docked at Boston to discharge cargo, and Priestley remained on board. At this point, he was interviewed by a journalist from a local News Syndicate who subsequently published an article, which suggested that the author disliked Boston and New York and thought of the United States 'in a bad way with afflictions of silly, childish movies, bad plays and cheap novels'. Priestley was furious when he heard about the article, denying outright that he had said any such thing. He complained to the head of the News Syndicate in New York, who agreed to withdraw the article, but by then 'the mischief was done'. Indeed, the incident earned a four-page description and denial 6 years later in *Midnight on the Desert,* where he suggested that the article had exerted a serious enough impact to warrant that he was 'still occasionally referred to as the English writer who does not like America'.[123] In a similar tone, Priestley claimed in 1938 that the critics who savaged *Time and the Conways* made several references to the ' "famous" interview'.[124]

Priestley's denials would seem to have some justification, not least when he challenged the language attributed to him in the piece. That having been said, given his comments prior to travelling and his willingness to speak openly about what was on his mind, he may have inadvertently given some material that the journalist was able to turn into the offending article. Indeed, he almost admitted as much when he wrote to his friend Hugh Walpole that 'as you supposed, my tongue got me into trouble right from the start...I think I ought to have taken a short course in American visiting technique from you before I started off'.[125] Priestley's troubled relationship with the press continued, as we have seen, after the war.

As the mass society developed, accelerated by World War II and post-war affluence, and via the Cold War, the United States' influence became stronger. Priestley became more critical of the United States and less convinced of its progressive potential. *Journey Down a Rainbow* illustrated this in the mid-1950s, but a more critical approach was apparent during the war, as the belief that the British people had shaken off the torpor of the 1930s and were now capable of defining their own future offered an alternative path to a modern order dominated by the United States. As he wrote to his friend Hugh Walpole, he 'would like to see Western Europe step out of this war morass, federate itself on a decent democratic basis, and then produce a civilisation that made America look like a rusty Ford car'.[126]

As the war came to an end, Priestley's disillusionment at what he saw as the failure of the progressive spirit was compounded by the emergence of the Cold War. As we have seen, Priestley disliked the anti-Sovietism in US foreign policy and the way the world was dividing into two oppositional blocs. This altered his impression of the United States itself. In *The Secret Dream*, if we recall, he depicted an America where the dream of liberty had stalled and anti-communism held sway, leading to a potential for a 'fascist economy' where 'the most appalling inequality will be confirmed in fact even if still denied in theory'.[127] Of course, the pamphlet was appealing for Britain, the Soviet Union and the United States to rediscover the best of their traditions, but the criticism of the United States stood in contrast to Priestley's more sympathetic writing from the 1930s.

Concern at American influence on Britain was also growing and would culminate in Priestley's describing the tentacles of Admass as the 'great invader'. In 1948, he wrote in the *New Statesman* about their 'invasion' by 'American Big Business Culture' utilizing 'cinemas and theatres, the columns of the popular press, radio programmes and dance halls'. This America was overwhelming the influence of the other, decent literary America and 'was beginning to insinuate itself into the dreams of our adolescents...with the result that, sooner or later, and probably quite soon, this America is accepted by millions here as the promised land'.[128] Priestley's fictional work portrayed a similar picture. In *Festival at Farbridge*, Theodore Jenks, who has just returned from the East Indies, is shocked to discover how Americanized Britain has become. Hence, the tabloid newspaper the *Daily Echo* was 'always saying it believes Britain and at the same time it always behaves as if it were a suburb of New York'. The press conference for the vacuous film star

Ilba Cram left Jenks bemused. When Lionel tells him that 'this is part of English life', Jenks replies, 'I call it American life. And I can't see why anybody wants it here'. The opening in Leicester Square of Cram's new film, *Hometown Kid*, suggested a more sinister turn of events. 'He had seen plenty of crowds before...but this was different, new and evilly strange, outside any tradition of human assembly, all dark and blind, somehow mechanical'. Even 'the people who thought they were pulling the strings here, manipulating the mass so that they came crowding and screaming to this place, were themselves only marionettes whose strings vanished into a darkness of mysterious and menacing power'.[129]

Jenks was of course a fictional character, and the metaphysical element of the above provided dramatic emphasis. However, it reflected Priestley's concerns, which were voiced so strongly in his writing and his eventual description of Admass. That brings us back to Priestley's denial in November 1955 that he was anti-American. As we have seen, Priestley did know the United States well, and he was aware of the complexity of the country and how it had changed since the 1930s. He was idiosyncratic and sometimes provocative in his approach to the country, and it is also true that while he claimed that *Journey Down a Rainbow* attacked a system rather than the nation, the form of the mass society Priestley described was born in the United States, and it spread American values outside its borders. As he put it 7 months earlier in the same journal, when talking about Billy Graham, 'America calls the tune we all dance to, in every possible sense of that expression', using very similar words to *Journey Down a Rainbow*.[130]

However, while the vibrant America Priestley liked was shrinking in the face of Admass, Priestley was able to see that it still existed. In February 1951, he wrote in the *Daily Herald* about an American bar with a television on that no one was watching, drunken singing, a fortune-teller, a young couple in love and more women than men drinking. Noting the ethnic mix of the clientele, Priestley suggested that 'this was America, and the ends of the earth had gathered here'. He added, 'very American too was the truly democratic, free and easy atmosphere of the place, and for my part I regard the atmosphere, so difficult to create elsewhere, as one of America's greatest possessions'.[131] His concern that this was not lost conveyed his admiration of the United States and explains why he was so irritated by the suggestion that he was anti-American. Priestley was fascinated by the United States, and as a genuine friend, he was concerned when it did not match up to the values that it was meant to stand for. *Journey Down a Rainbow* and his other writings offer a valuable insight into the United States at a key time in its history, reflecting part of a bigger movement where intellectuals questioned the mass society. They may have overstated the case, but Priestley and his fellow critics were right to ask the question about how much was being lost and what was being gained instead. The same debates were taking place in Britain, and still are, and Priestley's words still have a resonance within them.

Late Priestley

When the move to 'Kissing Tree House', in Alveston near Stratford upon Avon, was first considered in the early summer of 1959, J. B. Priestley was concerned that people would laugh at him.[1] Alveston was a small, genteel, almost stereotypically 'English' village, different even to the Isle of Wight and certainly a long way from either the bustle of London or the vibrancy of early twentieth-century Bradford. However, it did have the advantage of being near to the birthplace of Priestley's hero Shakespeare, and when the couple duly moved in at the end of August 1959, alternating with the flat in Albany, the house provided particular privacy and stability for Priestley until his death 25 years later.[2] The author was 64 at the time of the move and had just published one of his most important works, *Literature and Western Man* (1960), an impressive survey of the western cannon that displayed Priestley's wide intellectual engagement with literature and simultaneously confounded the opinion of those who described him as middlebrow. Other important works were to follow, which testified to Priestley's continued intellectual curiosity and the consistent quality of his best writing. Continuities also remained in his approach to politics, the Cold War, the United States and the rejection of the deracinating effects of the mass society, and his elevation to the role of elder statesman of British letters not only added a degree of gravitas to his work, and occasionally nostalgia, but also, in turn, led to a generally more sympathetic reception from critics.

Of course, to Priestley's chagrin, praise was not universal even for his stronger works, and he was underwhelmed by the reception for *Literature and Western Man*, particularly from some critics who did not necessarily appreciate his stepping on what they saw as academic turf, and the book's progress was accompanied by predictable concerns about lack of sales and poor reviews. Acknowledging the generally good reviews of the book in the United States, Priestley told Davison in April 1960 that he was 'much disappointed by the major reviews, which seemed to me stupid and carping, unable to understand the nature of the book', unlike their counterparts in Britain.[3] The following month, he reported in a more sanguine mood that the book was 'much admired' but 'hadn't really got going' in terms of sales. He added, however, that he was paid well and enjoyed writing the book.[4]

Literature and Western Man was certainly an achievement, covering literature over 500 years to the mid-twentieth century, eschewing the critics and celebrating the liberating, democratic nature of great art. It was situated in the crisis of Western life, which Priestley saw all around him, and it came as no surprise that contemporary literature came off second best to the earlier greats. Mixing political and Jungian ideas, Priestley wrote, 'the modern age shows us how helpless the individual is when he is in the power of his unconscious drives and, at the same time, is beginning to lose individuality because he is in the power of huge political and social collectives'. In this 'schizophrenic' age of 'inner despair' and 'appalling catastrophes', writers had become 'one sided', unable to reconcile the outer and inner world, and instead obsessed with the 'mysterious recesses of the personality'. While admiring their talent, Priestley saw the results as removed from the ordinary experience. 'Modern literature means little or nothing to the mass of the people, the very people in danger of losing true individuality'. [5] The sparkling accounts of Shakespeare, Dickens, Tolstoy and others were underlined in the concluding lines, when Priestley argued that the more rounded, richer literature of Shakespeare and others offered a way forward for contemporary art that reflected a more vibrant experience, 'a rich, new life, sometimes tragic, other times careless and gay'.[6]

Other important works from this period included the novels *Lost Empires* (1965), with its clever evocation of music hall and the troubled relationship of its central characters, and *The Image Men* (1968), a 300,000-word epic that satirized the growing public relations industry. Priestley and his fans were particularly fond of both books, and the author was once again disappointed when sales, and interest, did not meet expectations. Concerned about returns of *Lost Empires* in the United States, Priestley complained in similar terms to those he had been making since the 1930s: 'I can no longer make headway these days with the American reading public and publishers. Most of these days my books are out of print and not even in paperbacks'. He continued, 'though I'm no communist, they think far more about me in Russia, than they do in America'.[7] Priestley was also disappointed with the lack of interest in *The Image Men*, which had okay sales but was not seen as an 'important' novel. He pointed out that the publishers were printing 70,000 copies of his *The Prince and Pleasure and His Regency* (1969), a book which '20 or 30 men' could have written, yet 'nobody else could have written *The Image Men*'.[8]

His autobiographical writing continued with *Margin Released* (1962) and his final book, *Instead of the Trees* (1977), plus a variety of thrillers, historical 'coffee table books' such as the book on the Regency, *The Edwardians* (1970) and *Victoria's Heyday* (1972). Collected essays, travel books and a meditation on the passing of time, and death, *Over the Long, High Wall* (1972) (published when Priestley was 78), all reveal intellectual vigour and a continuity in elements of Priestley's thought.[9] This included his interest in politics.

Although his strong support of Labour had fractured in the 1950s, he remained on good terms with leading Labour figures.[10] He also supported Labour in the

1964 election criticizing the 'cynical rate race' of the Conservatives' years in power.[11] He mocked those who sought to run the country like a business, running public services for a profit like it was 'some kind of commercial concern'. 'It is our home', he wrote in the *New Statesman*, 'we don't just work here, we all live here'. Accepting that 'expensive and ubiquitous' government was here to stay, he mocked the Conservatives for selling private enterprise in elections while running 'a kind of socialist government' when in office. 'It seems to me', he wrote, 'that Mr. Wilson and his friends live here in a sense in which Mr. Macmillan and his friends don't live here'.[12] Priestley's support for Labour remained qualified, and he was critical of both their failure to deliver the vibrant politics that he supported and their connected failure to take on board unilateral disarmament.[13]

Added to this was his own personal concern with taxation, which inevitably took on a political dimension when the Labour Government sought tax increases. Writing to his former wife, Jane Priestley, he listed a litany of financial issues, including Roy Jenkins' increase in death duties, which he thought would hit him 'badly'. 'Labour still think they are "soaking the rich" ', he wrote, 'whereas the really rich always escape and it is self-employed successful professional men like me who really take a hiding'.[14] He made a similar argument in the *Sunday Times* 7 years later, commenting that 'I cannot be expected to admire a State performing the role of an ill-mannered highwayman'.[15]

Priestley's dislike of big organizations, including trade unions, became stronger as the post-war consensus began to fragment. The industrial unrest of the late 1960s and 70s that accompanied this process did little to impress the ageing author. The big trade unions were 'absurdly arrogant and need taking down a few pegs', he wrote in March 1971, and he saw communist influence in the trade union struggles with the Heath Government.[16] The re-election of a Labour Government did nothing to halt Priestley's criticisms. 'This government doesn't make me cheerful, it is afraid of the trade unions', he told his daughter Mary in May 1975, [17] going further in a letter to Peter Davison, which suggested that the country was effectively being run by shop stewards. 'We now have a New Left, which is Marxist, intolerant, ready to abuse any power it gets, with which I am entirely out of sympathy – they aren't my kind of people'.[18]

Priestley suggested that part of the problem for mid-1970s Britain was a lack of self-discipline. He argued that before 1940, people had been 'disciplined by circumstance', something which had been ended by the creation of the welfare state. However, he argued, self-discipline had not filled the gap, leading to selfishness and 'silliness' rather than good citizenship. This could create a 'wasteland', where radical students were not interested in learning but demonstrating and 'drop-of-a-hat strikers' and selfish trade union leaders pushed for wage increases whether they were affordable or not. These were daft types 'who think England is gaily floating when in fact is already half-sinking'.[19] And the working class were more to blame for this situation. Repeating earlier arguments, which saw him prioritizing the middle class, Priestley suggested that the working class people were 'overpaid and underworked', whereas the middle class had agency and potential.[20]

These sentiments were not uncommon in this period and certainly were shared by many conservatives, who saw the collapse of the consensus as a sign of the failure of welfare and social democratic policies more generally. It is difficult to situate Priestley in this company, however, as his critique of the welfare state showed continuities with his longstanding suspicion of state activity and his celebration of the vitality of the individual, community and a localized culture, not a capitulation to market forces and greater inequality. 'Even now', he wrote, 'I for one don't propose we return to the ruthless discipline of circumstance we were right to abolish', arguing instead that people needed to develop a 'sense of responsibility towards the community'.[21]

His anger at Labour, however, surpassed even the disillusionment of the 1950s, as he wrote at the start of 1976 that 'for the first time in my life I am feeling more sympathy with the Tories than with a Labour Government'.[22] Shortly afterwards, he told Peter Davison that the 'curse' of ideology 'among' the government and 'their bureaucrats' was leading towards 'totalitarianism' and that he had consequently 'voted Tory for the very first time in my life', as the latter offered 'choices' in 'education, health etc', which he claimed 'Labour is busy obliterating'.[23]

Alongside British politics, Priestley also remained interested in the United States, American politics and the Cold War. He was less than impressed by John F. Kennedy, who he described as lacking 'any political philosophy, and real statesmanlike ideas, any depth to challenge the electorate' after seeing the Kennedy-Nixon television debates in 1960.[24] Priestley was in the United States for the 1960 election, as he had been for the preceding two elections in the 1950s. He would also see Lyndon Johnson win in 1964, and he told Davison that, while the pattern had happened, rather than been planned, he would like to keep it up for the 1968 election. 'I think I'd like Humphrey to win', he wrote, in part because he was 'not a rich man like Kennedy and Rockefeller, nor a political thug like Nixon'. Interestingly, he suggested that the anti-war liberal, Eugene McCarthy, who would lose out to Humphrey at the tumultuous 1968 Democratic convention in Chicago, was 'probably the best human being among them', although he doubted he would be able to deal with the 'political machinery'.[25]

Priestley's interest and grumpy affection for the United States were captured in *Trumpets Over the Sea*, which had the descriptive subtitle, *Being a Rambling and Egotistical Account of the London Symphony Orchestra's Engagement at Daytona Beach, Florida in July–August 1967*. The book fulfilled its subtitle and conveyed Priestley's love of classical music and his mixed feelings about the United States. New York was 'slithering downhill', but he was determined to be fair to Daytona Beach, although in the setting, 'an author trying to be reasonable between hard covers was about as much in demand as an alchemist or a lecturer in Hegelian metaphysics'. [26] He found the heat too much, was bemused by the commercial exploitation of the area and even managed to get his hand shut in a car door. When encouraged to seek medical assistance, he demurred due to his dislike of the 'American Medical Association and its scale of fees'. [27]

The music was the star of the book, and Priestley had his doubts about whether the Americans in Daytona could really appreciate such great art. Describing the reaction to a concert conducted by Andre Previn, he suggested that behind the applause 'was a hollowness, a faintly chilly indifference, as if people were outside the essential experience, just tasting it; all of which, I feel is particularly character-istic of American life in the urban and ex-urban middle-income brackets'. [28]

A visit to a burnt out plantation on the Halifax River left him to ponder the generous hospitality he had encountered on his various visits to the United States, concluding that there was a ruthless element within this due to 'a want of empa-thy, a lack of imagination' that prevented Americans from seeing things 'from your point of view'. Thinking more broadly, Priestley developed this argument to explain what he saw as the United States' aggressive foreign policy. 'I asked myself', he wrote, 'if it wasn't precisely this underlying weakness, finally allowing ruthlessness to break through, that explains the failure of America in so many parts of the world, where after what seems like base ingratitude, revolt follows apathy or derision'.[29]

Trumpets Over the Sea was written with wry humour and was appreciative as well as critical of the experiences in Florida in 1967. Priestley's mocking tone, however, ruffled feathers and led to problems 4 years later, when he set off the lat-est instalment in the 'Priestley as anti-American' saga. For reasons best known to himself, in December 1971, Priestley allowed the publication of a short article for the *New York Times* entitled 'The Meaning of Brown Eggs'. The article, excerpted from a longer piece in the *New Statesman*, suggested that the British preferred brown eggs, whereas in the United States, they were 'despised' and white eggs favoured. This was representative of 'the invisible realm where our lives are shaped', and the brown egg represented a non-mass-produced rusticity that belonged 'to the enduring dream of the English who ever since the Industrial Revolution have created wretched towns chiefly because they never really accepted urban life, always hoping to move sooner or later to the country'. Americans disliked brown eggs for their rusticity and thought that white eggs suggested 'hygiene and purity'. Not pulling his punches, Priestley suggested that this related to 'the weakness of American civilization, and the reason why it creates so much discontent, is that it is so curiously abstract. It is a bloodless extrapolation of a satisfying life'. Striking a post-modern note in this regard, he concluded that advertisers and others defined consumption, so 'you dine of the advertiser's "sizzling" and not the make in the steak', and 'sex is discovered in manuals, not in bed'.[30]

Priestley's article drew a vigorous response that lasted well into the new year. Erica Jong called the piece 'English jingoism disguised as social comment', while another commentator countered that 'if Americans do learn about sex from manuals rather than in bed, we are one up on the English who never seem to think about it at all'. Others meanwhile, perhaps missing Priestley's metaphorical point, argued that brown eggs were in fact popular in New England.[31] E. B White wrote a more considered and humorous reply that explained his own preference for brown eggs and that white eggs were related to the widespread presence of the White Leghorn hen that laid white eggs. He also asked the pertinent question as to 'Why is it, do you suppose, that an Englishman is unhappy until he has explained America?'[32]

As the debate continued, one reader tried to inject a dose of realism asking whether 'at risk of being a kill-joy, I believe if *The Times* devoted as much space to writers professing love for brown people instead of for brown eggs we would all be much better off. Englishmen and Americans could better use their wit to examine their prejudices toward their fellow men'.[33] He had a point.

An interesting postscript to the 'egg debate' came with the publication of *Outcries and Asides* (1974), which gathered together shorter published and unpublished pieces. Priestley included the article on brown eggs but added a note that explained how his humorous piece had been misunderstood, leading to him being 'bombarded by cables and long-distance phone calls'. 'A new young writer could almost have based a career on these brown and white eggs', he wrote, before explaining why he did not reply to any of his critics. It was 'a lot of silly fuss, just a storm in an egg cup'.[34] This response captures the ongoing difficulty of Priestley's relationship with the United States and his willingness from his first contacts with the country onwards to shoot from the hip, without always realizing the consequences of what he had said or written. After all, Priestley may have been intending to be humorous, but in the process, he did write about the 'weakness' of American civilization and its 'bloodless extrapolation of a satisfying life', which was anything but light hearted and conveyed his longstanding dislike of Americanized mass culture.

Whether born in the United States or definitively American, Priestley's concerns about the 'Admassian' nature of popular culture continued into the 1960s and 70s. This was apparent in many of his works, including *Trumpets Over the Sea*, and was at the root of the discussions in *Literature and Western Man*. Priestley's views remained consistent in this regard, as in his discussion of 'Show-Biz' in *Outcries and Asides*. 'Show-Biz', he suggested, was not about talent and instead was 'apt to ruin talent while it inflates and shockingly overestimates very small and dubious talent'. This was thanks to 'its deals and busy publicity men and its almost hypnotic influence on the mass media'. Citing Tony Hancock, who Priestley suggested had 'great talent' but was 'neurotically divided and self-destructive' through his dislike of showbiz, he thundered 'it has contrived a vast idiot's dream-land of money and fame', which dominated television and produced programmes that were 'one fifth talent and four-fifths showbiz'. This was very reminiscent of Priestley's attack on television in *Journey Down a Rainbow*. However, it is also interesting to note Priestley's appreciation of Hancock, suggesting that he could differentiate between the one-fifth and the four-fifths.[35]

Priestley satirized Admassian public relations and advertising in *The Image Men*, which told the story of the likeable rogues, Professor Cosmo Saltana and Dr. Owen Tuby, who invent the notion of 'social imagistics', which concerned the 'selection, creation, projection of suitable and helpful public images'.[36] The result-ing 'Institute of Social Imagistics' is based first at the new University of Brockshire and then moves into the world of public relations. The book's humour revolves around the likeability of the two main characters and their enjoyment of life – par-ticularly through drink and love – and the gullibility of the customers who seek their services. Long, and occasionally rambling, the book was prescient about the shallow, publicity-hungry nature of the modern university as well as public and political life more generally. It also presented an established Priestley message. As John Atkins put it, 'the novel has a message. It's a fake world, with fake values, and fake men rigging fake expertise'.[37]

If Priestley's frustration with the modern world continued unabated, the issue of nostalgia also became more of an issue in his work. *Bright Day* had shown a sense of loss about the past but the need to critically engage with the present and future, but his later works had less faith in the latter. Of course, there was certain inevitability about this, as given Priestley's age, and his experiences of the dizzying changes of the twentieth century, an element of nostalgia was somewhat inevita-ble. However, it is important that historians and critics do not read back nostalgia into his earlier work from his later works, particularly from the important volume of memoirs, *Margin Released* (1962).[38]

The latter was an impressive work chronicling his life as a writer, divided into three parts that had previously been published in a different form in the *Sunday Times*.[39] The first part, 'The Swan Arcadian', looked at his experience in Brad-ford between 1910 and 1914, echoing in many ways the description of Bradford explored so powerfully before in fictional form in *Bright Day*. The second part, 'Carry on, Carry on!', looked at the war and immediate aftermath, and the final section, 'I Had the Time', explored his experience as a writer between 1920 and 60.

It was the first section in its presentation of a culturally rich, in parts cosmopol-itan and classless, Bradford before the deluge of World War I that a sense of loss came through most strongly. After describing how everything changed with the war, including culture, 'regional self-sufficiency' and even time itself ('perhaps the very hours began shrinking during the murderous imbecility of the First World

War'), he wrote, these years 'set their stamp on me...I belong at heart to the pre-1914 North Country. Part of me is still in Bradford, can never leave it, though when I return there now I wander about half-lost, a melancholy stranger. I am in the right place but not at the right time'.[40] Later, in the final section, he made a similar point, discussing his writing of essays in the 1920s, he described how 'half of me was still living in the years 1910–14, when I was growing up and first trying to write. (One part of me, perhaps going down the deepest, will always belong to these years.)' And as the 'new critics' became more influential with their elitist and miserabilist views, 'I was out of date before I even began'.[41] Writing about the present day, he made a very similar point. 'Just recently a young critic, rather an ass, announced that I was out of date. But I am further out of date than he imagines, for in my attitude toward work I belong in the eighteenth century, when authors were expected to write anything from sermons to farces'.[42]

A dislike of the modern world was at the heart of these comments, but there is also an almost painful sense of loss in the description of Bradford. Readers and critics also suggested that nostalgia played a role in Lost Empires. This probably came as no surprise, given the book's focus on music hall. Certainly, the sense of a watershed in World War I is apparent, as when Herncastle looks back at pre-war music hall and comments, 'I was at once haunted by a bright lost world that had taken my youth with it'.[43] There was also the expected critique of modern life, including Herncastle suggesting in one of the scenes dealing with sex that 'nakedness was an extraordinary revelation' before 1914, unlike the present day where there was a 'world of nudes and semi-nudes...so often exposed and browned that their skin seems like a kind of clothing'.[44] However, the story, including the darker side of music hall, offers a less poignant view of the past than was presented in Margin Released or fictional memories of Bright Day. Priestley certainly refuted this view of Lost Empires. Discussing the depiction of Delius' work as 'nostalgic', he noted that the latter word was 'the most overworked term of our recent time; thus a novel of mine, Lost Empires, about life in the music halls, had nostalgic pasted on to it, simply because I set its action back in 1913–14, when there was not a glimmer of true nostalgia in any page of it'.[45]

Lost Empires, particularly through the character Uncle Nick, also illustrated Priestley's continued interest in the issue of time and consciousness. Indeed in the very start of the book, Herncastle tells Priestley, in a fictional conversation, that 'time comes curving back to you, as if you weren't getting further and further away from it but coming nearer to some of it?'[46] Priestley's interest in time had been well established in his work from the 1930s, in his time plays, volumes of autobiography and novels and his contacts with Oupensky, Dunne and Jung. Towards the end of his life, his interest in time became stronger, not least because he was now facing up to his own mortality. This was most obvious in Man and Time (1964) and Over the Long High Wall (1972), although it was also apparent in virtually all his works from this period, including, as we have seen, *Margin Released* and *Literature and Western Man*.

Man and Time is an interesting work that saw Priestley swallow his misgivings about science and try to build an objective view of the relationship between man and time. He did, however, hold his hand up in the introduction admitting 'unlike most writers on Time who pretend and may have even deluded themselves into believing that they are purely objective, I will confess to prejudice, bias, an approach to some extent directed by feeling'.[47] The book dealt with various historical and philosophical approaches to time and included a section on precognitive dreams and telepathy. This was based upon a series of letters that had been sent to Priestley after he had appealed for viewers' experiences that challenged the ' "common-sense" ideas of Time' when he appeared on the BBC TV programme 'Monitor' in 1963.[48] The book concluded with the suggestion that 'our lives are not contained within passing time' and that humans exist in more than one dimension of time. 'Ourselves in times Two and Three cannot vanish into the grave: they are already beyond it even now'.[49] What follows is a rather confusing meditation on the 'Self' and 'Individuation', which is less than clear, and it is difficult not to agree with Brome's suggestion that 'the analysis left an uneasy feeling that he had not thought through the detailed consequences of such a theory'.[50]

Over the Long High Wall was a more sombre reflection on time, and its relationship to both life and death, and the need for society to think clearly about these issues. The book, in many ways, summarizes Priestley's views on this subject and links, as he had done before, with what he saw as the philosophical or mystical crisis and the more obvious political, economic and moral crises of the age. He concluded that there was a chance for readers to embrace the 'magical gift' of 'our consciousness' and look over the 'long high wall, the passing-time wall' or walk through it to a 'far wider view and sunlit horizon' and a liberated consciousness.[51] Although the book was not a religious statement, it sprang from similar roots, and its mysticism, apparent in much of Priestley's work, sat somewhat uneasily with his down-to-earth, plain speaking engagement with the more conventional world. It also had little impact on the reading public or critics.[52]

If Priestley remained uneasy about modern society on a variety of levels, he received a warmer response from the press and public in his later years, even if he still grumbled about critics. His 70th birthday drew praise from various quarters. *The Times* celebrated this occasion in an editorial entitled 'The Disappearing All-rounder' and declared that 'he is a man of letters in the good old sense of the phrase. We rejoice in him all the more because so few of his kind are left'.[53] From the other side of the political spectrum, Kingsley Martin in the *New Statesman* remembered meeting Priestley at Cambridge around 1920 and complemented him on having kept his 'red brick personality'. He noted, 'you stand in the public mind as a Yorkshire stalwart, a good trencherman, a Falstaffian character, who smokes a pipe and won't stand any nonsense', a view which he suggested accorded in many ways to the private character. Martin praised his independence of mind, willingness to innovate and successful writing and complemented his wartime radio postscripts and role in CND. He did point out that he was glad Priestley had 'not gone soft', although he added, 'even though you sometimes sound like a disgruntled capitalist who objects to paying his income tax'.[54] Heinemann honoured him on his 75th birthday with a party at the Savoy in 1969, which included family friends, and included Ralph Richardson performing the final scene of *Johnson Over Jordan*. The BBC also produced a tribute to him.[55]

He was given the freedom of Bradford in September 1973, bringing to a close his often troubled relationship with his home city, and he also, having previously rejected public honours, accepted an 'Order of Merit' in 1977, finding the queen 'charming'.[56] His 80th birthday celebrations in 1974 had again drawn together his family, friends and professional contacts and saw another crop of favourable press coverage, from both sides of the Atlantic, a radio programme and a production of *Eden End* at the National Theatre.[57] In an interview for the radio show, Priestley trod a familiar path on high brows, modern avant garde art and the fact that he was 'an old-fashioned English nineteenth century radical'. He also mentioned that he was writing another time play and that he was 'the most experimental dramatist this country's ever produced'.[58]

Priestley's play never surfaced, and his last publication was a final volume of autobiography, *Instead of the Trees* (1977), that was interesting but re-trod old ground, including frequent complaints about taxation.[59] He was able to live comfortably at Kissing Tree House on the proceeds of his writings, until his death on 14 August 1984. *Instead of the Trees* brought to close a remarkable variety and quantity of publications, which often displayed a lively imagination and a critical engagement with the modern world. Priestley's later works fit into this pattern, and the best of them stand alongside the best of his earlier work. Priestley was talented and hard working, and it is remarkable that he maintained his commitment to writing as long as he did but also that his ideas remained so relevant. Certainly, age eventually took its toll, and anger sometimes got the better of him. However, works such as *Lost Empire* and *Margin Released* are, and will remain, read and admired and represented a remarkable continuity with the ideas contained within his earlier writing.

Conclusion

Priestley had been receiving a kinder press in his later years, and the obituaries of February 1984 showed a degree of sympathy and understanding that had sometimes been lacking when he was alive. *The Times* described him as a 'many sided writer and extrovert public figure', before giving a positive and detailed appraisal of his life. It concluded that he was a great entertainer, a very English 'moralist' and the 'complete antithesis of the Organisation Man'. It continued, 'the independence of mind, egalitarian, non-conformist, together with a temperament innately romantic, is the constant element of his work. He expressed it in a prose of such sinew and liveliness that it is possible to say of him that he never wrote a dull sentence'.[1]

Priestley had always had an autobiographical element in his writing, and in his later years, an honest appraisal, sometimes side-by-side with self-deprecation, was present, often with posterity in mind. *Margin Released* conveyed Priestley's independence, the fact that he felt he had written too much, and his distance from the commercial and literary elements of twentieth century. As he put it, 'I was out of date before I even began'.[2] He also repeated his belief that his plays were his greatest achievements, offering an experimental angle and reaching heights that could not be scaled with fiction. Looking back on a production of *Time and the Conways* in Vienna in 1946, he recalled how the setting and the memory of writing the play had an 'overwhelming' impact. 'Perhaps it is more sensible to write books and not plays, but it is not out of books such moments arrive, beautiful and terrible'.[3]

Concluding *Margin Released*, Priestley suggested that 'irony' was a key part of his reminiscences. Among other things he claimed he was English, yet appreciated more on foreign shores, that 'he was too conventional for the avant-garde, too experimental for Aunt Edna', that he was a 'lowbrow to highbrows, a highbrow to lowbrows'. He went on to suggest that he was attacked when his writing became more political and that he had a 'reputation…for an almost ferocious aggressiveness', when he claimed he was nothing of the sort. He concluded in an elegiac way that his work 'has gone to many places, injured nobody, debased no civilised values' and that unlike people who wanted to write but never got round to it, he had made use of his time, concluding 'the use I made of it might have been better, it might have been worse'.[4]

The 83-year-old Priestley made similar points in *Instead of the Trees*. 'I have written too much', he conceded again, before bemoaning the lack of recognition in British theatre, and he stated that he 'had been a best-seller and a worst-seller' and that 'in 1940 I was one of the most popular men in the country, and about ten years later judging by the way everything I did was clobbered, one of the most unpopular men in the country', both of which he put down to experience. He went on to point out how 'long, thick and rich' his experiences had been. Married three times, he had been wounded in World War I and had travelled widely. 'I have been bored in Samarakand and amused in Pittsburgh', he suggested among a list of other destinations, even reminding the reader that he had been met by a crowd in southern Chile who thought he was Elvis Presley.[5]

Priestley was certainly right to point out the richness of his experience, as not only was he a writer who was also a public figure, but he did live a full life. He was certainly not an isolated artist who could only communicate through his work. His appeal was built around his direct, non-pretentious style and an honesty about the world as he saw it and about himself. In this sense, Priestley sometimes sold himself short. He did write a lot, probably too much, certainly enough for two or three lifetimes for some writers, but without the luxury of inherited money or a private income, he had little choice in this regard. He was a self-made man, and justifiably proud of this. His willingness to accept that he was not an intellectual, nor that his work displayed genius, was more questionable. Anthony Burgess addressed this issue, recalling how Priestley had told him that he was not a genius but had 'talent'. Burgess disagreed, suggesting that he 'had genius and that it was never sufficiently appreciated'. He continued, 'my generation had been warned off him by the intellectuals who derided or patronised him', but that Priestley 'was an intellectual himself, a man of wide erudition, the width of whose reading and understanding of what he read can be seen in his admirable *Literature and Western Man*'.[6]

There was a lot of truth in this. Priestley was often a great writer, and he was also intellectually engaged with the world. He was well read and frequently wrote with great skill and imagination, including a great command of language. *English Journey, An Inspector Calls, Bright Day, Journey Down a Rainbow* and *Margin Released*, to name five, were all brilliantly realized and exceptionally well-written works. Add to that the beautifully crafted postscripts, or the *New Statesman* article that helped launch CND, and you get politically astute and influential writing. How is any of this not intellectual? Priestley did not come up with elaborate social and political blueprints, nor did he look down on his audience, but those are not a pre-requisite for intellectual endeavour. He chose to write for the people, not just about them, and he called it as he saw it, whether it was inequality, privilege or the loss of individuality and vitality in the all-encompassing mass society. His approach to the latter revealed that he was much more than an English writer, or more accurately, that his Englishness was outward looking and his experiences while travelling, particularly in the United States, influenced his ideas and sharpened his analysis, leading to his formulation of Admass. The latter was a considered and perceptive idea that anticipated later debates on globalization.

Of course, as this book has shown, Priestley was idiosyncratic. He could be grumpy and polemical, and he was sometimes myopic about his own sense of privilege as a wealthy writer. His dismissal of class in favour of his preferred 'people' was in many ways characteristic of nineteenth-century radicalism, and his vision of the people was arguably more imagined rather than real. His dislike of trade unions and elements of the post-1945 Labour reforms, including aspects of the NHS, were also deeply felt, but he did not effectively spell out how ordinary people could achieve the greater equality they deserved without such measures. However, he was, by no means, the only intellectual who was better at identifying problems rather than solving them. And indeed, later radicals would rethink the Labourist values of the 1940s, although it seems unlikely that Priestley would have had much time for the some of the solutions favoured, for example, by New Labour.

Priestley disliked the big and the impersonal, because he was concerned with the individual, community and the vitality of life. He saw the mass society as draining the colour out of life, robbing people of their very humanity, including their initiative. As he put it in *Journey Down a Rainbow*, 'having disinherited ourselves, we keep on inventing new ways of forgetting what we once had and who we were'.[7] Priestley wrote to stop people forgetting and to celebrate the possibility of life lived well, 'a rich new life, a life sometimes tragic, at other times careless and gay'.[8] Priestley's vision of a better life, not wasted human potential, lay at the heart of his writing and his politics, and it is for this, as a decent, democratic, radical English intellectual, that he deserves to be read and remembered.

Notes

Notes to Introduction

1 *Times*, 16 Aug 1984, p. 12.
2 Bell A. O. *The Diary of Virginia Woolf, Vol. 3, 1925-30* (London, Harcourt and Brace, 1980), p. 318.
3 Vincent Brome, *J. B. Priestley* (London, Hamish Hamilton, 1988); John Braine, *J. B. Priestley* (London, Weidenfeld and Nicolson, 1979); Susan Cooper, *J. B. Priestley: Portrait of an Author* (London, Heinemann, 1970); John Atkins, *J. B. Priestley: The Last of the Sages* (London: John Calder, 1981); Dorothy Collins, *Time and the Priestleys: The Story of a Friendship* (Stroud, Alan Sutton, 1994): Judith Cook, *Priestley* (London, Bloomsbury, 1997).
4 The best example of this was the Chris Waters' interesting, 'J. B. Priestley, 1894-1984: Englishness and the Politics of Nostalgia', in Susan Pedersen and Peter Mandler (eds.), *After the Victorians: Private Conscience and Public Duty in Modern Britain* (London, Routledge, 1994), pp. 209–28.
5 Stefan Collini, *Absent Minds* (Oxford, Oxford University Press, 2006).
6 John Baxendale, *Priestley's England: J. B. Priestley and English Culture* (Manchester, Manchester University Press, 2007), p. 4; John Baxendale, ' "I had seen a lot of Englands": J. B. Priestley, Englishness and the People', *History Workshop Journal*, 51 (2001), pp. 87–111; Maggie B. Gale, *J. B. Priestley* (Abingdon, Routledge, 2008); Holger Klein, *J. B. Priestley's plays* (London, MacMillan, 1988) and *J. B. Priestley's Fiction* (Frankfurt, Peter Lang, 2002); Roger Fagge, 'J. B. Priestley, the 'Modern' and America', *Cultural and Social History*, 4,4 (Dec 2007), pp. 481–494.'From *Postscripts* to Admass: J. B. Priestley and the Cold War World', *Media History*, 12, 2 (Aug 2006), pp. 103–16; Kevin Davey, *English Imaginaries: Six Studies in Anglo-British Modernity* (London, Lawrence and Wishart, 1999); Sian Nicholas, ' "Sly Demagogues" and Wartime Radio: J. B. Priestley and the BBC', *Twentieth Century British History* 6, 3 (1995), pp. 247–66.

Notes to Chapter 1: Priestley, Politics and Class

1 On nostalgia see Chris Waters, 'J. B. Priestley, 1894–1984: Englishness and the politics of nostalgia', in Susan Pedersen and Peter Mandler (eds.), *After the Victorians: Private Conscience and Public Duty in Modern Britain* (London, Routledge, 1994), pp. 209–226, and David Smith, 'Churchill's Wartime Rival', *The Historian*, 44 (Winter 1994), pp. 12–15. Kevin Davey, *English Imaginaries: Six Studies in Anglo-British Modernity* (London, Lawrence and Wishart, 1999), p. 56.

2   J. B. Priestley, *Midnight on the Desert: A Chapter of Autobiography* (London, Heinemann, 1937), p. 136.

3   J. B. Priestley, *Margin Released: A Writer's Reminiscences and Reflections* (London, Heron Books, n.d. Orig. London, Heinemann, 1962), p. 140.

4   On Priestley's struggle before 1929, see Priestley to A.D. Peters, 25 May 1928, Uncatalogued Mss., A.D. Peters Files, J. B. Priestley Papers, Harry Ransom Research Center, University of Texas at Austin ('Priestley Papers' hereafter).

5   Priestley to Hugh Walpole, 9 Aug 1933, Letters from Priestley in other collections, Priestley Papers.

6   Priestley to Walpole, 24 July 1936, ibid.

7   Emerson Bureau flyer for Priestley lecture tour (1936). The lectures on offer were 'How shall we live?', 'The American Responsibility' and 'A writer looks at the world.' Folder 2, J. B. Priestley Correspondence with Edward Davison, Uncat Za Mss., Beinecke Library, Yale ('Davison Correspondence' hereafter).

8   Priestley, *Margin Released*, p. 229.

9   J. B. Priestley, *The Good Companions* (London, Heinemann, 1929), pp. 405, 409.

10 'T'Match' was originally published in *Apes and Angels* (1928). See Susan Cooper's preface to J. B. Priestley, *Essays of Five Decades* (selected with a preface by Susan Cooper) (London, Heinemann, 1969), p. xi.

11 Priestley to Eugene Saxton, 6 Oct 1933?, Catalogued Mss of J. B. Priestley, Priestley Papers.

12 Priestley, *Margin Released*, pp. 70–71; Priestley, *Midnight on the Desert*, p. 132.

13 *Sunday Telegraph*, 25 Nov 1962, p. 4.

14 Priestley, *Midnight on the Desert*, p. 135.

15 Priestley described the socialism that he grew up with in Bradford as 'liberalism with the starch out of it.' *Margin Released*, p. 71. See E.F. Biagini and A.J. Reid (eds.), *Currents of Radicalism: Popular Radicalism, Organized Labour and Party Politics in Britain, 1850–1914* (Cambridge, Cambridge University Press, 1991), on the continuing strength of popular liberalism in British radicalism.

16 Priestley, *Midnight on the Desert* , pp. 132–43. Priestley suggested that this description of his ideal state was based upon series of radio broadcasts given in London 'some years before', Ibid. p. 135.

17 James Hinton, 'Voluntarism versus Jacobinism: Labour, Nation and Citizenship in Britain, 1850–1950', *International Labour and Working Class History* 48 (1995), p. 77, Alastair J. Reid, *Social Classes and Social Relations in Britain, 1850–1914* (Basingstoke, MacMillan, 1992), p. 56.

18 J. B. Priestley, *Let the People Sing* (London, Mandarin, 1996. Orig., London, Heinemann, 1939), p. 188.

19 See, for example, Priestley's description of Stockton. J. B. Priestley, *English Journey* (London, Heron Books, n.d. Orig London, Heinemann, 1933), pp. 343–8.

20 J. B. Priestley, 'Freedom –English style', *The Star*, 24 July 1936, p. 4.

21 Priestley, *Midnight on the Desert*, p. 304.

22 Ibid., p. 303.

23 Priestley, *Margin Released*, pp. 28–9; *English Journey*, p. 197.

24 For Priestley on Settlement Houses, see *English Journey*, pp. 304, 325, 332.

25 J. B. Priestley, *Rain Upon Godshill: A Further Chapter of Autobiography* (London, Heinemann, 1939), p. 121. *Good Companions*, pp. 33, 239,333.

26 Priestley, *Rain Upon Godshill*, p. 255.

27 Priestley, *English Journey*, pp. 298–300.

28 Priestley, 'Freedom – English style', p. 4.

29 Priestley to Walpole, 21 Apr 1933. Letters from Priestley in Other Collections, Priestley Papers. Priestley's dislike of communism was such that he suggested Communism 'produced Fascism', in *The Sunday Chronicle*, 22 Oct 1933, p. 9.

30 See Chapter one of Andrew Miles and Mark Savage, *The Remaking of the British Working Class, 1850–1940* (London, Routledge, 1994).

31 Ross McKibbin, 'Class and Conventional Wisdom: The Conservative Party and the "Public" in Inter-war Britain', in McKibbin, *The Ideologies of Class: Social Relations in Britain, 1880–1950* (Oxford, Clarendon, 1990), pp. 271–5.

32 Priestley, *English Journey*, p. 29.

33 Priestley, *Good Companions*, p. 19.

34 Priestley, *English Journey*, p. 193.

35 Ibid.

36 Priestley, *Margin Released*, p. 7.

37 Ibid., pp. 11–12; Judith Cook, *Priestley* (London, Bloomsbury, 1997), pp. 5–7. J. B. Priestley, 'My Father', *Daily Telegraph*, 25 Nov 1962, pp. 4–5.

38 Priestley, *Margin Released*, p. 63.

39 Priestley, *Rain Upon Godshill*, p. 253.

40 Priestley, *Margin Released*, p. 63.

41 J. B. Priestley, *An Inspector Calls* (London, Samuel French, 1945), p. 22. Although inspired by memories from his Bradford youth, Priestley set the play in the North Midlands.

42 Priestley, *Margin Released*, pp. 63–4.

43 Ibid., pp. 7, 105.

44 Priestley to Jonathan Priestley, 17 Dec 1915. Catalogued Mss., Priestley Papers.

45 Priestley, *Margin Released*, p. 137.

46 Ibid., pp. 144–5; J. B. Priestley, *Instead of the Trees: A Final Chapter of Autobiography* (London, Heinemann, 1977), pp. 134–7.

47 Priestley to Peter Davison, 1 Aug 1970, Folder 6, Davison Correspondence.

48 J. B. Priestley, *Angel Pavement* (London, Heron Books, n.d. Orig., London, Heinemann, 1930), p. 115.

49 Ibid., p. 555.

50 Ibid., p. 588.

51 J. B. Priestley, *When we are Married and other Plays* (Harmondsworth, Penguin, 1969 edn. *When we are Married* Orig, London, Heinemann, 1938), p. 41.

52 On *Time and the Conways*, see David Hughes, *J. B. Priestley: An Informal Study of His Work* (London, Rupert Hart-Davis, 1958), pp. 143–5 and Gareth Lloyd Evans, *J. B. Priestley: The Dramatist* (London, Heinemann, 1964), pp. 91–103.

53 J. B. Priestley, 'Time and the Conways' in *Plays I* (London, Heron Books n.d., Orig. published as *The Plays of J. B. Priestley Volume 1* (London, Heinemann, 1948), p. 143. After Carol complements Beevers on charades, he comments, 'They didn't go in for those sort of things in my family', p. 183.

54 Ibid., 189.

55 Ibid., p. 195.

56 Priestley, *English Journey*, p. 233.

57 Ibid., p. 131.

58 Ibid., pp. 125–6.

59 Priestley to Walpole, 29 March 1928, Letters from Priestley in other collections, Priestley Papers.

60 Priestley, *Rain Upon Godshill*, pp. 253, 241.

61 Priestley to Davison, 9 March 1927, Folder 1, Davison Correspondence.

62 Cook, *Priestley*, pp. 123–4.

63 Peter Davison, *Half Remembered* (New York, Harper and Row, 1973), p. 104.

64 Priestley to Mary Priestley, 16 Feb. 1947, Catalogued Mss., Priestley Papers; Cook, *Priestley*, p. 208.

65 Vincent Brome, *J. B. Priestley* (London, Hamish Hamilton, 1988), p. 326.

66 Priestley, *Rain Upon Godshill*, pp. 241–2, 262–71.

67 Ibid., p. 208, although in February 1939 he told Walpole that the play was in trouble because the cheaper seats were filled but expensive 'fashionable' ones were not. Priestley to Walpole, 28 Feb1939, Letters from Priestley in other collections, Priestley Papers. By July 1939, he confirmed in a letter to Davison that this was the reason for the play's closure. Priestley to Davison, 3 July 1939, Folder 2, Davison Correspondence.

Notes to Chapter 2: Priestley and England Between the Wars

1 In his first radio postscript of 5 June 1940, Priestley suggested that 'when I say "English" I really mean British'. J. B. Priestley, *Postscripts* (London, Heinemann, 1940), p. 2.

2 Priestley to Davison, 11 Oct 1939, Folder 2, Davison Correspondence.

3 These included *The English Comic Characters* (London, The Bodley Head, 1925); *The English Novel* (London, Ernest Benn, 1927); *English Humour* (London, Longmans Green and Co, 1929); his introduction to *The Beauty of Britain* (London, Batsford, 1935) and his editing of *Our Nation's Heritage* (London, J. M. Dent 1939), as well as the novels including of course, *The Good Companions* (London, Heinemann, 1929), and *Let the People Sing* (London, Heinemann, 1939), and many of the plays including the political satire *Bees on the Boat Deck: A Farcical Comedy in Two Acts* (London, Heinemann, 1936).

4 See Martin Wiener, *English Culture and the Decline of the Industrial Spirit,1850–1950* (Cambridge, Cambridge University Press, 1981); Christopher Shaw and Malcolm Chase (eds.), *The Imagined Past: History and Nostalgia* (Manchester, Manchester University Press,1989); Robert Colls and Philip Dodd (eds.), *Englishness: Politics and Culture, 1880–1920* (London, Routledge, 1986). Patrick Wright's, *On Living in an Old Country: The National Past in Contemporary Britain* (London, Verso,1985) presented the 'Deep England' thesis (an idea 'hastily translated' from French according to Peter Mandler, 'Against "Englishness": English Culture and the Limits to Rural Nostalgia, 1850–1940', *Transactions of the Royal Historical Society*, 6th Series, 7 (1997), pp. 155–75, p. 175) . Wright's book however, whether we agree with its conclusions or not, provided a fascinating and intellectually adventurous approach to the subject.

5 Angus Calder, *The Myth of the Blitz* (London, Cape, 1991), p. 181; P. Dodd, 'The views of travellers: travel writing in the 1930s', in P. Dodd (ed.), *The Art of Travel: Essays on Travel Writing* (London, Frank Cass 1982), p. 127; David Smith, 'Churchill's Wartime Rival', *The Historian*, 44 (Winter 1994), pp. 12–15.

6 Ibid., p. 13.
7 Chris Waters, 'J. B. Priestley, 1894–1984: Englishness and the politics of nostalgia', in Susan Pedersen and Peter Mandler (eds.), *After the Victorians: Private Conscience and Public Duty in Modern Britain* (London: Routledge, 1994), pp. 209–28, p. 211. See also p. 219.
8 Mandler, 'Against "Englishness"', pp. 170, 173.
9 Alison Light, *Forever England: Femininity, literature and Conservatism between the Wars* (London, Routledge, 1991); David Matless, *Landscape and Englishness* (London, Reaktion Books, 1998); David Edgerton, *England and the Aeroplane: An Essay on Militant and Technological Nation* (Basingstoke, Macmillan, 1991); Philip Williamson, *Stanley Baldwin: Conservative Leadership and National Values* (Cambridge, Cambridge University Press, 1999). See also Mandler, 'Against "Englishness"', pp. 170–5.
10 John Baxendale, ' "I had seen a lot of Englands": J. B. Priestley, Englishness and the People', History Workshop Journal, 51 (2001), pp. 87–111, p. 89. For a fuller discussion, see John Baxendale, *Priestley's England: J. B. Priestley and English Culture* (Manchester, Manchester University Press, 2007), pp. 76–104.
11 Baxendale, "I had seen a lot of Englands", p. 89. Mandler, 'Against "Englishness"', pp. 170–5.
12 J. B. Priestley, *Midnight on the Desert: A Chapter of Autobiography* (London, Heinemann, 1937), p. 36. Priestley similarly described himself as a townsman who loved the county, in postscript of 25 Aug 1940. *Postscripts*, p. 55.
13 Priestley, *The Beauty of Britain*, p. 2.
14 Priestley, *Our Nation's Heritage*, p. x; Priestley's preface 'On England' to *The Shell Guide to England*, (ed. John Hadfield) (London, Michael Joseph, 1970), p. 11; J. B. Priestley, *English Journey* (London, Heron Books, n.d. Orig London, Heinemann, 1933), p. 83.
15 ibid., 113.
16 Priestley, *The Beauty of Britain,* p. 9. He later described the 1930s destruction of the environment in even less flattering terms, as 'the most determinedly tasteless of all our decades.' Priestley, 'On England', p. 9.
17 Priestley, *The Beauty of Britain*, p. 6.
18 Priestley, *Our Nation's Heritage*, pp. 165–6.
19 Priestley, *The Beauty of Britain* , p. 3.
20 *The Star*, 18 Sept 1936, p. 4.
21 *English Journey*, pp. 7–66. Quotes, pp. 58, 66.
22 Mandler, 'Against "Englishness"', pp. 163–7.
23 The Star, 18 Sept 1936, p. 4.
24 *Sunday Graphic,* 30 October 1938, pp. 20–21. For Priestley's objections to hunting , see *English Journey*, p. 117.
25 Ibid., p. 196.
26 Priestley to Davison, 9 April 1940. Folder 2, Davison Correspondence.
27 Priestley, *English Journey*, pp. 388–9.
28 Ibid., pp. 398–9.
29 Ibid., pp. 399–401.
30 Ibid., pp. 401–3.
31 Ibid., pp. 403–5.
32 Ibid., p. 406.
33 Ibid., pp. 406–12.

34 Ibid., pp. 114–5.

35 Ibid., p. 301.

36 Ibid., pp. 209–10.

37 Ibid., p. 310.

38 Ibid., pp. 314, 407. See similar sentiments ibid., p. 409.

39 Ibid., pp. 172–3.

40 Ibid., p. 286.

41 Ibid., pp. 410–11. Priestley believed that this continued into the present, and quoted a wool merchant in Bradford who told him that the idea that the city was 'making money again' was wrong. In fact, 'what bit o' money is being made's going to t'banks. It's banks' at's making money'. Ibid., p. 163.

42 Ibid., pp. 285–6, 411.

43 J. B. Priestley, *Rain Upon Godshill: A Further Chapter of Autobiography* (London, Heinemann, 1939), p. 251.

44 Ibid., p. 251.

45 Ibid., pp. 227–8.

46 Ibid., pp. 243–8; *Sunday Graphic* , 30 Oct 1938, pp. 20–1.

47 J. B. Priestley, *Margin Released: A Writer's Reminiscences and Reflections* (London, Heron Books, n.d. Orig. London, Heinemann, 1962), pp. 30–1.

48 See 'An Outpost' a draft of an essay, eventually published in T. Michael Pope, *The Book of Fleet Street* (London, Cassell, 1930), pp. 174–82. A.D. Peters Files, Priestley Papers.

49 P to 'Roughhead', 9 July 1928, Ibid.

50 Priestley, *English Journey*, pp. 162–3.

51 J. B. Priestley, *Wonder Hero* (London, Heinemann, 1933), pp. 221–2.

52 Priestley, *Rain Upon Godshill*, pp. 224–5, 236–9.

53 Ibid.,pp. 234–6, 227–228.

54 Ibid., pp. 225–6.

55 Priestley to Davison, 1 Feb [1937?], Folder 2, Davison Correspondence.

56 Priestley, *Rain Upon Godshill*, p. 206.

57 Priestley, *Margin Released*, p. 118.

58 Priestley, *Rain Upon Godshill*, p. 218.

59 *Sunday Graphic*, 30 Oct 1938, pp. 20–1.

60 J. B. Priestley, *Let the People Sing* (London, Mandarin, 1996. Orig., London, Heinemann, 1939), p. 160.; *English Journey*, pp. 405–6, where Priestley praised some of the younger people he had met, who had the 'strength' but not the weakness of the third 'new' England. 'They are good citizens and as yet we have no city worthy of them.'

61 Priestley to Davison, 27 June 1932, Folder 1, Davison Correspondence.

62 Priestley, *English Journey*, p. 417.

63 Priestley, *Rain Upon Godshill*, p. 217.

64 Priestley, *English Journey*, p. 416; See also p. 115.

65 Priestley, *Rain Upon Godshill*, pp. 23–4.

66 James Hinton, 'Voluntarism versus Jacobinism: Labour, Nation and Citizenship in Britain, 1850-1950', *International Labour and Working Class History* 48 (1995), p. 73.

67 As early as 1920 Wells argued that Britain, France and the US shared a common radical heritage, which could benefit the world . H.G. Wells, *Outline of History: Being a Plain History of Life an mankind* (London, Cassell, 1920). See also Roger Fagge, ' "The finest or

the damndest country in the world ?": British Radicals and America in the 1930s', in C. Armstrong, R. Fagge and T. Lockley (eds), *America in the British Imagination* (Newcastle, Cambridge Scholars Press, 2007), pp. 168–81.

68   Miles Taylor, 'Patriotism and the Left in Twentieth-Century Britain', *The Historical Journal* 33, 4 (1990), pp. 980–3.

69   Priestley, *English Journey*, pp. 160–1; *Margin Released*, p. 65.

70   'This Jew Business', *The Star*, 10 July 1935, p. 4; 'Jew-Baiting', *News Chronicle* 17 July 1939, p. 10; Priestley, *Midnight on the Desert*, pp. 155–6.

71   Priestley, 'Jew Baiting', p. 10.

72   Priestley to Mrs. Harold Laski, 9 Sept 1930. Uncatalogued Mss. Priestley Papers.

73   Priestley, 'This Jew Business', p. 4, and *Midnight on the Desert*, 156.

74   See for example, J. B. Priestley, *Angel Pavement*, (London, Heron Books, n.d. Orig., London, Heinemann, 1930), pp. 182–3, 192,254, 425–6, 452, and 589.

75   Priestley, *English Journey*, p. 242.

76   Ibid., p. 243.

77   Ibid., pp. 248–9.

Notes to Chapter 3: Priestley, the 'People' and the Second World War

1   Peter Hennessy, *Never Again: Britain 1945–1951* (London, Jonathan Cape, 1992), p. 318.

2   J. B. Priestley, 'Journey into Daylight', *The Listener*, 17 May 1945, p. 543.

3   Priestley to Walpole, 13 Sep 1939. Letters from Priestley in other collections, Priestley papers.

4   Priestley to Davison, 11 Oct 1939, Folder 3, Davison Correspondence.

5   Ibid.

6   Priestley to the Davisons 27 Jan 1940. Ibid. *Music at Night* was written for, and first performed at, the Malvern Festival in 1938. Neither the Malvern or Westminster productions were well received by critics. See the Introduction to J. B. Priestley, *Plays I* (London, Heron books, n.d., Orig. published as *The Plays of J. B. Priestley Volume 1* (London, Heinemann,1948)), p. xi–x. The difficulties of putting on a new play were also becoming apparent to Priestley. Having just finished *Ever Since Paradise*, he told Walpole in January 1940 that it was almost impossible to cast plays at that point, and that 'serious theatre is now non-existent'. Priestley to Walpole, 30 Jan 1940. Letters from Priestley in other collections, Priestley Papers.

7   Priestley to Cass Canfield, 29 April 1940. Priestley originally described the proposed novel to Canfield in February. See Priestley to Cass Canfield, 29 April 1940. Catalogued Mss., Priestley Papers.

8   Alan Day, *J. B. Priestley: An Annotated Bibliography: A Supplement* (Slad, Ian Hodgkins and Co, 2001), pp. 21–22. See also Priestley to Sylvia and Mary Priestley, 26 July 1940 Catalogued Mss., Priestley Papers. See also Priestley to A.D. Peters, 11Nov 1940. Priestley had hoped that 'Let the People Sing' might be made into a film, but this didn't happen. Priestley to A.D. Peters, 9 April 1940, A.D. Peters Files, Priestley Papers.

9   He wrote *An Inspector Calls* in autumn 1944, and *Bright Day* was also written 'towards the end of the war'. J. B. Priestley, *Margin Released: A Writer's Reminiscences and Reflections* (London, Heron Books, n.d. Orig. London, Heinemann, 1962), p. 195; Vincent Brome, *J. B. Priestley* (London, Hamish Hamilton, 1988), pp. 283, 285.

10 Priestley to Walpole, 30 Nov 1939, Letters from Priestley in other collections, Priestley Papers.
11 Priestley to the Davisons, 27 Jan 1940, Folder 2, Davison Correspondence.
12 The rather contradictory approach was illustrated in 1932 when discussing the Great Depression in a letter to Davison. He also complained about the amount of tax he had to pay. Priestley to Davison, 6 Jan 1932. Folder 1, ibid.
13 Asa Briggs, *The BBC: The first fifty years* (Oxford, Oxford University Press, 1985), p. 191; Sian Nicholas, ' "Sly Demagogues" and Wartime Radio: J. B. Priestley and the BBC', *Twentieth Century British History*, 6, 3, p. 254; Day, *J. B. Priestley: An Annotated Bibliography* (London, Garland, 1980), p. 21; J. B. Priestley, *Britain Speaks* (Harpers, New York, 1941).
14 'Civilization can defend itself as fiercely as barbarism can attack', Broadcast of 30 May 1940, Priestley, *Britain Speaks*, pp. 1-7.
15 Angus Calder, *The People's War* (London, Pimlico, 1992), p. 110.
16 Postscript for Wednesday 5 June 1940, Priestley, *Postscripts*, pp. 1-4.
17 Postscript for Sunday 9 June 1940, ibid., pp. 5-8.
18 Postscript for Sunday 16 June 1940, ibid., pp. 9-13.
19 Ibid., p. 55.
20 Postscript for Sunday 23 June 1940, ibid., pp. 14-18.
21 Postscript for Sunday 4 August 1940,ibid., pp. 44-48.
22 The political right of course saw the conflict in a similar light, but drew more conservative conclusions. Churchill for example talked of 'Christian civilisation' and 'the long continuity of our institutions and our Empire' in his broadcast of 18 June, 1940. Quoted in Richard Weight, *Patriots: National Identity in Britain, 1940-2000* (London, Macmillan, 2002), p. 2.
23 Postscript for Sunday 30 June 1940, Priestley, *Postscripts*, pp. 19-23.
24 Postscript for Sunday 1 September 1940, ibid., pp. 60-65.
25 Postscript for Sunday 8 September, ibid., pp. 67-68.
26 Postscript for Sunday 15 September 1940, ibid., p. 715.
27 Postscript for Sunday 14 July 1940, ibid., pp. 29-33.
28 Postscript for Sunday 21 July 1940, ibid., pp. 34-38.
29 Billingham had been requisitioned in autumn 1940. Jane Priestley to the Davisons, 11 Sep 1940 and 30 Nov 1940, Folder 2, Davison Correspondence.
30 Postscript for Sunday 21 July 1940, Priestley, *Postscripts*, pp. 34-38.
31 Postscript for Sunday 28 July, 1940 ibid., 39-43. Sunday 4 August 1940, pp. 44-48 made a broader case for avoiding the mistakes of the interwar years. It also, with its mention of a fortune teller, hinted at the mystical feel of the Margate discussion.
32 Postscript for Sunday 22 September 1940, ibid., p. 79. He was referring to the village of Broxwood, where Jane Priestley was running a home for mothers and children who had been bombed out of the East End. Vincent Brome, *J. B. Priestley*, pp. 244-245; Priestley to Peters, 25 Nov 1941, A.D. Peters Files, Priestley Papers.
33 Postscript for Sunday 22 September 1940, Priestley, *Postscripts*, pp. 76-80.
34 Postscript for Sunday 6 October 1940, ibid., pp. 86-90.
35 Postscript for 25 August 1940, ibid., p. 57.
36 Postscript for Sunday 20 October 1940, ibid., pp. 97-8; 96-100.
37 Priestley to A.D. Peters, 11November 1940, A.D. Peters Files, Priestley Papers.

38 *Daily Mail*, 2 July 1940, quoted in Asa Briggs, *The History of Broadcasting in the United Kingdom, Volume III: The War of Words* (Oxford, Oxford University Press, 1970), pp. 210–211.

39 Storm Jameson to Priestley, 30 June 1940, Catalogued Mss, Letters to J. B. Priestley, Priestley Papers.

40 Lord Kennet to Priestley, 4 July 1940, ibid.

41 Ernest Bevin to Priestley, 9 August 1940, ibid.

42 Edward Davison to Priestley, 1 September 1940, Folder 2, Davison Correspondence.

43 George Bernard Shaw to Priestley, 1 August 1940, Letters to J. B. Priestley, Priestley Papers.

44 Briggs, *The History of Broadcasting in the United Kingdom, Volume III*, p. 211–212; Sian Nicholas, "Sly Demagogues", pp. 256–257.

45 Postscript for Sunday 20 October 1940, Priestley, *Postscripts*, p. 98.

46 Priestley to Walpole, 24 October 1940. Letters from Priestley in other collections, Priestley Papers.

47 Priestley to Harold Laski, 22 Dec 1940, Catalogued Mss., Priestley Papers.

48 Priestley was also angry with the BBC over their 'discourteous' failure to reply promptly to a suggestion he had made for a series of special feature shows. See ibid.

49 Judith Cook, *Priestley* (London, Bloomsbury, 1997), pp. 186–187; Sian Nicholas, "Sly Demagogues", pp. 258–259.

50 Priestley to Cass Canfield, 29 April 1941, Catalogued Mss., Priestley Papers.

51 Priestley to Walpole, 12 May 1941, Letters from Priestley in other collections, ibid.

52 Priestley, *Margin Released*, pp. 221–222.

53 Brome, *J. B. Priestley*, p. 251; Sian Nicholas, "Sly Demagogues", p. 260.

54 Ibid., pp. 259–261.

55 Ibid., p. 266.

56 Ibid., p. 261.

57 Jane Priestley to the Davisons, 30 Nov 1940, Folder 2, Davison Correspondence.

58 He had only moved into the hotel that day, as he wanted to be near the BBC. He spent the afternoon in his room, before being called in by the BBC 'overseas' service. 'I wasn't too pleased about it' he told overseas listeners the following day, 'because Monday was one of my free nights and I hoped to get to bed early.' Broadcast of 17 Sep 1940, *Britain Speaks*, pp. 235–236.

59 Sian Nicholas, "Sly Demagogues", p. 260.

60 Priestley, *Margin Released*, p. 223.

61 Coughlin began broadcasting in the late 1920s, and by 1930 had 30 to 40 million listeners. Drawing on the US 'populist' tradition he attacked Wall Street and British financiers, and favoured an inflationary economic policy. Initially a supporter of the New Deal, by 1934 he became a prominent critic, having established 'The National Union of Social Justice' to further his beliefs, and added an illiberal dose of anti-Semitism into his speeches and writings. See Michael E. Parrish, *Anxious Decades: America in Prosperity and Depression, 1920–41* (New York, Norton, 1992), pp. 325–328.

62 In *Margin Released* he described the postscripts as being 'ridiculously over-praised'. See pp. 220–221.

63 Calder, *The People's War*, p. 253.

64 Ibid., 253; Diana Collins, *Time and the Priestleys: The Story of a Friendship* (Stroud, Allen Sutton, 1994), p. 92; Priestley to Hugh Walpole, 14 December 1940, Letters from Priestley in other collections. Priestley Papers.

65 Priestley to Canfield, 29 April 1941. Catalogued Mss., ibid.

66 The pamphlet had actually been commissioned by Collins, as a part of series negotiated with the 'Author's National Committee'. Priestley had been involved in the latter earlier in 1940 (and in its predecessor, the 'Author's Planning Committee' in 1939) in an attempt at organising writers behind the war effort. See Brome, *J.P. Priestley*, pp. 256-8; Cook, *Priestley*, pp. 190-191. By 6 December 1940 Priestley told Walpole that he had done little 'lately' on the Committee because he had been 'very busy' and he was 'no longer' getting 'enquiries about jobs from authors'. Priestley to Walpole, 6 December 1940, Letters from Priestley in other collections, Priestley Papers.

67 See Priestley to Cass Canfield,16 Nov 1941, Catalogued Mss., ibid.

68 Paul Addison, *The Road to 1945: British Politics and the Second World War* (London, Jonathan Cape 1977), p. 158.

69 Collins is interesting on the relationship between the two men, having known them both. Collins, *Time and the Priestleys*, pp. 94-95.

70 Calder, *The People's War*, pp. 289-299; 546-550; Steven Fielding, Peter Thompson and Nick Tiratsoo, *"England Arise!" The Labour Party and Popular Politics in 1940s Britain* (Manchester, Manchester University Press, 1995), pp. 54-55; Addison, *The Road to 1945*, pp. 159-163. Both Brome and Cook wrongly suggest that Commonwealth was formed in July 1941. See Brome, *J. B. Priestley*, p. 260 and Cook, *Priestley*, p. 193.

71 Fielding et al, 'England Arise!', p. 55; Calder, *The People's War*, pp. 548-549.

72 J. B. Priestley, 'Preface' to Richard Acland , *How It Can Be Done: A Careful Examination of the Ways in which we can, and cannot, advance to the kind of Britain for which many hope they are fighting* (London, Macdonald and Co. 1943), pp. 5-13.

73 Ibid.

74 'Democratic England has arrived', *London Calling*, 28 May 1942, pp. 3-4; Brome, *J. B. Priestley*, pp. 262-276.

75 Brome, *J. B. Priestley*, p. 258.

76 J. B. Priestley, *Out of the People* (London, Collins in association with William Heinemann Ltd., 1941), p. 13.

77 Ibid., pp. 14-17.

78 Ibid., p. 27.

79 Ibid., pp. 18-20.

80 Ibid., p. 32.

81 Ibid., p. 8, 12, 87.

82 Ibid., p. 69.

83 Ibid., p. 36.

84 Ibid., p. 109, 50, 69.

85 Ibid., pp. 50-62.

86 Ibid., p. 59.

87 Ibid., pp. 60-61.

88 Ibid., p. 60.

89 Priestley made it clear that it was the value religion placed upon the individual human life that mattered, rather than clericalism or religious fundamentalism. Ibid., p. 52.

90 Ibid., pp. 71–73.
91 Ibid., pp. 74–77.
92 Ibid., p. 64.
93 Ibid., pp. 66–67.
94 Ibid., pp. 82–85.
95 Ibid., pp. 83–85.
96 Ibid., p. 89.
97 Ibid., p. 91.
98 Ibid., pp. 92–93.
99 Ibid., pp. 93–95.
100 Ibid., p. 97.
101 Ibid., pp. 99–100.
102 Ibid., p. 68.
103 Ibid., p. 112.
104 Ibid., pp. 112–116.
105 Ibid., pp. 118–127.
106 Ibid., pp. 119–120.
107 Ibid., pp. 121–122.
108 Ibid., p. 32.
109 Ibid., p. 121.
110 Ibid., p. 122.
111 Ibid., p. 112.
112 Priestley, *Out of the People*, pp. 86–87.
113 George Orwell, *Coming up for Air* (London, Penguin, 1962. Orig. London, Gollancz, 1939), pp. 25, 192, 176–180, 209, 124–131.
114 Ibid., pp. 215, 158.
115 Ibid., p. 158.
116 Christopher Hitchens, *Orwell's Victory* (London, Allen Lane, 2002), pp. 113–114.
117 George Orwell, *The Lion and the Unicorn: Socialism and the English Genius* (London, Secker and Warburg, 1962. Orig. S and W, 1941), pp. 93–94.
118 Ibid., p. 54.
119 Ibid., pp. 55–57.
120 Ibid., p. 67.
121 Ibid., p. 58.
122 Ibid., p. 87.
123 Ibid., p. 74.
124 Ibid., pp. 20–21.
125 Ibid., pp. 14, 15, 20, 35.
126 Ibid., p. 27.
127 Ibid., pp. 76–81.
128 Ibid., p. 84.
129 Ibid., pp. 76–77.
130 Ibid., p. 49.
131 Ibid., p. 86.
132 Ibid., p. 85.
133 Ibid., pp. 17, 30–31.

134 Ibid., p. 37, p. 76. Hitchen's respect for Orwell's writings on Empire is such that he situ-
     ates Orwell as one of the 'founders of the discipline of post-colonialism' as well as being
     one of the 'literary registers of the historic transition of Britain from an imperial and
     monochrome (and paradoxically insular) society to a multicultural and multi-ethnic one.'
     Orwell's Victory, p. 32.

135 Orwell wrote of the Home Guard that it 'swells to a million men in a few weeks, and is
     deliberately organised from above in such a way that only people with private incomes can
     hold positions of command.' Orwell, *The Lion and the Unicorn*, p. 58.

136 Ibid., pp. 74–75.

137 Ibid., p. 75.

138 Ibid., p. 86.

139 Bernard Crick, *George Orwell: A Life* (London, Penguin, 1980), p. 409.

140 Orwell, *The Lion and the Unicorn*, p. 78.

141 'Vision, Not Hate, Will Win the War', *New York Times Magazine*, 18 October 1942, p. 3.

142 Orwell, *The Lion and the Unicorn*, p. 96.

143 A similar point is made in David Gervais, *Literary Englands: Versions of Englishness in
     Modern Writing* (Cambridge, Cambridge University Press, 1993), p. 179.

144 Hitchens, *Orwell's Victory*, p. 114.

145 Priestley, 'This England at Zero Hour', *Reynold's News*, p. 2. See also, 'Democratic England
     Has Arrived', *London Calling*, 28 May 1942, pp. 3–4.

146 Priestley's *Black out in Gretley: A Story of and for Wartime* (London, Heinemann, 1942)
     was a wartime thriller dealing dealing with fifth columnists. An effective and enjoyable
     novel with insights into the wartime experience, it nevertheless was not intended as a
     heavyweight novel.

147 J. B. Priestley, *Daylight on a Saturday: A novel about an aircraft factory* (London, Heine-
     mann, 1943), p. 2.

148 Ibid., pp. 10–11.

149 Ibid., pp. 28–30, 89.

150 Ibid., pp. 59, 244–7.

151 Ibid., p. 248.

152 Ibid., pp. 75, 78–79.

153 Ibid., pp. 25–26.

154 Ibid., pp. 213–224.

155 Ibid., p. 5.

156 Ibid., p. 229.

157 Ibid., pp. 159, 134, 159, 219, 225–227, 260.

158 Ibid., p. 220.

159 Ibid., p. 194.

160 Ibid., pp. 108–9, 252.

161 Ibid., p. 292.

162 Ibid., p. 303.

163 Ibid., p. 305.

164 Ibid., pp. 305–6.

165 J. B. Priestley, 'They Came to a City' in *The Plays of J. B. Priestley Vol III* (London: Heine-
     mann, 1950) (orig. pubd. In *Three Plays* (London, Heinemann, 1943), p. 184.

166 Ibid., pp. 146, 144, 147.

167 Ibid., pp. 190–191.

168 Ibid., pp. 199–200.

169 Ibid., p. 201.

170 For example, J. B. Priestley, *Here are Your Answers* (London, Commonwealth, 1944) which offered similar arguments to *Out of the People*, although with a somewhat harder political edge. The play *Desert Highway* (London, Heinemann, 1944), written for the army explored the role of soldiers across different time-periods. 'Let's have less about them, more about us', *Reynold's News*, 4875, 6 Feb 1944, p. 6; 'Show them the Real Britain in Shirt-sleeves', *News Chronicle*, 29 Jan 1945, p. 2 were two examples among many other pieces of journalism.

171 *Margin Released*, p. 192.

172 J. B. Priestley, *Letter to a Returning Serviceman* (London: Home and Van Thal, 1945), p. 23, 31.

173 Priestley, *The Plays of J. B. Priestley, Vol. III*, p. xii.

174 *Margin Released*, p. 195. He told Davison that he was 'in the middle of a new novel' in October 1944. Priestley to the Davisons, 20 Oct 1944, Folder 2, Davison Correspondence

175 Ibid.

176 See Postscript for Sunday 20 October 1940, Priestley, *Postscripts*, pp. 97–98; 96–100.

177 Priestley's contribution was titled, 'It is easy to play tricks with words – as the Tories are doing.' *Reynolds News*, 1 July 1945, p. 4.

178 Brome, *J. B. Priestley*, p. 281.

179 For an overview of this debate, see Sonya O. Rose, *Which People's War? National Identity and Citizenship in Wartime Britain, 1939-45* (Oxford, Oxford University Press, 2003). See Addison, *The Road to 1945*; Calder, *The People's War*; and Hennessey, *Never Again* for the best, and in many ways still relevant, arguments in favour of a consensual 'people's war.' For a more critical emphasis upon divisions and indifference during wartime, see Fielding et al., *"England Arise!"*; A. Mason and P. Thompson, 'Reflections on a Revolution? The Political Mood in Wartime Britain', in N. Tiratsoo (ed.), *The Atlee Years* (London, Continuum, 1991), and S. Fielding. 'What the People Want? The Meaning of the 1945 General Election', *Historical Journal*, 35 (1992), pp. 623–9. Other important works include James Hinton, *Women, Social Leadership and the Second World War: Continuities of Class* (Oxford, Oxford University Press, 2002); Stephen Brooke, *Labour's War: The Labour Party and the Second World War* (Oxford, Oxford University Press, 1992).

180 James Hinton, 'Voluntarism versus Jacobinism: Labour, Nation and Citizenship in Britain, 1850–1950', *International Labour and Working Class History* 48 (1995), p. 80.

Notes to Chapter 4: The Disillusioning of Mr. Priestley

1 J. B. Priestley, *Thoughts on the Wilderness* (London, Heinemann, 1957), p.vii.

2 Priestley to Natalie Davison, 3 May 1946, Folder 2, Davison Correspondence.

3 Priestley to Edward Davison, 16 Sep 1946, ibid.

4 J. B. Priestley, *Instead of the Trees: A Final Chapter of Autobiography* (London, Heinemann, 1977), pp. 95–6. In 2006 Tom Priestley told an audience celebrating the republication of *Bright Day* that, 'a lot of it echoes my own father's experiences in his youth…It's about memory, about the way our past becomes our present and the future. It's also about the

Yorkshire character.' *http://www.bbc.co.uk/bradford/content/articles/2006/10/12/timothy_ west_ilkley_feature.shtml* (visited 18 September 2009).

5 J. B. Priestley, *Bright Day* (London, Penguin, 1951, Orig. London, Heinemann, 1946), p. 11.
6 Ibid., pp. 10–15. Quote, p. 12.
7 Ibid., p. 16.
8 Ibid., p. 110.
9 Ibid., p. 101.
10 Ibid., p. 48.
11 ibid., p. 169.
12 Ibid., p. 73.
13 Ibid., p. 23.
14 Ibid., pp. 40–1.
15 Ibid., p. 23.
16 Ibid., pp. 287–8.
17 Ibid., pp. 11–12.
18 Ibid., p. 145 Priestley's dislike of Ragtime was repeated elsewhere, most notably in J. B. Priestley, *Margin Released: A Writer's Reminiscences and Reflections* (London, Heron Books, n.d. Orig. London, Heinemann, 1962), pp. 66–7.
19 Priestley, *Bright Day*, p. 38.
20 Ibid., p. 22.
21 Ibid., p. 38.
22 Ibid., pp. 58–9.
23 Ibid., p. 60.
24 Ibid., p. 23, 47.
25 Ibid., pp. 22, 123.
26 Ibid.,p. 178.
27 As he recalls getting to know the Alingtons and their friends, Dawson notes 'Behind the feeling that all this was new and strange was a mysterious conviction that I had at last arrived where I belonged.' Ibid., p. 49.
28 Ibid., pp. 212–13 and 227.
29 Ibid., p. 226.
30 Ibid., p. 246.
31 Ibid., pp. 270–1.
32 Ibid., pp. 273–4.
33 Ibid., p. 277.
34 Ibid., p. 283.
35 Ibid., p. 287.
36 Ibid., p. 290.
37 Ibid., pp. 293–4.
38 Priestley, *Instead of the Trees*, p. 96.
39 Priestley, Introduction to *The Plays of J. B. Priestley Vol. III* (London, Heinemann, 1950), pp. xii–xiii. See Maggie B. Gale, *J. B. Priestley* (Abingdon, Routledge, 2008), pp. 142–4 on the critical reception for the play.
40 Priestley intro to *The Plays of J. B. Priestley, Vol. III* p. xii, Gale, *J. B. Priestley*, pp. 151–2; Priestley, *Margin Released*, p. 199.

41 Laurence Olivier to Priestley, 21 August 1947. Terrence Rattigan also praised the play. Terence Rattigan to Priestley, 22 August 1947, Catalogued Mss, Letters to J. B. Priestley, Priestley Papers.

42 Priestley, intro to *The Plays of J. B. Priestley, Vol. III* pp. xii–xiii. John Braine, *J. B. Priestley* (London, Weidenfeld and Nicolson, 1979), p. 129. See Priestley to Davison, 29 September and 26 October 1955, Folder 4, Davison Correspondence. A handwritten note in the A.D. Peters Files, presumably written by Peters described *Mr. Kettle and Mrs. Moon* as 'a financial success, but a mediocre play.' A.D. Peters Files, Priestley Papers.

43 Priestley, intro to *The Plays of J. B. Priestley, Vol. III* p. xiii; Vincent Brome, *J. B. Priestley* (London, Hamish Hamilton, 1988), p. 223.

44 Ibid., p. vii, See Gale, *J. B. Priestley* on Theatre finance and management, pp. 29–35.

45 Brome, *J. B. Priestley*, p. 224; Dulcie Gray, *J. B. Priestley* (Stroud, Sutton, 2000), p. 75. Weaker plays included Priestley's *Golden Door*, which had to be partially rewritten after the author met with Ralph Richardson who was to star in the play. Priestley to Davison, 3 April 1951, Folder 3, Davison Correspondence.

46 Priestley to Davison, 4 June 1950, ibid.

47 Priestley to Davison, 19 April 1953, ibid. On difficulties with *A Dragon's Mouth*, see Priestley to Davisons, 26 April 1952, Jacquetta Hawkes to Natalie Davison, 8 May 1952, ibid.

48 Priestley to Peters, 23 August 1951, A.D. Peters Files, Priestley Papers.

49 Peters to Priestley, 24 August 1951, ibid.

50 Priestley to Natalie Davison, 27 November 1953, Folder 3, Davison Correspondence.

51 Brome, *J. B. Priestley*, pp. 368–9.

52 Priestley to Davisons, 24 July 1949; Priestley to Davison, 4 June 1950; Priestley to Davison, 4 Nov 1950, Folder 3, Davison Correspondence.

53 Brome, *J. B. Priestley*, pp. 298–9.

54 Priestley told Davison *Jenny Villiers* was 'best forgotten', Priestley to Davison, 21 August 1949, Folder 3, Davison Correspondence.

55 Priestley to Davison, 4 November 1950, Priestley to Peters, 16 June 1950, A.D. Peters Files, Priestley Papers.

56 Priestley to Davison, 4 June 1950, Folder 3, Davison Correspondence.

57 Priestley to Davison, 11 June 1951, ibid.

58 Priestley, *Margin Released*, pp. 194–5.

59 Priestley to Davison, 1 May 1951, Folder 3, Davison Correspondence. Brome, *J. B. Priestley*, pp. 336–7; Gray, *J. B. Priestley*, p. 75.

60 Priestley to Davison, 26 December 1953 and 24 February 1954, Folder 3, Davison Correspondence.

61 *Evening Standard*, 5 June 1953. Press cutting in ibid.

62 See Priestley to Natalie Davison, 23 June 1953, ibid. For the break-up, see Gray, *J. B. Priestley*, pp. 59–69; Brome, *J. B. Priestley* , pp. 301–366; Judith Cook, *Priestley* (London, Bloomsbury, 1997), pp. 213–44. For Jane's account of the breakdown of the marriage, see her letter to Edward Davison, nd (1951?) Folder 3, Davison Correspondence.

63 Jacquetta Hawkes, *A Quest for Love* (London, Chatto and Windus, 1980), pp. 204–20; Dorothy Collins, *Time and the Priestleys: The Story of a Friendship* (Stroud, Alan Sutton, 1994), pp. 155–87; Gray, *J. B. Priestley*, p. 69.

64 Priestley to Mary Priestley, 12 August 1953, Catalogued Mss, Priestley Papers. The family had purchased two farms under Jane's initiative, and against Priestley's advice. Brome, *J. B. Priestley*, p. 347.

65 Priestley to Davisons, 22 February 1953 and 5 February 1953, Folder 3, Davison Correspondence.

66 Priestley to Davisons, 5 March, 1953; 19 March 1953 and 24 March 1953, ibid.

67 Priestley to Davisons, 22 January 1953, ibid.

68 Priestley Preface to Fenner Brockway, *Socialism over Sixty Years: The Life of Jowett of Bradford, 1864–1944* (London: Allen and Unwin, 1946), pp. 11–12.

69 J. B. Priestley, *The Secret Dream: An Essay on Britain, America and Russia* (Turnstile Press, London, 1946), pp. 12–13.

70 Priestley to Davison, 16 Sept. 1946, Folder 2, Davison Correspondence.

71 Priestley, 'Cantankery I', *New Statesman* 15 May 1948, p. 390 and 'Cantankery II', *New Statesman*, 22 May 1948, pp. 408–9.

72 'Cantankery I', p. 390; 'Cantankery II', pp. 408–9.

73 *Sunday Pictorial*, 23 January 1949, p. 5.

74 Ibid.

75 *Tribune*, 28 January 1949, pp. 1–2.

76 Ibid.

77 *Sunday Pictorial*, 6 February 1949, p. 6.

78 Ibid.

79 Priestley to Peters, 24 March 1949, A.D. Peters Files, Priestley Papers.

80 Priestley to Davison, 21 August 1949, Folder 3, Davison Correspondence.

81 'To All Women', Labour Party Election pamphlet, 1949, University of Warwick Library, pamphlets 50/14.

82 Priestley to Davison, 16 January 1950, Folder 3, Davison Correspondence.

83 Clement Atlee to Priestley, 17 January 1950, Catalogued Mss., Letters to J. B. Priestley, Priestley Papers.

84 Harold Laski to Priestley, 18 January 1950; Herbert Morrison to Priestley, 13 December 1949, ibid. Bliss was awarded a knighthood in 1950.

85 Clement Atlee to Priestley, 11 April 1951, ibid.

86 Priestley, 'On with the Festivals', *The Listener*, 10 May 1951, pp. 739–40.

87 J. B. Priestley, *Festival in Farbridge* (London, Heinemann, 1951), p. 25.

88 Priestley to Davison, 1 May 1951, Folder 3, Davison Correspondence.

89 Priestley to Davison, 7 August 1951, ibid.

90 Ibid.

91 *The Times*, 7 October 1950, p. 7; 11 October 1950, p. 7; and 14 October 1950, p. 7.

92 Priestley to the Davisons, 12 January 1952, Folder 3, Davison Correspondence.

93 Priestley to Davison, 7 Feb 1952, ibid.

94 Priestley to Davison, 19 April 1953, ibid.

95 Priestley to Davison, 27 May 1955, Folder 4, Davison Correspondence.

96 Priestley to the Davisons, 26 April 1952, Folder 3, ibid.

97 Priestley to the Davisons, 9 October 1953, ibid.

98 Ibid.

99 J. B. Priestley, *Thoughts in the Wilderness*, pp. vii–viii.

100 Ibid., p. 1–7.

101   Ibid., p. 18.
102   Ibid., pp. 4–5.
103   Ibid., p. 38.
104   Ibid., pp. 47–53, 221.
105   Ibid., pp. 8–13.
106   Ibid., pp. 11–12.
107   Ibid., p. 34.
108   Ibid., p. 124.
109   Ibid., pp. 14–17.
110   Ibid., See pp. 42–6 on 'Time'; p. 66 on Jung, pp. 34–39 on Eros.
111   Malcolm Muggeridge to J. B. Priestley, 7 September 1953, Catalogued Mss, Letters to J. B. Priestley Papers, Priestley Papers.
112   Hugh Gaitskell to J. B. Priestley, 25 June 1956, ibid.
113   John Campbell, *Nye Bevan and the Mirage of British Socialism* (London, Weidenfeld and Nicolson, 1987), pp. 191–5.
114   J. B. Priestley, *Russian Journey* (Issued under the auspices of the Writers Group of the Society for Cultural Relations with the USSR, 1946), p. 4. On war damage in Kiev, see p. 13. On Leningrad, see p. 29.
115   Ibid., pp. 3, 7, 30.
116   Ibid., pp. 30–31.
117   Ibid., pp. 8, 30, 34.
118   Ibid., p. 33.
119   Ibid., pp. 36–7.
120   Ibid., pp. 38–40.
121   Thomas Natfali, 'George Orwell's List', *New York Times*, 29 July 1998. *http://www.netcharles.com/orwell/ctc/docs/list.htm* (visited 26 January 2010); Timothy Garton Ash, 'Orwell's List', *The New York Review of Books*, 50, 14 (25 Sep 2003). *http://www.nybooks.com/articles/16550.* (visited 22 January 2010).
122   Priestley, *Russian Journey*, p. 37.
123   Ian MacDonald, *The New Shostakovich* (London, Pimlico, 2006. Orig. London, Fourth Estate, 1990), pp. 1–17.
124   Walter LaFeber, *America, Russia and the Cold War, 1945–2002* (Boston, McGraw-Hill, 2004).
125   J. B. Priestley, *The Secret Dream: An Essay on Britain, America and Russia* (London, Turnstile Press, 1946), pp. 4–13.
126   Ibid., pp. 14–26.
127   Ibid., pp. 34–6.
128   Ibid., pp. 37–8.
129   Priestley to Davison, 16 September 1946, Folder 2, Davison Correspondence.
130   Priestley to Jane, 9 November 1947, Catalogued Mss., Priestley Papers.
131   Priestley to Davison, 4 June 1950, Folder 3, Davison Correspondence.
132   Priestley to Davison, 13 August 1950, ibid.
133   Priestley, *Thoughts in the Wilderness*, pp. 34–39.
134   Ibid., pp. 73–79.
135   Ibid., pp. 27–33.
136   Priestley, *The Plays of J. B. Priestley, Vol. III* , p. 343.

137 See introduction, ibid., pp. xiii–xiv.

138 Ibid., p. xiii.

139 Ibid., p. 443.

140 Ibid., p. 443.

141 Ibid., pp. 472–3.

142 Ibid.

143 Paul Boyer, *By the Bomb's Early Light: American Thought and Culture at the Dawn of the Atomic Age* (New York, Pantheon, 1985) Although about the US, this is the best book on the cultural consequences of the early atomic age.

144 Priestley, *Thoughts in the Wilderness*, p. 16.

145 *Reynold's News*, 1 Dec 1957.

146 J. B. Priestley and Jacquetta Hawkes, *Journey Down the Rainbow*, (London, Heron Books, n.d.; Orig. London, Heinemann, 1955), pp. 223–7.

147 *New Statesman*, 2 Nov 1957, pp. 554–6. On Bevan's views See John Campbell, *Nye Bevan and the MIrage of British Socialism*, pp. 330–40.

148 *New Statesman*, 2 Nov 1957, pp. 554–6.

149 Ibid.

150 Ibid.

151 Ibid.

152 Priestley to Davison, 2 December 1957, Folder 4, Davison Correspondence.

153 Ibid., p. 549.

154 Hinton, James, *Protests and Visions: Peace Politics in Twentieth Century Britain* (London, Hutchinson Radius, 1989), pp. 152–60; Collins, *Time and the Priestleys*, pp. 13–16.

155 Ibid., p. 17.

156 Collins, Diana, *Time and the Priestleys*, pp. 17–23; Priestley to Davison, 30 Jan 1958, Folder 4, Davison Correspondence. For transmission date etc of 'Domesday for Dyson', see *http://ftvdb.bfi.org.uk/sift/title/551342?view* ī *transmission*(visited 6 Feb 2010).

157 Collins, *Time and the Priestleys*, pp. 18–23; Cook, *Priestley*, pp. 260–1. Priestley to Davison, 30 May 1958, Folder 4, Davison Correspondence.

158 Priestley to Lesley Davison, 10 April 1958, ibid.

159 Priestley to Davison, 10 May 1958, ibid.

160 See Hawkes to Natalie Davison, 10 March 1959 on CND being 'torn by dissension', ibid. Cook, *Priestley*, pp. 261–2.

Notes to Chapter 5: Priestley, Admass and the United States

1 Priestley to Natalie Davison, 20 July 1954; Priestley to Edward Davison, 6 October 1954, Folder 3, Davison Correspondence.

2 Priestley to Edward and Natalie Davison, 12 Nov 1954; Hawkes to Natalie Davison, 16 November 1954, ibid.

3 Priestley to Edward and Natalie Davison, 26 November 1954, ibid.

4 J. B. Priestley and Jacquetta Hawkes, *Journey Down the Rainbow*, (London, Heron Books, n.d.; Orig. London, Heinemann, 1955), p. xi.

5 ibid., pp. xii–xiii.

6 J. B. Priestley, *English Journey* (London, Heron Books, n.d. Orig. London, Heinemann, 1933), p. 402.

7 Priestley and Hawkes, *Journey Down a Rainbow*, xiii.

8 Ibid., pp. 51–2.

9 Ibid., pp. 52–3.

10 Ibid., pp. 45, 146–8, 154, 215–19.

11 Ibid., p. 9, 46.

12 Ibid., pp. 98–9.

13 Ibid., pp. 179–80.

14 Ibid., pp. 223–6.

15 Ibid., p. 19, 210.

16 On McCarthyism, see Richard M. Fried, *Nightmare in Red: The McCarthy Era in Perspective* (Oxford, Oxford University Press, 1990) and M. J. Heale, *McCarthy's Americans: Red Scare Politics in State and Nation, 1935–1965* (Basingstoke, Macmillan, 1998).

17 Priestley and Hawkes, *Journey Down a Rainbow*, p. 37.

18 Ibid., pp. 220–22.

19 Rebecca West to Priestley, 22 June 1955, Catalogued Mss., Letters to J. B. Priestley, Priestley Papers. The enmity that arose from this issue was such that Dulcie Gray recalls Priestley refusing to talk to Rebecca West when she mistakenly invited both of them to her house. Dulcie Gray, *J. B. Priestley* (Stroud, Sutton, 2000), p. 44.

20 Ibid., pp. 31, 130–4.

21 Ibid., pp. 144–5.

22 Ibid., p. 145.

23 Betty Friedan, *The Feminine Mystique* (New York, W.W. Norton, 1963), see Chapter 1 in particular.

24 Ian Hamilton selected Priestley's writing on a football match in *The Good Companions*, as part of his influential collection, *The Faber Book of Soccer* (London, Faber, 1992), pp. 35–37. Charlie Habble was a keen amateur footballer in Priestley, *Wonder Hero*. (London, Heinemann, 1933).

25 Priestley and Hawkes, *Journey Down a Rainbow*, pp. 75–86.

26 Ibid., pp. 77–78.

27 Ibid., p. 78.

28 Ibid., p. 195.

29 Ibid., p. 195.

30 Ibid., pp. 197–99.

31 Ibid., p. 201.

32 Ibid., p. 202.

33 Ibid., pp. 202–7.

34 Ibid., p. 265, 275.

35 Ibid., p. 282, 264.

36 Ibid., p. 282.

37 David Reisman, with Nathan Glaze, and Reuel Denney, *The Lonely Crowd: A study of the Changing American Character* (New Haven, Yale University Press, 1961 edn. Orig. 1950), pp. 17–24.

38 Wright Mills C. *White Collar: The American Middle Classes* (New York, Oxford University Press, 1951); C. Wright Mills, *The Power Elite* (New York, Oxford University Press, 1956).

39 William Whyte, *The Organization Man* (New York, Simon and Schuster, 1956), pp. 8–14.

40   Ibid., p. 298.

41   John Keats, *Cracks in the Picture Window* (Boston, Houghton-Mifflin, 1956). Lewis Mumford's most famous work is *The City in History* (New York, Harcourt, Brace and World, 1961).

42   J. K. Galbraith, *The Affluent Society* (Harmondsworth, Penguin, 1984 edn. Orig. Boston, Houghton Mifflin, 1958), p. 192.

43   Arthur Miller *Death of a Salesman* (New York, The Viking Press, 1949); John Updike *Rabbit Run* (New York, Alfred A. Knopf, 1960); Jack Kerouac *On The Road* (New York, The Viking Press, 1957); J. D. Salinger *The Catcher In The Rye* (Boston, Little, Brown and Co., 1951).

44   On Pollock, see Kirk Varnedoe and Pepe Karmel (eds), *Jackson Pollock: New Approaches* (New York: Museum of Modern Art, 2000). For Parker, Ross Russell *Bird Lives: The High Life and Hard Times of Charlie 'Yardbird' Parker* (London, Quartet Books, 1972). 'Invasion of the Body Snatchers' (Don Siegel, 1956). For an interesting discussion of the film see Peter Biskind, *Seeing is Believing: How Hollywood Taught us to Stop Worrying and Love the Fifties* (London, Bloomsbury, 2000 edn. Orig, New York, Henry Holt and Co., 1983), pp. 137–44.

45   On British television see Ed Buscombe, *British Television: A Reader* (Oxford, Oxford University Press, 2000). For the US see Erik Barnouw, *Tube of Plenty: The Evolution of Television* (New York, Oxford University Press, 1975).

46   Richard Hoggart *The Uses of Literacy* (Harmondsworth, Penguin, 1957); Dominic Sandbrook, *Never Had It So Good: A History of Britain from Suez to the Beatles* (London, Abacus, 2006), pp. 391–3.

47   Herbert Gans, *The Levittowners: Ways of Life in a New Suburban Community* (London: Allen Lane, 1967), p. 213. Sandbrook, *Never Had It So Good*, pp. 409–53. On the US, see James Gilbert, *A Cycle of Outrage: America's Reaction to the Juvenile Delinquent in the 1950s* (New York, Oxford University Press, 1986).

48   Priestley and Hawkes, *Journey Down a Rainbow*, p. 273.

49   Barnouw, *Tube of Plenty*, pp. 133–4, 172–83.

50   Gans, *The Levittowners*, pp. 280–98.

51   Priestley to Mary Priestley, 3 October 1954, Catalogued Mss., Priestley Papers.

52   Priestley to Davison, 2 March 1955, Folder 4, Davison Correspondence.

53   Priestley to Davison, 25 March 1955, ibid. Programme information from http://www.imdb.com/name/nm0697362/filmoseries#tt1586243 (visited 15 April 2010).

54   Priestley to Davison, 14 January 1956, Folder 4, Davison Correspondence.

55   Priestley to Richard Church, 10 April 1956, Catalogued Mss., Priestley Papers.

56   *Radio Times*, 29 November 1957, *http://www.luiserainer.net/The-Stone-Faces.php* (visited 17 May 2011).

57   Priestley to Davison, 9 October 1957, Folder 4, Davison Correspondence.

58   Priestley also mentioned that 'many of our friends are mixed up with this commercial TV now being organised.' Priestley to Davison, 2 March 1955, ibid.

59   Priestley to Davison, 2 December 1957, ibid.

60   Priestley to Davison, 14 September 1958, ibid; Alan Day, *J. B. Priestley: An Annotated Bibliography* (London, Garland, 1980), p. 268. http://www.bbc.co.uk/bradford/content/articles/2008/09/26/priestley_lost_city_reaction_feature.shtml (visited 16 April 2010).

61 Day, *J. B. Priestley: An Annotated Bibliography*, p. 264; Priestley to Davison, 5 Jan 1958; Priestley to Davison, 30 Jan 1958, Folder 4, Davison Correspondence.

62 Priestley to Davison, 10 May 1958, ibid.

63 Priestley, 'The Writer in a Changing Society', republished in *Thoughts in the Wilderness* (London, Heinemann, 1957), p. 237.

64 Ibid., pp. 11–12.

65 Ibid., pp. 101–6.

66 Priestley to Davison, 19 January 1955, Folder 4, Davison Correspondence.

67 *Dallas News*, 2 January 1955. Press cutting in ibid.

68 Priestley to Davison, 8 September 1956, ibid.

69 Priestley to J. Lehmann, 4 October 1955, Letters from Priestley in other Collections, Priestley Papers. See similar comments in Hawkes to Edward Davison, 9 November 1955, Folder 4, Davison Correspondence.

70 Priestley to Davison, 7 April 1956; See also Priestley to Natalie Davison, 26 October 1956, ibid.

71 Priestley, 'Who is Anti-American', *New Statesman*, 5 Nov 1955, reprinted in *Thoughts in the Wilderness*, pp. 148–9.

72 Ibid., pp. 149–50.

73 Ibid., pp. 148–54.

74 J. B. Priestley, *Margin Released: A Writer's Reminiscences and Reflections* (London, Heron Books, n.d.; orig. London, 1962), pp. 124–5.

75 Priestley, needless to say, was not impressed with the performance. He also drew more dramatic lessons from the sound of the music, suggesting it represented the corrosive elements of modernity: ibid., pp. 66–8. See also J. B. Priestley, *Delight* (London, n.d.; orig. London, 1949), pp. 63–5.

76 J. B. Priestley, *Midnight on the Desert: A Chapter of Autobiography* (London, Heinemann), p. 37.

77 Ibid., pp. 286–7. Priestley told Edward Davison that they had a 'grand time' on the visit, but offered a less majestic account. 'I had a huge comical mule that never turned corners properly but always looked right over the precipices, as if fascinated by the depths below and wondering whether to take himself—and me—down there in one leap. He was a great and indiscriminate eater too, and our theory was that he was partly responsible for the size of the Grand Canyon, and that he had enlarged it considerably during our trip.' Priestley to Davison, 17 March [1936?] Folder 1, Davison Correspondence.

78 Priestley to Davison, 26 Nov 1936, Folder 2, Davison Correspondence.

79 Priestley to Davison, 4 Dec 1935, ibid., Priestley to Davison, 19 Mar 1937, ibid. See also Jane Priestley to the Davisons, 1 Dec 1935, Folder 1, ibid. Priestley described how in 1937 'I came back to this Arizona country almost like coming back home.' J. B. Priestley, *Rain Upon Godshill: A Further Chapter of Autobiography* (London, Heinemann, 1939), p. 109.

80 Priestley, *Midnight on the Desert*, p. 91. Priestley was similarly appreciative of the scenery and 'vintage air' of rural New York. Priestley, *Rain Upon Godshill*, p. 6.

81 On Lawrence, see Peter Conrad, *Imagining America* (London, Routledge, 1980), pp. 159–93.

82 Priestley, *Midnight on the Desert*, p. 101.

83 Ibid., pp. 101–5.

84 Priestley, *Midnight on the Desert*, p. 105.

85 Priestley, *Rain Upon Godshill*, p. 109.

86 Priestley to Davison, 31 Jan 1951, Folder 3, Davison Correspondence; *Daily Herald*, 13 Feb 1951, p. 4.

87 Wells H. G. wrote a letter to the *New York Times* in 1919, starting 'Greetings to the great English-Speaking Republic which has solved itself, and must now help the world solve its problems of diversity and unity and republican freedom with honour and stability.' H. G. Wells, *The Correspondence of H. G. Wells, Volume 3*, ed. David C. Smith (London, Pickering and Chatto, 1998), pp. 21–2. See also H. G. Wells, *The Future in America: A Search after Realities* (London, 1906) and Michael Foot, *H. G: The History of Mr. Wells* (London, Doubleday, 1995), pp. 233–4.

88 Priestley, *Midnight on the Desert*, pp. 85–9.

89 Ibid., pp. 88–9.

90 Ibid., pp. 116–25.

91 Ibid., pp. 110–12.

92 'The smashing return of Roosevelt is excellent', Priestley wrote following Roosevelt's re-election. Priestley to Davison, 5 Nov 1936, Folder 2, Davison Correspondence—an opinion shared with other British radicals, including Vera Brittain, *Testament of Experience: An Autobiographical Story of the Years, 1925–50* (London, Virago, 1978; orig. London, Gollancz 1957), pp. 183–4 and of course, H.G. Wells, *Experiment in Autobiography: Discoveries and Conclusions of a Very Ordinary Brain, Vol II* (London Faber, 1984 edn. Orig., London, Gollancz/Cresset Press, 1934), pp. 794–8.

93 Priestley, *Midnight on the Desert*, pp. 124–5.

94 Ibid., pp. 113–14.

95 Ibid., pp. 124–32.

96 Priestley, *Rain Upon Godshill*, pp. 90–1.

97 See Priestley to Jane, 19 Feb 1931, Catalogued MS., Priestley Papers.

98 Priestley, *Rain Upon Godshill*, pp. 65–6. Priestley shared his dislike of New York with Edward Davison: 'You are like me in this—that you can only find yourself in America so long as you leave New York with its gin-and-taxi atmosphere a long way behind.' Priestley to Davison, 25 Feb 1936, Folder 1, Davison Correspondence. See also Davison to Priestley, 11 Nov 1935, ibid.

99 Priestley, *Midnight on the Desert*, pp. 173–5.

100 Priestley to Davison, 3 Nov [1937?], Folder 2, Davison Correspondence.

101 Ibid., Priestley, *Rain Upon Godshill*, p. 71.

102 Priestley, *Midnight on the Desert*, p. 174.

103 These included 'Sing As We Go' (Gaumont British, 1934), and the John Grierson documentary, 'We Live in Two Worlds' (GPO, 1937). See Alan Day, *J. B. Priestley: An Annotated Bibliography*, pp. 265–7. For a broader discussion of Priestley's attitude to film and the mass media, see Roger Fagge, 'From the Postscripts to Admass: J. B. Priestley and the Cold War World', *Media History*, 12, 2 (August 2006), pp. 103–15.

104 Priestley, *Midnight on the Desert*, pp. 166–173.

105 Priestley, J. B., *Rain Upon Godshill*, pp. 78–82.

106 Priestley, *Midnight on the Desert*, pp. 184–5. See Priestley, J. B., *English Journey*, p. 121. For Hollywood's impact on provincial theatre, see ibid., p. 197. Hollywood's influence over young film goers was satirized in various novels, including Priestley, J. B., *Let the People*

Sing (London, Heinemann, 1939), p. 84. See also, Priestley to Davison, 10 Feb 1938, Folder 2, Davison Correspondence.

107 Priestley, *Margin Released*, pp. 215–18; Priestley to Davison, 26 Nov [1934?], Folder 2, Davison Correspondence; Priestley to A. D. Peters, 23 Dec 1935, A. D. Peters Files, Priestley Papers.

108 J. B. Priestley, *Angel Pavement* (London, Heron Books n.d.; orig. London, Heinemann, 1930), pp. 508–14.

109 Ibid., pp. 523–46. Priestley does provide a sting in the tail, however, ending the chapter with the sentence 'Perhaps this was the best day's work in one or other of their lives; or perhaps the worst', p. 546.

110 Priestley, *English Journey*, p. 4.

111 Priestley to Davison, 28 Dec 1927, Folder 1, Davison Correspondence. See similar sentiments in Priestley to Natalie Davison, 4 Dec 1927, ibid.

112 Priestley to Davison, 22 Nov [1929?], Folder 1, Davison Correspondence. As late as August 1930, six months before his first visit, Priestley was claiming that he felt 'a certain distinction now about not having been to America'. Priestley to Davison, 19 Aug 1930, ibid.

113 Priestley to Davison, 28 Dec 1929, ibid.

114 Priestley, *Rain Upon Godshill*, p. 20; Priestley, *Midnight on the Desert*, pp. 29–34; Priestley, *Margin Released*, p. 190.

115 Priestley, *Midnight on the Desert*, p. 44.

116 Priestley to Davison, 10 Feb 1938, Folder 2, Davison Correspondence.

117 Priestley, *Rain Upon Godshill*, pp. 35–7.

118 Priestley to Davison, 4 Dec 1938, Folder 1, Davison Correspondence.

119 Priestley to Peters, 16 Sept 1936, A. D. Peters Files, Priestley Papers.

120 Priestley to Davison, 4 Dec 1938, Folder 1, Davison Correspondence. See also Priestley to Hugh Walpole, 8 Dec 1937, Folder 1, Letters from J. B. Priestley in other collections, Priestley Papers.

121 Priestley, *Rain Upon Godshill*, p. 116.

122 Priestley to Edward Davison, 14 Jan. 1956.

123 Priestley, *Midnight on the Desert*, pp. 18–21.

124 Priestley to Davison, 10 Feb 1930, Folder 2, Davison Correspondence.

125 Priestley to Hugh Walpole, 25 Feb 1931, Letters from Priestley in other collections, Priestley Papers.

126 Priestley to Walpole, 30 Nov 1939, ibid.

127 J. B. Priestley, *The Secret Dream: An Essay on Britain, America and Russia* (London, Turnstile Press, 1946), p. 26.

128 *New Statesman*, 28 August 1948, p. 172.

129 J. B. Priestley, *Festival at Farbridge* (London, Heinemann, 1951), pp. 46, 56, 57.

130 *Thoughts in the Wilderness*, p. 114.

131 *Daily Herald*, 2 Feb 1951, p. 4.

Notes to Chapter 6: Late Priestley

1 Hawkes to Natalie Davison, 4 June 1959, Folder 5, Davison Correspondence.
2 Priestley to Edward Davison, 9 Aug 1959, ibid.

3   Priestley to Davison, 21 April 1960, ibid.

4   Priestley to Davison, 30 May 1960, ibid.

5   J. B. Priestley, *Literature and Western Man* (London, London Heinemann, 1960), pp. 443–4. Vincent Brome, *J. B. Priestley* (London, Hamish Hamilton, 1988), pp. 413–18.

6   Priestley, *Literature and Western Man*, pp. 445–6.

7   Priestley to Davison, 6 Feb 1967, Folder 5, Davison Correspondence.

8   Priestley to Davison 26 Apr 1969, 24 May 1969, ibid.

9   For thrillers, see *Saturn Over the Water: An Account of His Adventures in London, South America and Australia by Tim Bedford* (London, Heinemann, 1961) and *The Shapes of Sleep: A Topical Tale* (London, Heinemann, 1962). Collected essays *Outcries and Asides* (London, Heinemann, 1974). For travel, see *A Visit to New Zealand* (London, Heinemann, 1974) and *Trumpets over the Sea: Being a Rambling and Egostistical Account of the London Symphony Orchestra's Engagement at Daytona Beach Florida in July-August 1967* (London, Heinemann, 1968). The above are only a selection of the variety of work that Priestley produced in these years.

10 For example, the Crossmans came to dinner at Kissing Tree House at the time of the CND campaign. Jacquetta wrote, 'we had some good political talk, but kept off the precise topic of nuclear disarmament.' Hawkes to Edward Davison, 11 May 1960, Folder 5, Davison Correspondence.

11 Priestley to Davison, 30 July 1962, ibid.

12 J. B. Priestley, 'Dark Junction', *New Statesman*, LXVI, 4 Oct 1963. Reprinted in Priestley, *The Moments and Other Pieces* (London, Heinemann, 1966), pp. 24–7.

13 See, for example, Priestley 'Ambience or Agenda', *New Statesman*, LXIII, 2 Feb 1962, Reprinted in Priestley, *The Moments*, pp. 7–9.

14 Priestley to Jane, 23 Sept 1968, Catalogued Mss, Priestley Papers.

15 Priestley, 'Mr. Healey should heed the squeaking pips', *Sunday Times*, 6 Apr 1975, p. 17.

16 Priestley to Peter Davison, 15 Mar 1971; 25 Nov 1973; 2 Jan 1974, Folder 6, Davison Correspondence.

17 Priestley to Mary Priestley, 1 May 1975, Catalogued Mss., Priestley Papers.

18 Priestley to Peter Davison, 7 Apr 1975, Folder 6, Davison Correspondence.

19 Priestley, 'The English Disease', *Sunday Times*, 15 June 1975, p. 17.

20 Cutting Robert Mitgang, 'J. B. Priestley, the Octogenarian offers a bit of advice on writing', *New York Times*, 1977/8? in Folder 5, Davison Correspondence. Priestley, 'Middle Class Awakening', *Sunday Times*, 16 Mar 1975, p. 16.

21 Priestley, 'The English Disease', p. 17.

22 Priestley to Peter Davison, 28 Jan 1976, Folder 6, Davison Correspondence. This was not strictly true because Priestley had, of course, been sympathetic to the Conservatives for a brief period in the 1950s.

23 Priestley to Peter Davison, 6 May 1976, ibid.

24 He rated Kennedy more highly than Nixon though. Priestley to Davison, 3 Oct 1960, Folder 5, Davison Correspondence.

25 Priestley to Davison, 26 May 1968. Priestley made the visit the following autumn. Priestley to Davison, 12 Oct 1968, ibid.

26 Priestley, *Trumpets over the Sea*, p. 11, 13.

27 Ibid., pp. 11–42; 44.

28 Ibid., p. 33.

29 Ibid., p. 77.

30 Priestley, 'The Meaning of Brown Eggs', *New York Times*, 17 Dec 1971, p. 41. Excerpts from same titled article in the *New Statesman* 82, 10 Dec 1971, p. 815.

31 Letters page, *New York Times*, 28 Dec 1971, pp. 29–30.

32 Ibid., 31 Dec 1971, p. 19.

33 Ibid., 10 Jan 1972, p. 32.

34 Priestley, *Outcries and Asides*, pp. 124–6.

35 Ibid., pp. 108–9.

36 J. B. Priestley, *The Image Men* (London: Allison and Busby,1968), p. 16. (Originally published in two volumes as *Out of Town* and *London End* (London: Heinemann, 1968).

37 John Atkins, *J. B. Priestley: The Last of the Sages* (London: John Calder, 1981), p. 200.

38 Chris Waters, 'J. B. Priestley, 1894–1984: Englishness and the politics of nostalgia', in Susan Pedersen and Peter Mandler (eds.), *After the Victorians: Private Conscience and Public Duty in Modern Britain* (London, Routledge, 1994), pp. 209–28.

39 *Sunday Times*, 25 June 1961–1 April 1962.

40 Priestley, *Margin Released*, pp. 28–32.

41 Ibid., p. 155–6.

42 Ibid., p. 180.

43 J.B Priestley, *Lost Empires: Being Richard Herncastle's Account of His Life on the Variety Stage from November 1913 to August 1914. Together with a Prologue and Epilogue* (London, Heinemann, 1965), p. 23.

44 Ibid., p. 152.

45 Priestley, *Trumpets over the Sea*, p. 93.

46 Priestley, *Lost Empires*, p.xi.

47 J. B. Priestley, *Man and Time* (London: Bloomsbury, 1989 edn. Orig London, Aldus, 1964), p. 12.

48 Ibid., 187.

49 Ibid., p. 306.

50 Ibid., pp. 306–8; Brome, *J. B. Priestley* , p. 432–5. See also Atkins, *J. B. Priestley*, pp. 163–9 and John Baxendale, *Priestley's England: J. B. Priestley and English Culture* (Manchester, Manchester University Press, 2007), pp. 187–8. Maggie B. Gale, *J. B. Priestley* (Abingdon, Routledge, 2008), pp. 89–106.

51 J. B. Priestley, *Over the Long High wall: Some Reflections and Speculations on Life, Death and Time* (London, Heinemann, 1972), p. 142.

52 John Braine, *J. B. Priestley* (London, Wiedenfeld and Nicolson, 1979), p. 149.

53 *Times*, 14 Sep 1964, p. 7.

54 Kingsley Martin, 'Birthday Letter', *New Statesman*, 11 Sept 1964, p. 354.

55 Judith Cook, *Priestley* (London, Bloomsbury, 1997), pp. 277–8.

56 Priestley to Peter Davison, 13 Dec 1977, Folder 6, Davison Correspondence.

57 Priestley to Peter Davison, 18 Sep 1974; Evelyn Ames to Peter Davison, 8 Oct 1974. Copy of Evelyn Ames speech at 80th celebration in ibid. Ray Gosling in the *Times*, 12 Sept 1974; Richard Eder, *New York Times*, 6 Apr 1974, p. 6; David Hughes 'Union Jack' *Guardian*, 14 Sept 1974.

58 *The Listener*, 12 Sept 1974, pp. 335–38.

59 See, for example, Priestley, *Instead of the Trees*, p. 46 for complaints about taxation.

Notes to Conclusion

1 The *Times*, 16 Aug 1984, p. 12. See also ibid., p. 24, and Beryl Bainbridge, 'Priestley: A Message of All Times', *Times*, 17 Aug 1984, p. 8.
2 J. B. Priestley, *Margin Released: A Writer's Reminiscences and Reflections* (London, Heron Books, n.d. Orig. London, Heinemann, 1962), p. 156.
3 Ibid., p. 211.
4 Ibid., pp. 230-1.
5 J. B. Priestley, *Instead of the Trees: A Final Chapter of Autobiography* (London, Heinemann, 1977), pp. 126-7. See also *Margin Released*, p. 182.
6 Quoted in Dorothy Collins, *Time and the Priestleys: The Story of a Friendship* (Stroud, Sutton, 1994), pp. 239-40.
7 J. B. Priestley and Jacquetta Hawkes, *Journey Down the Rainbow*, (London, Heron Books, n.d.; Orig. London, Heinemann, 1955), p. 282.
8 J. B. Priestley, *Literature and Western Man* (London, London Heinemann, 1960), p. 446.

Bibliography

MANUSCRIPTS

J.B. Priestley Correspondence with Edward Davison, Beinecke Rare Books and Manuscript Library, Yale University
J.B. Priestley Archive, Harry Ransom Research Center, University of Texas at Austin

NEWSPAPERS AND MAGAZINES

Daily Herald
Daily Telegraph
Dallas News
Evening Standard
Guardian
Listener
London Calling
New Statesman
New York Times
News Chronicle
Reynold's News
Star
Sunday Chronicle
Sunday Graphic
Sunday Pictorial
Sunday Telegraph
Sunday Times
Times
Tribune

BOOKS, ARTICLES AND PAMPHLETS

Acland, R. *How It Can Be Done: A Careful Examination of the Ways in Which We Can, and Cannot, Advance to the Kind of Britain for Which Many Hope They Are Fighting* (London, Macdonald and Co., 1943).

Addison, P. *The Road to 1945: British Politics and the Second World War* (London, Jonathan Cape, 1977)

Ash, T. G. 'Orwell's List', *The New York Review of Books*, 50, 14 (25 September 2003)

Atkins, J. *J.B. Priestley: The Last of the Sages* (London, John Calder, 1981)

Barnouw, E. *Tube of Plenty: The Evolution of Television* (New York, Oxford University Press, 1975)

Baxendale, J. ' "I had seen a lot of Englands": J.B. Priestley, Englishness and the People', *History Workshop Journal*, 51 (2001)

—. *Priestley's England: J.B. Priestley and English Culture* (Manchester, Manchester University Press, 2007)

Bell, A. O. *The Diary of Virginia Woolf, Vol 3, 1925–1930* (London, Harcourt and Brace, 1980)

Biagini, E. F. and Reid, A. J. (eds), *Currents of Radicalism: Popular Radicalism, Organized Labour and Party Politics in Britain, 1850–1914* (Cambridge, Cambridge University Press, 1991)

Biskind, P. *Seeing Is Believing: How Hollywood Taught Us to Stop Worrying and Love the Fifties* (London, Bloomsbury, 2000 Ed.; Orig. New York, Henry Holt and Co., 1983)

Boyer, P. *By the Bomb's Early Light: American Thought and Culture at the Dawn of the Atomic Age* (New York, Pantheon, 1985)

Braine, J. *J.B. Priestley* (London, Weidenfeld and Nicolson, 1979)

Briggs, A. *The History of Broadcasting in the United Kingdom, Volume III: The War of Words* (Oxford, Oxford University Press, 1970)

—. *The BBC: The First Fifty Years* (Oxford, Oxford University Press, 1985)

Brittain, V. *Testament of Experience: An Autobiographical Story of the Years, 1925–1950* (London, Virago, 1978; orig. London, Gollancz, 1957)

Brockway, F. *Socialism Over Sixty Years: The Life of Jowett of Bradford*, 1864–1944 (London, Allen and Unwin, 1946)

Brome, V. *J.B. Priestley* (London, Hamish Hamilton, 1988)

Brooke, S. *Labour's War: The Labour Party and the Second World War* (Oxford, Oxford University Press, 1992)

Buscombe, E. (ed.) *British Television: A Reader* (Oxford, Oxford University Press, 2000)

Calder, A. *The Myth of the Blitz* (London, Cape, 1991)

Campbell, J. *Nye Bevan and the Mirage of British Socialism* (London, Weidenfeld and Nicolson, 1987)

Collini, S. *Absent Minds* (Oxford, Oxford University Press, 2006)

Collins, D. *Time and the Priestleys: The Story of a Friendship* (Stroud, Alan Sutton, 1994)

Colls, R. and Dodd, P. (eds), *Englishness: Politics and Culture, 1880–1920* (London, Routledge, 1986)

Conrad, P. *Imagining America* (London, Routledge, 1980)

Cook, J. *Priestley* (London, Bloomsbury, 1997)

Cooper, S. *J.B. Priestley: Portrait of an Author* (London, Heinemann, 1970)

Crick, B. *George Orwell: A Life* (London, Penguin, 1980)

Davey, K. *English Imaginaries: Six Studies in Anglo-British Modernity* (London, Lawrence and Wishart, 1999)

Davison, P. *Half Remembered* (New York, Harper and Row, 1973)

Day, A. *J.B. Priestley: An Annotated Bibliography* (London, Garland, 1980)

—. *J.B. Priestley: An Annotated Bibliography: A Supplement* (Slad, Ian Hodgkins and Co., 2001)

Dodd, P. 'The views of travellers: travel writing in the 1930s', in Dodd, P. (ed.), *The Art of Travel: Essays on Travel Writing* (London, Frank Cass, 1982)

Edgerton, D. *England and the Aeroplane: An Essay on Militant and Technological Nation* (Basingstoke, Macmillan, 1991)

Fagge, R. 'From Postscripts to Admass: J.B. Priestley and the Cold War World', *Media History*, 12, 2 (August 2006)

—. 'J.B. Priestley, the 'Modern' and America', *Cultural and Social History*, 4, 4 (December 2007).

—. ' "The finest or the damndest country in the world ?": British Radicals and America in the 1930s', in Armstrong, C., Fagge, R., and Lockley, T. (eds), *America in the British Imagination* (Newcastle, Cambridge Scholars Press, 2007)

Fielding, S. 'What the People Want? The Meaning of the 1945 General Election', *Historical Journal*, 35 (1992)

Fielding, S., Thompson, P., and Tiratsoo, N. *'England Arise!' The Labour Party and Popular Politics in 1940s Britain* (Manchester, Manchester University Press, 1995)

Fried, R. M. *Nightmare in Red: The McCarthy Era in Perspective* (Oxford, Oxford University Press, 1990)

Galbraith, J. K. *The Affluent Society* (Harmondsworth, Penguin, 1984 Ed.; Orig. Boston, Houghton Mifflin, 1958)

Gale, M. B. *J.B. Priestley* (Abingdon, Routledge, 2008)

Gans, H. *The Levittowners: Ways of Life in a New Suburban Community* (London, Allen Lane, 1967)

Gervais, D. *Literary Englands: Versions of Englishness in Modern Writing* (Cambridge, Cambridge University Press, 1993)

Gilbert, J. *A Cycle of Outrage: America's Reaction to the Juvenile Delinquent in the 1950s* (New York, Oxford University Press, 1986)

Gray, D. *J.B. Priestley* (Stroud, Sutton, 2000)

Hamilton, I. *The Faber Book of Soccer* (London, Faber, 1992)

Hawkes, J. *A Quest for Love* (London, Chatto and Windus, 1980)

Heale, M. J. *McCarthy's Americans: Red Scare Politics in State and Nation, 1935–1965* (Basingstoke, Macmillan, 1998)

Hennessy, P. *Never Again: Britain 1945–1951* (London, Jonathan Cape, 1992)

Hinton, J. *Protests and Visions: Peace Politics in Twentieth Century Britain* (London, Hutchinson Radius, 1989)

—'Voluntarism versus Jacobinism: Labour, Nation and Citizenship in Britain, 1850–1950', *International Labour and Working Class History*, 48 (1995)

—*Women, Social Leadership and the Second World War: Continuities of Class* (Oxford, Oxford University Press, 2002)

Hitchens, C. *Orwell's Victory* (London, Allen Lane, 2002)

Hoggart, R. *The Uses of Literacy* (Harmondsworth, Penguin, 1957)

Hughes, D. *J.B. Priestley: An Informal Study of His Work* (London, Rupert Hart-Davis, 1958)

Keats, J. *Cracks in the Picture Window* (Boston, Houghton-Mifflin, 1956)

Kerouac, J. *On The Road* (New York, The Viking Press, 1957)

Klein, H. *J.B. Priestley's Plays* (London, MacMillan, 1988)

—*J.B. Priestley's Fiction* (Frankfurt, Peter Lang, 2002)

Labour Party, 'To All Women' (London, Labour Party, 1949)

LaFeber, W. *America, Russia and the Cold War, 1945–2002* (Boston, McGraw-Hill, 2004)

Light, A. *Forever England: Femininity, literature and Conservatism between the Wars* (London, Routledge, 1991)

Lloyd Evans, G. *J.B. Priestley: The Dramatist* (London, Heinemann, 1964)

MacDonald, I. *The New Shostakovich* (London, Pimlico, 2006; Orig. London, Fourth Estate, 1990)

McKibbin R. (ed.) 'Class and Conventional Wisdom: The Conservative Party and the "Public" in Inter-war Britain', *The Ideologies of Class: Social Relations in Britain, 1880–1950* (Oxford, Clarendon, 1990)

Mandler, P. 'Against "Englishness": English Culture and the Limits to Rural Nostalgia, 1850–1940', *Transactions of the Royal Historical Society*, 6th Series, 7 (1997)

Mason, A. and Thompson, P. 'Reflections on a Revolution? The Political Mood in Wartime Britain', in Tiratsoo, N. (ed.), *The Atlee Years* (London, Continuum, 1991)

Matless, D. *Landscape and Englishness* (London, Reaktion Books, 1998)

Michael F. *H. G: The History of Mr. Wells* (London, Doubleday, 1995)

Miles, A. and Savage, M. *The Remaking of the British Working Class, 1850–1940* (London, Routledge, 1994)

Miller, A. *Death of a Salesman* (New York, The Viking Press, 1949)

Mumford, L. *The City in History* (New York, Harcourt, Brace and World, 1961)

Nicholas, S. ' "Sly Demagogues" and Wartime Radio: J.B. Priestley and the BBC', *Twentieth Century British History*, 6, 3 (1995)

Orwell, G. *Coming up for Air* (London, Penguin, 1962; Orig. London, Gollancz, 1939)

—*The Lion and the Unicorn: Socialism and the English Genius* (London, Secker and Warburg, 1962; Orig. London, S and W, 1941)

Parrish, M E. *Anxious Decades: America in Prosperity and Depression, 1920–1941* (New York, Norton, 1992)

Priestley, J. B. *The English Comic Characters* (London, The Bodley Head, 1925)

––*The English Novel* (London, Ernest Benn, 1927)

—*English Humour* (London, Longmans Green and Co, 1929)

—*The Good Companions* (London, Heinemann, 1929)

—*Angel Pavement* (London, Heron Books, n.d.; Orig. London, Heinemann, 1930)

—*English Journey* (London, Heron Books, n.d.; Orig. London, Heinemann, 1933)

—*Wonder Hero* (London, Heinemann, 1933)

—*The Beauty of Britain* (London, Batsford, 1935)

—*Bees on the Boat Deck: A Farcical Comedy in Two Acts* (London, Heinemann, 1936)

—*They Walk in the City: The Lovers in the Stone Forest* (London, Heinemann, 1936)

—*Midnight on the Desert: A Chapter of Autobiography* (London, Heinemann, 1937)

—*When We Are Married and Other Plays* (Harmondsworth, Penguin, 1969 Ed.; *When We Are Married*, Orig. London, Heinemann, 1938)

—*Rain Upon Godshill: A Further Chapter of Autobiography* (London, Heinemann, 1939)

—(ed.) *Our Nation's Heritage* (London, J.M. Dent, 1939)

—*Let the People Sing* (London, Mandarin, 1996; Orig. London, Heinemann, 1939)

—*Postscripts* (London, Heinemann, 1940)

—*Britain Speaks* (Harpers, New York, 1941)

—*Out of the People* (London, Collins in association with William Heinemann Ltd., 1941)

—*Black out in Gretley: A Story of and for Wartime* (London, Heinemann, 1942)

—*Daylight on a Saturday A novel About an Aircraft Factory* (London, Heinemann, 1943)

—'They Came to a City', *The Plays of J.B. Priestley Vol III* (London: Heinemann, 1950; orig. published as *Three Plays*, [London, Heinemann, 1943])

—*Here Are Your Answers* (London, Common Wealth, 1944)

—*Desert Highway* (London, Heinemann, 1944)

—*Letter to a Returning Serviceman* (London: Home and Van Thal, 1945)

—*An Inspector Calls* (London, Samuel French, 1945)

—*The Secret Dream: An Essay on Britain, America and Russia* (Turnstile Press, London, 1946)

—*Russian Journey* (Issued under the auspices of the Writers Group of the Society for Cultural Relations with the USSR, 1946)

—*Bright Day* (London, Penguin, 1951; Orig. London, Heinemann, 1946)

—*Plays I* (London, Heron books, n.d.; Orig. published as *The Plays of J.B. Priestley Volume 1* [London, Heinemann, 1948])

—'Time and the Conways', *Plays I* (London, Heron Books n.d.; Orig. Published as *The Plays of J.B. Priestley Volume 1* [London, Heinemann, 1948])

—*Festival at Farbridge* (London, Heinemann, 1951)

Priestley, J. B. and Hawkes, J. *Journey Down the Rainbow*, (London, Heron Books, n.d.; Orig. London, Heinemann, 1955)

—*Thoughts on the Wilderness* (London, Heinemann, 1957)

—*Literature and Western Man* (London, London Heinemann, 1960)

—*Saturn Over the Water: An Account of His Adventures in London, South America and Australia by Tim Bedford* (London, Heinemann, 1961)

—*The Shapes of Sleep: A Topical Tale* (London, Heinemann, 1962)

—*Margin Released: A Writer's Reminiscences and Reflections* (London, Heron Books, n.d.; Orig. London, Heinemann, 1962)

—*Man and Time* (London: Bloomsbury, 1989 Ed.; Orig. London, Aldus, 1964)

—*Lost Empires: Being Richard Herncastle's Account of His Life on the Variety Stage from November 1913 to August 1914 Together with a Prologue and Epilogue* (London, Heinemann, 1965)

—*The Moments and Other Pieces* (London, Heinemann, 1966)

—*Trumpets Over the Sea: Being a Rambling and Egostistical Account of the London Symphony Orchestra's Engagement at Daytona Beach Florida in July–August 1967* (London, Heinemann, 1968)

—*The Image Men* (London: Allison and Busby, 1968; Orig. published in two volumes as *Out of Town* and *London End* (London: Heinemann, 1968).

—*Essays of Five Decades* (selected with a preface by Susan Cooper) (London, Heinemann, 1969)

—Preface 'On England' to *The Shell Guide to England*, in J. Hadfield (ed.) (London, Michael Joseph, 1970)

—*Over the Long High Wall: Some Reflections and Speculations on Life, Death and Time* (London, Heinemann, 1972)

—*Outcries and Asides* (London, Heinemann, 1974)

—*A Visit to New Zealand* (London, Heinemann, 1974)

—*Instead of the Trees: A Final Chapter of Autobiography* (London, Heinemann, 1977)

Reid, A. J. *Social Classes and Social Relations in Britain, 1850–1914* (Basingstoke, MacMillan, 1992)

Reisman, D. et al. *The Lonely Crowd: A Study of the Changing American Character* (New Haven, Yale University Press, 1961 Ed.; Orig. Yale University, 1950)

Rose, S. O. *Which People's War? National Identity and Citizenship in Wartime Britain, 1939-1945* (Oxford, Oxford University Press, 2003)

Russell, R. *Bird Lives: The High Life and Hard Times of Charlie 'Yardbird' Parker* (London, Quartet Books, 1972)

Salinger, J. D. *The Catcher in the Rye* (Boston, Little, Brown and Co., 1951)

Sandbrook, D. *Never Had It So Good: A History of Britain from Suez to the Beatles* (London, Abacus, 2006)

Shaw, C. and Chase, M. (eds), *The Imagined Past: History and Nostalgia* (Manchester, Manchester University Press, 1989)

Smith, D. 'Churchill's Wartime Rival', *The Historian*, 44 (Winter 1994)

Taylor, M. 'Patriotism and the Left in Twentieth-Century Britain', *The Historical Journal* 33, 4 (1990)

Updike, J. *Rabbit Run* (New York, Alfred A. Knopf, 1960)

Varnedoe, K. and Karmel, P. (eds), *Jackson Pollock: New Approaches* (New York: Museum of Modern Art, 2000)

Waters, C. 'J.B. Priestley, 1894–1984: Englishness and the politics of nostalgia', in P., Susan and M., Peter (eds), *After the Victorians: Private Conscience and Public Duty in Modern Britain* (London, Routledge, 1994)

Weight, R. *Patriots: National Identity in Britain, 1940–2000* (London, Macmillan, 2002)

Wells, H. G. *The Future in America: A Search After Realities* (London, 1906)

—*Outline of History: Being a Plain History of Life and Mankind* (London, Cassell, 1920)

—*Experiment in Autobiography: Discoveries and Conclusions of a Very Ordinary Brain, Vol II* (London Faber, 1984 Ed.; Orig. London, Gollancz/Cresset Press, 1934)

—*The Correspondence of H. G. Wells, Vol. 3*, D. C. Smith (ed.) (London, Pickering and Chatto, 1998)

Whyte, W. *The Organization Man* (New York, Simon and Schuster, 1956)

Wiener, M. *English Culture and the Decline of the Industrial Spirit, 1850–1950* (Cambridge, Cambridge University Press, 1981)

Williamson, P. *Stanley Baldwin: Conservative Leadership and National Values* (Cambridge, Cambridge University Press, 1999)

Wright, P. *On Living in an Old Country: The National Past in Contemporary Britain* (London, Verso, 1985)

Wright Mills, C. *White Collar: The American Middle Classes* (New York, Oxford University Press, 1951)

—*The Power Elite* (New York, Oxford University Press, 1956)

Index

Lightning Source UK Ltd.
Milton Keynes UK
UKHW020813020121
375999UK00004B/45